Contents

Come with me, on a journey beyond your horizon. Along wide open boulevards and narrow dark laneways. Through elegant terminals and contentious border crossings. As I try to make friends and detect conniving enemies. A miniscule figure in a capital metropolis, to unanimous prying eyes of a remote village. Give more than a pleasant courtesy smile, penetrate the local culture. To be a participant, rather than a spectator. Seek and ask questions, throw off the shackles, a challenge to endure.

Now, don't get apprehensive if you think the paragraph you've just digested has you popping-up in it. Sorry to disappoint, you are almost certainly wrong. For others who may feel they are not worthy of a mention, think again, but only you will know. Some of the names have been changed to prevent major embarrassment and also a bounty on my head. There was never any intention of writing anything. Flapping about on a Saturday afternoon I started scribbling from memory. If you experience monotony at anytime, hopefully it's just momentarily. If it's repetitive I apologize. If it's constant, then you are probably monotonous. Throw this literature in the garbage and write your own chapter.

How well do you mix on holiday? Or do we make excuses that you just went, to get away. Isn't it always to get away. So while you're in a foreign country you may as well try and make a few new acquaintances, most times it's a positive outcome. A trip overseas should be a bit more than been chauffeured around on a tourist bus taking snapshots of town squares and historical architecture. Release that free-spirit, for some it's been unnecessarily dormant which you know will make these moments more enjoyable. Arrive back with at least one interesting story for each day.

From my teenage era I was just as content venturing beyond my boundaries to socialize rather than to continually hang' local. For many a ten-day break on a sunshine island offers plenty of satisfaction, great for releasing the energy. But let's try and go a step further, make that a couple of steps further. A guided-tour is not exactly my thing, so individual preparation is a virtue if I'm to take the road less travelled. Four days was my shortest stay, eleven months being the longest in a country. Would friends, relatives or work colleagues come along? Not possible flying to places that are out-of-their comfort zone or applying for extended visas. Strolling solo around a foreign capital is certainly not the worst thing in the world, but there is better ways to enjoy it. So I began corresponding with citizens overseas. Building up genuine friendships in Brazil, Russia, Ukraine, Belarus, India, Malaysia, Hong Kong, New Zealand and Australia. Over a six-year period at the turn of the new millennium I would intermittingly 'hit the road' and see what happens. Sorry folks, before the vanity of selfies,' life was more spontaneous. I use my first and middle names throughout, so keep-up, don't get lost and have a sense-of-humour. In no particular sequence, here is an in-sight. There is a few grammar mistakes, see how many you can find.

India

I trudged off the plane feeling weary. There were mops, buckets, brooms with long handles, brooms with no handles. Cleaning products, aerosol cans, rags and sponges. It was the sanitation crew waiting to prepare the aircraft for the next departure. The arrivals hall at Indira Gandhi International airport in New Delhi was basic and certainly in need of a lick of paint. As I walked through the barrier, a new backpack strapped-up, one rugged-looking native shouts at me in his long drab brown smock and matching trousers. He sounds loud and crazy. [This airport added a beautiful new terminal in 2010, so it's quite modern today]. Then I see, the big grin, my friend Jimmy from Cork [Ireland]. We embraced and then hopped into a black and yellow taxi. Stopping at the exit gate, Jimmy has the appropriate paper filled-in which is necessary for the transport. "Indian bureaucracy, you'll see plenty of it," as a uniformed official checked the document.
"It's the Wacky Races and we're off, I love this," Jimmy nudging and pointing, as the driver turned onto the main road.
"Just watch how they drive."
We were into a journey with such a contrast to my everyday life. Trucks, buses, three-wheeled motor rickshaws, push-carts, bicycle rickshaws, all jockeying with us for a place on the road. Changing lanes which do not really exist, the markings have long faded.
As the traffic lights changed to red I observed society, sadly some are begging children, elderly folk, others with disabilities. One guy on crutches, another with deformed arms. Everywhere there are people standing, staring and carrying stuff on their heads, struggling to push an overloaded trolley. Men in sharp suits with briefcases, women with grocery bags, dressed in bright coloured saris. This is India, it could not be anywhere else. The realization will go far beyond your deepest imagination.
It was Jimmy's second visit to the Sub-continent. So for the first week he made most of the decisions.
We stayed in the Paharganj, a popular area for western tourists. He had arrived a week earlier by train from Mumbai [Bombay], having lounged around for two months on the beaches of Goa, on the south-west coast a common choice for holiday-makers especially during

the Christmas season. Now in New Delhi, this nation's capital, situated inland in the northern half of the country. That night I went to bed early, feeling ill from the effects of a delayed stopover. This is not the start I was anticipating. The flight from London to New Delhi via Dubai had a schedule one-hour stop. We landed on the tarmac at twelve midnight, departed at 8 a.m. No announcements were made through the night. Drinking coffee to enhance my vigor, browsing through the duty-free, the staff was all Philippine. Purchasing two bottles of vodka and one whiskey, a request from Jimmy. As a result of being awake all night, fatigue set-in, then flu. The London to Dubai leg was a full house. I was seated next to a Belgian doctor and his wife. He pointed out senior European golfers. Also a number of television crews. Coverage of the Dubai Golf classic was imminent. Professional players suffer ailments, back pain, wrist problems, shoulder agony. They will visit a local specialist wherever the venue is held, so the doctor set-up a travelling clinic to treat the golfers. He had a repertoire file on each client, performing the right treatment when necessary during a tournament. I prodded him on certain individuals who had questionable personalities, but he was not telling. As a teenager been a caddy, I experienced the direct scorn of a few grumpy players. "Where did that ball go, you were not even watching."
I should tell him, "there is a creek in my neck with all your slicing and hooking. Why not play a more suitable game like bowls, you would not spend so much time in the trees." But of course I bit my lip, embarrassed and red faced.
In Delhi our room has two single beds, an en-suite bathroom for two hundred and fifty rupees. Jimmy grabbed a bottle of vodka and went off with a couple of Irish guys from Dublin. Feeling sick, I tried to sleep. But there is constant noise from other guest rooms, traffic from the street and worst of all, dogs. They seem to be sending messages to each other. When one stops barking, another starts. I flicked through the television channels. To my surprise an English league game is in progress, the 'Liverpool derby.' But to watch this potential exciting match, I have to sit twelve inches from the screen, because in order to hold this channel I have to keep my finger on the button. I notified the porter, but his efforts were to no avail. I suggested wedging a piece of meat in-between the television knobs. He duly obliged, returning from the kitchen with small pieces of

chicken. Amazingly, it worked. I enjoyed an Everton victory. The voice of the co-commentator had me thinking, then I realized it is Tommy Smyth, plying his trade. Well known on Irish radio and Gaelic Park sports in New York. A native of my hometown, Dundalk. 'Cathamari hit the onion bag that night.'

The following day I went in search, of yet more medical personnel. The main street in the Paharganj is an engrossed thoroughfare. Silk clothing shops, photo stores, restaurants, cafes, travel agents, grocery marts, barbers and guest houses. I see a sign, Doctor Ravi's clinic. It's an open store front, one room of about twenty-feet by eight and a cubicle at the rear for his prescription assistant. No doors or windows, a steel shutter to pull down when closing. Standing on the edge of the steps, undecided whether to wait or not. There is a ticket machine on the wall, I pull one. Is this peak-time? About fifteen people are waiting.

'What happens now?' I'm thinking. Will this be the standard two-hour visit, fidgeting, turning, looking around. Should I leave, seek another clinic that will welcome me in open arms and have sympathy to my condition. My temperature is high, morale is low, the body is weak. Patience is a virtue. A voice rings out, peering over spectacles the doc hand signals me to the front. "Come, come," offering me a seat. He takes one more patient, then invites me to the 'treatment chair.' I explain my condition, where I'm from.

"I will give you medication, different from what you receive back at home. You will be fine in three days," the doc assured.

I received my remedy, paying 150 rupees, my lowest payment ever, to a doctor. Why is it, we suddenly feel a touch of rejuvenation when leaving a doctor's office. I meet Jimmy and head for a restaurant. Ordering soup, followed by mash potato, eggs and beans, the local cuisine can be tasted later.

"Indian medicine is like rocket fuel, you'll be better in two days," Jimmy trying to be positive.

"Ya know I have guilt in my veins, I jumped the queue, ahead of women and children. No, babies and pensioners. They are probably thinking, selfish arrogant tourist, showing no respect."

Jimmy looked at me. "It's like this, the doctor seen an opportunity to make money. For sure he has charged you about six times the normal fee. After a couple of weeks you will see women's true position. It's not an equal society."

"All the more reason not to accept the status quo," I shot back.

Strolling back to the hotel we bumped into Joe, from Limerick, [Ireland] Jimmy's travelling buddy for the past few weeks. Also Joe's cousin, Carolyn had arrived in India recently. They had bought train tickets for Rajasthan. The lads were planning to meet in Pushkar, on Thursday.

"That's too soon for me," I interrupted. "I'm not ready for any long journeys."

"For feck sake, you better be ready. Anyway it'll be more pleasant out of Delhi, down in the smaller towns," Jimmy speaking his mind, Joe nodding in agreement. The following day my health was vastly improved. 'God bless Indian medication.'

A visit to New Delhi train station was necessary, a fifteen minute walk. The area was over-run with people. Lucky for us there was a separate office for foreigners. But buying a ticket is not a simple procedure. A passport is needed and a money exchange receipt. Eight customers ahead of us, it would take more than one hour. Bureaucracy takes over, it was helpful to have Jimmy as my guide. But a Russian guy struggled to understand why he could not buy a ticket. Missing, was the money exchange document. It's not possible to buy a ticket and travel on the same day, another bloody rule, but I guess it's necessary with such a massive population. One hundred and forty rupees for an eight-hour journey, what a price. [About $5 U.S.]

Outside the railway station we stand and watched the activities. Taxis and rickshaws dropping-off and picking-up customers, entrepreneurs are applying their trade. A tea seller is near-by selling Chai, as the locals call it. A Sadhu claims one, he doesn't pay, barefooted, in orange robes with a small sack hooked on a long stick, looking aged. These holy men travel around the country for free, they probably deserve to.

Carts are being pushed, stacked with fruits and vegetables. Sacks of rice are plentiful. A man pulls-up on his bike, a few people gather round. Jimbob [as I sometimes call him] gives him a utility knife. The bike man has his back-wheel on a stand and is free-wheeling, creating a circular stone to spin. The stone is a sharpener, placed underneath the saddle, absolutely brilliant invention. Everyone seems to be on a mission, so much movement. We take a motor rickshaw to Connaught Place. Fifty rupees is the asking price, but Jimbob bargains like a natural and pays twenty. Connaught Place, a commercial area of New Delhi with minimal American influence that has Pizza Hut and MacDonald's. It's circular in shape with a large park in the middle, in which we enter. People are scattered, it seems subdued.

"Let's sit down," I suggest.

"No, they're gonna come," says Jimbob.

"What do you mean, who'll come?" I questioned.

"You'll see."

"Relax, chill-out" I enthused, as I stretched-out.

Three minutes later about ten people were smothering us, all with their own agenda. The shoe-shiner was the first on the scene. Feeling sorry for him I took off my boots and put them in his care. Caterpillars, bought from an ex-workmate at wholesale price because of a slight defect, or so I thought until this guy got hold of them. What was supposed to be a quick polish job, developed into a renovation. Replacing stitching, shaving the oversized sole tip, cutting the tongue shorter and changing the shabby laces. But his fee kept increasing. I looked to Jimmy for assistance.

"Fight your own battles, they'll take every rupee you have," lighting a cigarette in a nonchalant manner. We were surrounded, reminiscent of a Flea market, only the customers were the minority. The fruit vendor, Jewellery woman, Snake boy who wanted to put his five-foot pet around my neck for a photo, Fortune teller, Masseur, who persistently demanded my hand for a demonstration. I reluctantly agreed. Realizing he was no fake, cracking bones, moving flesh and tissue, my hand felt like brand new, loose and flexible. Producing a note book of recommendations, "What country you from?" then opening the appropriate page of satisfied customers from the Emerald Isle. Tom, 28 from Galway, Aiden, 30 a Dubliner. I flicked through, a page for each country. Just how authentic was his book of references.

A woman with cakes knelt in front of me, another with toys, young men with hand drums, tin whistles, razor blades, tee-shirts, socks, sunglasses. Should I be charitable and buy a few items, to give preference just wasn't possible. They had arrived like magic out of thin-air, as my buddy had warned. Another crowd had gathered watching the action. This would become the norm. Everywhere I went in this country, the natives, always watching.

In another area of the park, groups of men were playing cards, others were spectators. As Jimmy and I observed, we chatted with locals about their government and current issues. I was amused by their headshake. It's like they are saying 'no' but it means 'I understand.' For the next few weeks I would encounter this headshake, always having me to think, does he really know what I'm saying. Later we would develop this headshake, creating humour and confusion. Returning to our lodgings on a bicycle rickshaw, we seemed to go the long way. Our rider was constantly complaining about the police, a heavy stench of alcohol a new meaning to 'driving under the influence.' He looked over seventy.

"This guy will suffer heart-failure going up these hills," I protested, wanting to get off, Jimmy laughing continuously enjoying the ride. The following day, I was feeling a little healthier. Jimmy was off to wish a 'bon voyage' to the Dubliners, whom he met on the Mumbai-New Delhi train. They were on their way to Dharamsala, home to his holiness, the Dalai Lama.

I went looking for a book shop. Taken a busy road, open sewers were visible, garbage in abundance. Goats and cows were feeding off the rubbish. Five women came walking in the opposite direction, middle-aged, dressed in traditional saris, each a different colour, Red, green, blue, yellow and orange. They returned my smile, a picture of elegance and beauty.

I tried crossing the street, traffic was flowing at a brisk pace. Then I realized the traffic lights were not operating. 'Damn, this will take forever.'

'When in India, do as the Indians do.' I joined a group of locals crossing in conjunction, lane by lane. Dangerous but I was safely in the middle of the pack.

I was approached by a young man who was offering cheap travel packages. In his brother's office they showed me photographs of a house with hills and a lake in the background.

"It's four hours north, very beaut-i-full. We give very gud price sir." Persistent for a down payment, but I was not cracking. Then they showed me a brochure with many attractive pictures of the countryside. They had plenty to say, but I was pleasant and calm braking free from their clutches, excusing myself to make a private phone call.

Later an Irish guy who was touring by motorbike told me 'It's a scam. The catch is it will be a remote place with only one food store with high prices. You will have no other choice but to buy from this store. Transport will be almost non-existent, but expensive. Everything owned by the same guy.

That evening packed and ready to experience India's famous rail system. As we stood surveying the giant timetable, wearing a Guinness tee-shirt, I was approached by a Japanese guy.

"I love this beer, friend, one year in college in Derry," [a town in Ireland]. "I'm sorry there is no bar to have a drink, I could have sake," I replied.

An English chap interrupted, "anyone heading for Calcutta?"

Ike from Tokyo was. "Am over here, come join me mate."

"Your train is two hours late," as I pointed to the notice board.

"It's India," he shrugged.

****

Ajmer was our destination, an overnight journey south, arrival time 6 a.m. A Dutch couple was seated next to us, a second-class carriage. Six bunks in each bay, very open, no curtains or petitions. Indians don't travel light, much more than the kitchen sink. A couple was opposite us who were going to Mount Abu, popular with newlyweds. Jimmy copped it, so a small celebration was called. The Dutchman purchased sodas to mix with our duty-free whiskey.

The new bride was twenty-seven.

"Was this a bit late to tie-the-knot?"

"In the past, yes, but things are changing."

They responded accepting a soft-drink only. We teased and joked with them. "Whiskey helps your love-life, after three drinks, there is only one thing you will want to do, and it's not sleep."

They laughed shyly.

An over-weight man was sitting near-by, constantly staring at us. We offered him a drink, he refused. Jimmy and the Dutchman went for a smoke at the exit doors. The fat man disappeared in the same direction. When the lads returned, Jimmy whispered, "We were followed."

"I guess he really likes one of you, sleep with one eye open, I'm safe up in the top bunk," I joked.

Later I organized myself to bed-down for the night, using my day-pack covered by a towel as a pillow. Fat man had his steely eyes fixed in my direction, a rough, tough, stern looking character, showing no emotion.

He had me on-edge.

The feckin vendors made sure to interrupt my sleep. They're awake, so the whole train has to be also. Entering at station stops, creating a racket they were selling newspapers, food and chai [tea]. The chant is 'chai con chai,' loud and clear.

We arrived in Ajmer at 6:30a.m. I wasn't even sure if this was our stop. I didn't know the right name of the town. Jimmy rushed off, so I just followed. I don't think I said goodbye to the Dutch folk. Walking two blocks, we jumped on a bus, it was bright and sunny. Jimmy was repeating a trip he had made two years earlier. Pushkar, our final destination, problem was we were bloody going nowhere. The bus driver went all around town, several times. When the bus is full, it will leave. No, let me rephrase that. When the bus is packed to capacity, Indian-style, it will hit the road. People standing were crammed against each other. Squashed against a window and unable to offer my seat, a young school boy sat on my knee. A teacher next to us, "this is normal," she commented.

Pushkar is a beautiful scenic town with a lake in the middle surrounded by small mountains.

Our accommodation was at the south end of the main street. Single brick rooms, circling a court yard, haggled down from ninety to sixty rupees per night. Sixty...........this is why people extend their visas and stay three months longer. Why return to the rat-race of the western world.

After sleeping several hours, a quick bite to eat. Then off to climb one of the peaks with Jimmy, Joe and Carolyn, after an hour of panting before reaching the summit where a tiny stone-wall temple stood. Some westerners were meditating. A panoramic view as the sun was setting with the rumble of drums in the distance across the lake signalling night fall. This town is important to Hindus. The lake is sacred with bathing Ghats, many Sadhus are visible. A Brahma temple is near-by with its distinctive red spire. Priests offer you a blessing and tie a red ribbon on your wrist for a donation. I was invited by three local guys for a blessing by the water. Their hands-on aggressive method often results in foreigners retaliating on the same level. So I had to shove them off because of their persistence. The following day, I rented a bicycle, heading for the countryside. Teenagers on the way home from school began shouting at me. "Give me pen, give me pen." I bought some soft drinks and candy, their eyes lit up. But pens, pencils and note pads are helpful items for school kids in rural areas. The roads are narrow with little traffic, a calming influence away from the hustle and bustle of Delhi.

A passenger on my flight was enthusiastic about a drink called Bhang Lassi. "You must try it in India, it'll knock your socks off." He was an engineer on his way to Dhaka, the capital of Bangladesh to investigate irrigation and drainage systems.

"Flooding is a disastrous problem in that country. No one has come-up with a solution yet, the first person who does could become very wealthy."

Alcohol is sold covertly in Pushkar. I'm mystified what category Bhang Lassi's are in. I ordered one from the waiter who asked, "do you want a strong or weak one."

"I'll start with a weak drink."

Joe and Jimmy vociferously interrupted, "no, no, it must be strong." We were in the company of English and German travellers. The Bhang Lassi had a foul water taste, the juices from the leaves have a real potency. The others were knocking back duty-free vodka topped with coke in plastic cups.

I ordered another which I struggled to finish, the lads were watching. To leave a restaurant with food left on your plate. Throw a half-eaten bag of chips in the waste basket, a cup of coffee unfinished.

Opinions are not passed, a second thought is not given, but can't finish an alcohol beverage, that's outrageous. 'You're a wimp, soft, a light-weight,' are the comments that burn your ears.

Dieter was talking about Goa, how he bought a small amount of weed and one hour later the local cops came knocking on his room door investigating a disturbance.

"Luckily I had just passed the stuff onto a friend. For sure the seller had followed me back to my lodgings and then tipped-off the cops. The police did a quick search of my room, said they were looking for a knife."

Word among some travellers was, when in Goa, be careful who you buy a smoke from. Some of the dealers are friends with the local police.

"In Goa I seen some Israelis running from the police," says Joe.

"Yea, the younger ones cause trouble sometimes," Darren jumping in, "Giving bad manners to street vendors over the price of fruit, arguing with the motor-bike taxi drivers about the fare."

Sarah had been travelling by bus in Gujarat, known to be a dry state in reference to alcohol. "I awoke to discover this Indian guy fondling me. I pushed him away and shouted to attract attention. My friend Jackie came to the rescue. She is much bigger than me, sleeping in the seat behind. That guy quickly moved to the back of the bus, it was a horrible feeling."

Jimmy, Joe, Carolyn and myself headed off to a place called the 'German Bakery,' a chain of restaurants scattered around the sub-continent. Travellers judge these places as safe and hygienic to dine, western-style and slightly more expensive.

Browsing through the menu, suddenly my appetite disappeared, I was in cloud nine, I could barely speak. "See yas later," I mumbled, the Bhang-Lassi had kicked-in. Taking off to locate my bike, hidden in an alley-way, I stumbled around trying to recognize the appropriate alley, a clothing retailer pointing me in the right direction. The locals are always watching, a good thing this time. It was an effort to steer on a dimly lighted street. My wobbly control resulted in hitting a cow sitting with his mates blocking my passage, a bruised arm for me and the sacred animal unfazed, the locals on the sidelines just stood and laughed. As I entered my guesthouse, making a conscious but miserable effort to go quietly, the peddles catching on the steps at the front door.

"Are you o.k. sir?" a voice called out, inevitably.

"No problem, no problem," I shouted, ignoring eye contact with our landlord. Sprawled out in bed I was forcing my brain to relax and sleep, but it was racing. My head spinning one way, the walls the other, somewhere in a deep consciousness I didn't want to dose-off. After what seemed an eternity, the doors swung open. The light switch was flicked, then another one. Jimmy quickly correcting his mistake of turning-on the ceiling fan which my mosquito net was hooked onto. The net hung down over my bed, apologies, with laughter from Joe and Jimmy.

"Don't touch the net," I called out. "Look leave it, just leave it," I

13

stuttered as they tried to re-arrange it.

"What's wrong Sean, do you want a beer," called out Joe. I didn't respond. "We'll see ya tomorra," as they banged the door shut.

Ready to face a new day, an early morning cold shower did the trick, not that I had another option. You should see the toilet paper in India…….. there is none. Jimmy was sitting in the courtyard smoking a rolled-up cigarette. "Let's go for breakfast," he called out. "I'll just have a quick dump, do you have any toilet paper?" I asked.

"For feck sake Sean, you can't use it in this country."

"Of course I can."

Jimmy approached the lavatory in the corner.

"Don't use bog roll, you will create a blockage."

"Ah come on, you must have some in your room."

The high-pitched laugh came out, "I haven't used it in two months, do it the Indian way."

"What do you mean?" feeling stupid now.

"Ya see that bucket and tap, that's the toilet paper, it'll come natural after a while."

"Listen Jimbob, I'm going to introduce toilet roll to this country, we could start a business."

"No one will buy it, besides there is less waste this way."

A hole in the ground with a ceramic tile base with prints specifically moulded for your feet. One must squat. No western-style toilet bowls here. No miniature magazine racks for a comfortable read or long day-dreaming moments. Washing your waste down is also a necessity, whenever there is no handle flush.

I brushed my teeth at the courtyard sink which was thick with dirt.

"Is there a taboo on cleanliness?"

"As you can see Sean there is a lot of poverty, they don't have money for these products."

Brooms without handles were common, the stooping to sweep the floor would be back-breaking. Mops and sponges were less visible.

The nominated restaurant for breakfast had an obstacle. A large bull was blocking the entrance. Been familiar with this fascinating country, Jimmy would always take the lead. But not this time, his bravado suddenly disappeared. The bull took no notice of our intimidating stomps and shouts. A couple of whacks from the cook with a broomstick had him scampering away.

Porridge had become a regular order, keeping it simple and healthy.

Strolling to the north end of the main street to visit Joe and Carolyn, I checked the local stores on the way.

"What price is this?" a tee-shirt with a Rajasthan print of Elephants.

"One hundred rupees," the shopkeeper answered. "Very gud price, the right size for you."

"The price is too high," I countered.

"No, no this is very gud quality. One hundred rupee, is gud price. Simple, simple, yes for you," the shopkeeper tried to convince.

"Too high my man."

"What price then?"

"I'll give you fifty," shrugging my shoulders.

I made my way for the door, the shopkeeper followed me to the street.

"Give me gud price and it's yours."

"I'll come back later," I gestured.

"Come, come give me gud price my friend."

"I'll be back."

"O.K. my friend, I will be waiting."

I love the way the locals talk.

A few shops down Jimmy was looking at a necklace. Seventy rupees was the opening price. He bought three for one hundred. As we proceeded I notice a tee-shirt with Camel prints, the shop attendant was quickly on to me.

"One hundred rupees, Very gud price sir."

I smiled and nodded, the jargon was repeated. On the street I continued to haggle. I turned to look for Jimmy, nowhere to be seen. But a crowd of about ten natives had gathered to view the action. A local against a foreigner, it was stalemate.

Another man interrupted, "I am the owner of this store sir, I like your tee-shirt sir. Guinness, this is beer, am I correct sir."

"That's right, Irish beer. It's good for your heart, I'll get you some." I wisecracked. "Oh no, I do not drink alcohol, it makes me sleepy, give me head-ache sir."

"I like European clothing, can we do exchange sir."

"Sure my man, why not." So it's like an international football, swapping at the end of the game.

"It's fresh and clean, just washed yesterday," I assured.

"Remember Guinness is a health drink in Ireland."

"Oh sir it gives me a bad stomach, I drink it in England when I visited my brother."

"Listen, my friend, tell your brother to send you a keg of this beer. Then the whole town can taste the nourishment."

"A keg, what is this? sir."

"Just tell him. Hasta la vista, my man."

Guinness is an Irish success story. Unfortunately it is now in the hands of an overseas company that has little conscience, a one-track mind of profits only.

As I continued on my way down the street, I handed an old woman fifty rupee, as she held her hand out and then gave thanks. A few minutes later as I talked with German tourists, she returned to profusely touch and chant. Was she expressing gratitude again or asking for more. Slightly embarrassed but remaining sympathetic, my patience allowing her to conclude.

With many beggars it's impossible to give to everyone. Sometimes kids work for a pimp, who is nearby but difficult to notice for a traveller. So I made a decision, the elderly gets priority, too old to have a job.

I entered the archway to the 'Pushkar guesthouse,' flowers blooming along the pathway. It certainly looked more up-market than our residence. Jimmy was doing a roll-up, surprise, surprise. Carolyn was reading and Joe was puffing on a pipe, grinning.

"Are you all right now, Sean? More Bhang Lassi tonight, right."

"Sorry about last night folks, I lost the plot. That stuff is lethal."

"We had a good laugh watching you," Joe still grinning.

"There's always someone watching me. It's got to be the number one pastime in this country," being sarcastic behind my sunglasses.

I was introduced to the others sitting among my friends, three Israeli women who had just completed their military service, now on a six-month tour of this country, Nepal and Thailand. Two were in the medical services, the other in the secret-service. They had that distinctive curly hair, dark eyes and slightly prominent nose. They took off when five of their friends appeared, a common scene, many groups from this middle-east country.

"Listen Sean, we're riding out of town tonight," Jimmy moving his chair closer to the table.

"O.K. have my horse ready."

"Give us one hundred and twenty rupees and your passport, this guesthouse will organize the bus tickets," Jimmy explained.

"A feckin passport for everything, if you went to use a public toilet at a train station, I bet they would have an identity check. What about the Indians themselves, what do they use when buying a simple bus ticket?" I humorously ranted.

"We're the cowboys, the Indians are keeping tabs on us," Joe replied giggling.

I relaxed back into the chair, taking the warm sun on my face, collecting my thoughts.

"I haven't had a good curry yet," thinking of my stomach.

"Are you going to drink ten pints first, the way we do it back home."

"Well Jimbob, that's a bit hard when I haven't seen a pub yet."

"Me and Joe had plenty of tasty curries in Goa."

"Right, we'll all go to Goa especially for a curry," been sarcastic.

"What's the craic with you Carolyn, enjoying the holiday? I asked.

"Yea, we're getting around."

"What about Delhi," I shot back.

"I hate that place, the men always staring at you."

"Well, you're a novelty, blond hair, Caucasian, green eyes, very attractive to the local guys."

"Sean, I couldn't even walk down the street, men coming really close to me, asking, where you from? Come into my shop, sometimes they ask, are you married?"

"Right, in the next town, I will be your escort. If anyone approaches you, we are husband and wife, I will be your security," I offered.

'Hi, he's hitting on your cousin," Jimmy not letting it slide.

"Ahh, he's just been an idiot," Joe replied.

"Any other problems Carolyn," I asked.

"Getting use to the toilets, but you can't help with that."

"Joe has the solution to dirty toilets," Jimmy informed.

"Tell them what you did in Mumbai."

"It's not so interesting."

"Yea it is, go-waun, go-waun," Jimmy insisted.

"We were having dinner and a few beers one night, I went to the jacks, but it was absolutely filthy. I was not going to use them, it was

17

too much, but I had to go badly. So I went off down the street looking for other restaurants. I checked two, but the bloody toilets were locked, for customers only. Then I walked down this side-street, I noticed a guy in a squatting position, I went beyond him. Some cows were grazing on the rubbish; I used them as my cover. It was a residential area, but no one noticed."

"So the quiet streets are the public toilets," I said testing.

"I'm not proud of it, there was no other choice," Joe shrugging.

"Would you do that in the streets in Ireland?"

"Look, for feck sake I was desperate."

"Where are you off to now?" Jimmy mumbled at me with a fag in his mouth. "Gotta pack my stuff," I replied.

"But it's only just after four."

"I'm a punctual person, I prepare early. No last minute rushing," I emphasized.

"Sean, you were never on time in your life and tonight will be no different," Jimmy bellowed through his laughter.

"You're actually very rough looking, you make our group look like nomads," he continued.

"Alright, alright," gesturing with my hands. "I was under the weather for a few days, now I'm coming back to normal. A shave, a shower and a shit, a little nap, some grub and then I will be first on that bus."

"Listen, have you been to the barbers for a cut-throat job?" Jimmy asked. "Ahh, I don't need any of that, I can do it myself."

"Just try them once, it's great, I'm telling ya," he insisted.

I reluctantly went along to a local barber. As he sharpened his blade I wiped some of the shaving cream off, otherwise he was about to pare half my face. Then, a magical transformation, a meticulous grooming, twice, finishing off with massage treatment; my forehead, cheeks, neck and shoulders. Cracking sounds in the back of my head. Feeling like a new, much younger person, the simple pleasures in life. I walked out of there totally refreshed, it was absolutely brilliant. To grade the level of satisfaction, better than sex? let's not deliberate. It certainly is a top-five feel good factor, not that I'm an expert in mating. The Indian barbers are the easy winners in this category of the cut-throat activists.

At 10p.m. about fifteen travellers squeezed into a mini-bus to take us to Ajmer bus station. By midnight we were traversing west in the state of Rajasthan, destination Jaisalmer.

Jimmy would sleep on a bed of nails, in another world next to the window, not unlike my ex-house buddy, Richie Roach. I was drifting in and out of consciousness, at one stage I noticed the bus was stopped for a while. Quite a lot of noise outside, I went to investigate. We had a puncture. A 'town' of about five houses, the locals were on hand to help, despite the time of 3:20a.m.

Later I sat near the front observing the journey. For on occasions the ride was bumpy. The dark road was narrow in stretches which made it difficult with traffic coming in the opposite direction. The front man competent, keeping a swift steady speed.

A taxi ride from Jaisalmer bus station to our next place to explore resulted in Jimmy and myself arguing over the choice of guesthouses.

"Why can't we stay in this area," [by the bus station] I questioned.

"Look, let me decide, I have been here before," Jimmy growled.

His decision was right; minutes later on this hot sunny morning a magnificent fort came into view, way in the distance, across the dry flat landscape. An elevated structure, high garrison style walls, desert-like colour. It was now a residential area and we would stay inside this compound, where a funeral was in progress. We slipped down a side alley for breakfast, to avoid been disrespectful. Joe and Jimmy's second visit, they had accommodation arranged. I was a couple of alleys away, sixty rupees for a single room. I met Marlene for dinner, a German I had chatted with on the overnight bus. She was accompanied by Lara from Scotland. I had ordered Tandori chicken, rice with spicy vegetables. I introduced Carolyn to the girls who became more extrovert with her new gender friends.

A Camel trek was been organized, this is desert country so it's the thing to do. The following morning we loaded into a jeep and headed into the Rajasthan desert. Raj was the organizer, known by Jimmy. We stopped to pick-up a very attractive woman, a school teacher on her way to work, constantly at ease as we talked and joked with her, such a sweet personality.

Arriving at our starting point, an isolated village with mud houses. No electricity and water fetched from wells surrounded by dry sandy

ground. My first thought was, 'how do people survive here?'
I asked Raj. He explained, "In the wet season, maze is grown, also water melons are harvested. It looks like nothing now, but it's busy when the rains come."
The kids stared from a distance at first, they grew in confidence as we offered them some fruit and sweets. But the most frequent request was a pen followed by a plastic water bottle. In India, tap water is not safe for western folk. Mineral water should be used at all times even when brushing your teeth. I was drinking about four litres per day. But here in the open countryside, fresh well-water was not a problem. Raj's parents were from this village, he was not an official tour guide, but we were contented to give a little business. We had lunch in his parents' house, two large rooms with dry mud floors. We all sat on mats. They cooked outside with gas cylinders. We had salad of lettuce, onion, tomato and cucumber, potato curry and rice with Nan bread. At the village square nine Camels and their owners were waiting. Joe was brave enough, the first to step forward to mount this hump back animal as the master signalled his Camel to knell down on his front legs. Joe made an awkward attempt to climb aboard, but slid off and finished sitting on the animal's neck. We all laughed, some hysterically. The second effort was only slightly better, when the Camel stood upright, Joe somehow was facing his rear end. A standing ovation and the jokes started, "Backward Joe, hay take up the rear as a lookout for bandits."
No one in the group had been on a Camel before, so jaunting through the open wilderness was an unexpected adventure. Everyone on the first day was obliged to share a Camel with it's master. My partner was a small Sikh man decked out in his long white robes, a rugged beard and aluminous yellow turban. When we converged on a village, the tourist would dismount and walk through the community, basically a cluster of mud and straw houses.
 The guides took a detour round the perimeter and meeting us the other side. Curious stares from the children, we'd smile and wave at them. Beckoning them to us, their innocence would melt the toughest of hearts.
We set up camp at sundown and the guides lit fires to cook a local cuisine of Nan bread, curry, rice and lots of salad. No cutlery here, you eat with your hands. Jimmy had bought local whiskey, Joe and myself chipped-in. "This will keep the guides happy," mixing it with

water to ease the potency. A sing-song began around the camp fire, the Rajasthanies blasting out their own lyrics. We didn't waste the opportunity to cite Irish traditional ballads: the Button Pusher, Dicey Riley, Twice Daily, the Bumble Bee, plus a couple of pop songs, like 'Singing the blues, 'Dancing in the street,' I'm gonna be [500 miles]. By bedtime a resting place had been prepared, three blankets were sufficient, a cold wind blowing as expected in this open seclusion. Wild bush sheltered us on one side, the Camels on the other. During the night I awoke to the ocular proof of the planet's solar system. Breadth-taking would be modest. What any human sees on a clear night as they look to the heavens in a capital city, multiply this by one thousand, the result if that imagination is possible would be absolutely phenomenal. The only sound, heavy breathing from the animals, multitudes of stars dotted the sky. Caught in a moment of distant fear that drifting back to sleep would be difficult and remaining conscious to sustain and enjoy the realization. To click the camera, the beauty would not be justified. Too much disruption, to fetch that instrument, the level of bewilderment will drop. This is an ultimate, be spontaneous. To nudge a special individual lying inches away would be ideal, but it's Joe, sorry mate. Why can't it be someone who romances my heart, a soul mate, so I just lie there.

The next I know, a new dawn is beginning. Sub-consciously, perhaps I make a greater effort to be single rather than follow in the footsteps of my siblings and embrace matrimony. Taking advantage of my situation, no consultation if I get the notion to move east.........or west, to reside in a street three blocks away from my current residence or move across town. This is why I'm here. Right here, in an Indian desert, because this is the alternative, but not the only track. I could try being a monk or a full-time charity worker in a developing country. Now, that would be a genuine sacrifice, putting others first..............all the time.
At breakfast soup was served, also rice and vegetables, partly, last night leftovers. Marlene talked about the fabulous night sky, her slumber also interrupted. I assisted with the description as she pencilled it into her diary. Jimmy and Joe returned with Raj to his parents' village, some of the guides disappeared also. The rest of the group continued on the trek. It started strangely, upon arriving at the next hamlet. Tito who seemed to be the decision maker of the guides

beckoned Marlene to enter a house with him. "Sick baby in house," he mumbled. I give him aspirin and Lara offered medicine. Marlene emerged from the house a few minutes later.

"I don't understand there is no one sick in that house, just a woman baking bread."

We were a little puzzled, but the usual mystic story that tourists hear from Indian men who are looking for a way to squeeze money from them. Tito later used the medication to buy whiskey, an exchange deal. With less people in the group it was possible to ride a Camel solo. They are a phenomenal animal with the ability to carry heavy loads, travel for long distances through dry climates. Camels drink lots of water whenever possible and can store this water in their bodies for many days. An early lunch was called. The guides prepared food and knocked back the alcohol. I was hung-over, quite contented to laze under a tree in the shade. Later, afternoon pit stops at a watering station for the Camels. Local farmers giving the girls glinted looks. The mood of the younger guides was more upbeat whenever they shared a Camel with one of the women. Shouting and joking as if they had hit the jackpot. That night sitting around the camp fire Lara talked about the many Indian men who talked wrongly to women on the street.

"They ask loaded questions. Where are you from? Are you married? You are not married, you come here alone? There is a lack of pleasant conversation."

I pointed out, "it's a male dominated society. Walk the streets, what do you see? The wives, grandmothers are all at home doing the housework. The girls will go off and live with their husband's family. The sons stay and take care of their parents as they get older, it's economics. Look around, walk into shops, railway stations, go to a bank or post office, most employees are men."

"How about helping to form an organization; Women's civil liberties, the dowry must be abolished for starters," Lara been serious on the issue. Most westerners are touched in some way by what they see, experience and feel. The poverty is highly evident, the infrastructure is derelict.

"What's the best way to make a difference?" I threw out.

"Encourage a women's movement for equal rights," Carolyn suggested. "Perhaps take one person and be the sponsor for their education and let every tourist do the same," Lara coming-up with a personal idea.

Returning to Raj's village concluded our trek. The kids were out in droves to greet us, such joy to simply play with them. The countdown was on for Raj, his wedding approaching. He was twenty-seven, but looked forty, the desert sun does more damage than favours. We threw questions at him about his special day. Raj was positive and philosophical about the up-coming event.
"It is an arranged marriage. My bride-to-be is fifteen years-old, we got engaged when she was eleven."
Sighs of shock from the women.
"Have you ever met?" I asked.
"I don't know how she looks, when she enters the bedroom that will be my first real chance to see her properly."
"What happens if there is no attraction to each other?" coming from Carolyn.
"There has to be, if not in the beginning, then later," Raj shrugged.
"She is so young," Carolyn the brave one to say it.
"I will help her, the relationship will grow slowly," he responded.
In some countryside areas, the level of education is low. The family is happy for a daughter to get married, it can lessen the economic burden.
"At least the crazy idea of a dowry has been abolished. It's against the law, but some people still try to use it," Joe letting us know.
Sitting on a hump backed animal for three days, I almost lost my walking rhythm. Temporarily moving around with a banty-legged stance, suffering in silence with aches in my thighs, not to mention my ass.

In Jaiselmer over a few beers, Jimmy encouraged me to be independent. "Break from us if you wish."
He knows my personality.
Marlene and I discussed visiting Mount Abu, a mountain station on the border of Rajasthan and Gujaret. Splitting-up is healthy, gives people breathing space. Quality time is better than quantity time.
That night as I returned to my guest house I tread on a cow. Street lighting was almost non-existent. I knew the cows were blocking the path, taking shelter for the night, but a heavy darkness was confusing. Problems the next morning, when I went to meet Marlene

23

to catch the 6a.m. bus, literally having to bloody zigzag through about ten cows to reach her residence, on my guard that one would not douse me. As we made our way down the main street, a dog began barking. It soon accumulated, all emerging from different side streets in pursuit of us, seemingly the only two legged creatures alive. Contemplating running, surely they'd be on our heels in a flash. With our backpacks as a hindrance, a brisk pace, a safer option, a rickshaw taxi coming to the rescue as we hailed him. India has many dogs, lots roam freely. On hot days they are lounging in the shade, they come alive after dark. Many are scrawny, can be threatening in packs. Some carry rabies, a deadly disease of the nervous system. I met one unlucky English girl who got bitten by a dog. Her friend with written advice from a local doctor was administering two injections a day.

A thirteen-hour luxury coach journey to Mount Abu, well, I wish. The bus was an old bone-shaker, a rattling bumpy ride. I was hooked on a book, 'Freedom at Midnight,' the story of India's Independence. Jostled about in our seat, unable to hold anything steady, made reading arduous. We divert to playing cards and solving riddles. At the dusty small-town pit-stops we stocked-up on fruits, biscuits, pastries and water. Taking turns to do security with the luggage as the other answered nature's call. Youngsters gazing as cows, goats, dogs, chickens and the colourful peacocks roamed freely. The countryside looked parched, probably not enough rain. On the bus a middle-aged Sikh had his fifteen minutes of gawking every hour. Sitting five seats in front on the opposite side, he'd simply turn around and watch us for long periods.

"Which one is he looking at? It must be the blonde," I teased Marlene.

I made faces at the guy, giving him hand signals. First the victory salute, then the opposite vulgar sign. No reaction, a continuous stare, part of the culture.

We struggled through a cluster of taxi drivers at the Mount Abu bus station. Marlene was referring to the guide book.

"It's about ten minutes walk to the lake."

An elderly man joined us, hopping along playing his string instrument and chanting. I compensated him for his efforts.

In India this is known as a hill-top town. We checked into a guesthouse overlooking the lake, which makes the tourist area very attractive. Each morning I jogged around the lake, in the afternoon we tested our rowing skills.

One evening I was entering the grounds of our residence, teenagers were playing the national sport, cricket.

"Give me that bat there," placing myself in the crease.

The bowler steadied himself, taking a long run-up, throwing a couple of fast balls, which ended up in the yard next door, I guess that's a six each time, he wasn't getting me out.

One youngster asked, "are you from Ireland?"

"Shit, how'd you know that?" I answered.

"Oh we have Irish teachers in our school, you talk like them."

"Is that right, where is this school?"

"Three kilometres from here, it's easy to find."

The following morning I was having breakfast in a café which had a framed recipe of the cocktail 'Irish coffee' hanging on the wall. I enquired to the owner about serving this drink.

"That's a gift sir, from Saint Mary's, the Irish school."

Later I went to find the brothers from the 'ol country.' It was founded two hundred years ago by an Irish clergyman. I got friendly with a local man who said he 'was a helper at the school.' Nobody else was around to talk with, so I accepted his invitation for tea. He was elderly, had lots of knowledge about England.

"I have relatives there, in Birmingham and Leeds," he informed me. Introducing his granddaughter, Ashna, encouraging me to be her friend. Arrangements were made to meet Ashna for a meal the following evening. I was a little shocked by his frankness, but grandparents are normally more lenient than parents.

Initially she was shy, but grew in confidence as the evening progressed. Ashna was an accountant, originally from Kerala, a southern state. We ordered chicken jalfrezi, vegetable curry, pilau rice and Nan bread. It was Friday night, there were no bars or night-clubs, India is such a contrast to western life-styles. By 10p.m. I had escorted her to a taxi to return home.

Over the next few days my senior acquaintance was putting marriage ideas into my head.

"Hundreds of men would jump at this chance, she is perfect."

He wanted a western man to join the family. Relocating to his country was part of the deal.

"You are young, we could get you a job here. Settle down have children. You are wasting the best years of your life, marriage is good," he continued.

"Let me sleep on it."

"You do not like Indian woman," he seem to challenge. "Indian woman you do not like," he repeated.

"No, I do" stuttering, smiling, scratching my head. "Indian women look great, beautiful, we'll talk later," waving goodbye.

On occasions I might avoid a long term relationships. Marriage, the likelihood of this type of responsibility developing, if there is a slight murmur of wedlock, I'd be out-of-there, faster than a Japanese bullet train. Now, in this instance allowing myself to day-dream a little. In parts of this country, talk with a potential female for a couple of hours, 'a nod and wink' from her elders and that could be it, friendship, love, affection, desire, emotion, compatibility and arguments can all come later, perhaps this is a better way.

It's certainly cheaper to what I have been exposed to in my miniscule life. No expensive dinner dates. No late-night cinema movies. No bowling evenings or chit-chat and funny stories in the pub. No silly arguments about where to socialise.

There is no clear winner here. Or is there? Are 'western men' too soft?

The Holika festival had come around, celebrating the destruction of the evil demon, by lighting bonfires. 'Watch out tomorrow, coloured powder and water will be the ammunition, and you cannot call the police,' local people warned. I bought two bags of powder, red and green. With Marlene we headed for the town square at about 10a.m. Not getting very far, suddenly about twenty guys pounced. Water and powder came from all sides. I fired back, their attack seemed to increase. Then Marlene, let out an almighty roar. In a flash, everything ceased. They were stunned by her outburst. Red, green, yellow and blue powder clogged my ears, stuffed my nose, foul tasting in my mouth. A week later I was still washing this shit out of me. That's the way it was all day, locals getting destroyed in these messy battles. For days the coloured powder littered the town.

Sunsets are popular viewing in this country. We headed out the road, joined by Amanda, from Manchester, England.

"A.B.S. another bloody sunset," she called it. A van stopped and

26

offered us a lift, in exchange for a photo. The girls the obvious target, both blonde and blue eyed. Indians love a photo opportunity. Numerous times we were requested to face the lens. I got pulled-into a poesy shot, apparently the weakest link with nine males all sporting the 'manly moustache.' Hundreds of native tourists would gather to watch the sun's gloriously fading light from the valley and disappear behind the hills and mountains. All the people we mixed with were tourists. I don't know where they were during the day, as the town seemed only mildly busy.

We visited a Jain temple, it's carved pillars and figures of elephants in possession. Close-by was the Tejpul temple with it's delightful marble designs. No leather goods could be worn. Shoes, belts, handbags and wrist watches were left at the entrance.

Backpackers make hasty decisions. Marlene had planned to change her return flight to Germany, but the charges were ridiculous. In five days she had to be at New Delhi airport.

I was debating in my mind, should I go see my pensioner friend before leaving Mount Abu. Suddenly I noticed him, watching me as I went to pick-up my washing, clean and neatly folded, several items, at a cost of seventy rupees.

"Come, come" he called out and over chai we had a difference of opinion.

I told him, "if I was to live on the sub-continent, there'd be plenty of arguments with the male dominated society. Women need more liberty, be allowed to choose what they want and I also totally disagree with the caste system" [which is illegal now]. Previously, I kept our conversation light. Now I was direct and he was showing his disappointment in me. We came from different continents, different worlds and it was evident in our ideas on life. I wished him well.

****

Udaipur was our next 'port of call,' necessary to visit so to get a direct train to the capital. A city of four-hundred-thousand inhabitants, built in a romantic setting with a jungle of jumbled streets. It's full of elaborately decorated temples, Palaces and residential buildings. Our base was next to Lake Pichola. I rented a bicycle and each morning I'd spin around and watch the town come to life. Large separate gender groups of children congregating on street corners. In school uniform, blues, greys and purples the most common colours. Open back small canopy trucks packed with juveniles, clutching school bags. Motor rickshaws were in abundance with the same objective. Clicking my camera, the kids never wasting a chance to wave cheerfully. I visited the centre for performing arts. Painting and craft stalls, a mixture of local and international culture. I could hear music in the distance, one man with hand playing drums, another on the tin whistle, the third on the sitar. Four women dressed in tartan blue shawls were dancing in a gracious manner. Joining them at their request, adding a touch of traditional Irish jig, laughter, hand-clapping and feet stamping followed.

Later in the day I went to cash traveller's checks, two banks refused, not enough identification. Third time lucky, but the entire transaction took forty minutes and I was basically the only customer. Pacing around while I waited, two locals entered and departed in quick succession. Three people would handle my request. If one person was absent from their desk, well tough. Diligence seemed to be missing.

I'm sure they're more honest than some Irish bankers, who helped to sink their own country and got away with it. In reference to the financial crisis of 2008, which is current, a bank should lend money in a responsible manner, they failed to do this. Massive over leveraging is totally wrong. The politicians elected by the people allowed this bad behaviour to materialize. But it's not just bad behaviour, it's criminal activity and people involved should be prosecuted. Large fines should be implemented, assets stripped and prison, duplication across Europe in Spain, Portugal, Italy and Greece. The U.K. and U.S. also, who are cheating by printing money, this is capitalism collapsing, just seventeen years after communism failed. So the next time you are browsing the internet, check for the name of your local politician. He's probably doing a bad job, but is still getting paid, by you, the taxpayer. So start a petition for him to resign, spread the word, this puts his job, 'on the line.' Come on people, use your vitality.

The citizens of Iceland showed real courage, some bankers were sent to jail and British investors in Icelandic banks were bailed out by the British government, which means the taxpayer, but not the taxpayers of Iceland.

Some finance people would sell their grandmother for $10, if they could make 20% on the deal, many are not to be trusted.

As I walked out of that bank with my new baksheesh it's necessary for us Europeans to understand, job creation is essential. Six employees were behind the counter, not a woman in sight. In a country that had a woman prime minister, thirty years previous. Why does the female community continue to struggle with basic equality issues, especially in the countryside? Did Indira Gandhi do anything to help? For she was groomed from a young age to lead the country, by her father Nehru, who was the first prime minister of independent India in 1948.

Later Marlene, Amanda from Manchester who became a temporary friend and myself relaxed in a park. "It's too hot, I want to take off this sweater, but I know they will come," stressed Amanda. Ten minutes after her and Marlene doing so, wearing jeans and a vest, the men began to circle. About twelve, of different age groups, planting themselves at close proximity. Others walked passed not really going anywhere.

"Hay guys change into swimsuits, that'll get their temperatures soaring," I joked.

"Maybe that would get us arrested," quipped Marlene.

"It could create heart failure for the older men," responded Amanda. Bare arms and shoulders are rare in this country.

Amanda had slipped a note of 'bon voyage' under my room door. The landlady frowning a day later when enquiring about the girl in the blue pants, discovering by now she'd probably be in Jaipur, fourteen hours away. Five meals and two nights of accommodation unpaid, the sweet gabby blond did a runner.

Sometimes after dark there can be a void, what shall we do now? With night-clubs and bars almost non-existent, to play cards or a house board game, read or smoke a pipe. Alternatively, go to a restaurant, chat with other travellers, drink beer if it's available and watch Octopussy, a James Bond film made in this town. Then watch the Kingfisher beer bottles been snatched from the table with mumbled apologies, moments later gray suited men would enter. We wondered, are they off-duty police or government officials? These alcohol incidents happened in three different towns, perhaps, no license to sell lager.

Time was of the essence for Marlene, so she departed on a north bound train to the capital. Taking refuge from the mid-day heat in an Indian eatery, I exchanged pleasantries with patrons at the next table. Their questions came thick and fast about my country, job and family. They were army officers, having a break from border security.

"India doesn't have enemies, surely military activity is minimal," I tested.

"Oh no sir," with shock expressions. "We have many problems. Pakistan is a short drive from our station in Jaisalmer. We must be ready for any hostile movement. Look at the difficulties in Kashmir, up in the north."

"Come on guys, what about a peace treaty?"

"Sir, Pakistan will not agree, we have tried for many years." Geographically, Kashmir is divided between Pakistan and India. Today there are still problems in this region. Both countries want total control of this state. Miniature battles do occur with neither side gaining. Also some people want Kashmir to be totally independent. I was currently reading about India's independence and Pakistan becoming a country. Lord Mountbatten, the viceroy of India at that time is portrayed as heroic, courageous and honourable in the book. But in reality, another fine mess was created by British imperialism. Pakistan for the Muslims. India for the Hindus and Sikhs. Thousands were killed as they senselessly fought against each other making their way to their own side of the border. Outside the restaurant a vociferous crowd was gathering, we all went to have a look, a bull fight was in progress. No matador flashing red signals in opposition here. A straight head to head battle between two bulls. The crowd scurrying into shops, behind parked cars and climbing walls. Roars and cheers as they watched from a safer location. Then large sticks, aggressive whacks needed to separate them.

"The black one is a wild bull from the countryside," a local explained.

In a furious mood, not knowing which way he should turn next, the Black Country bull continued to be aggressive, but slowly and surely he was enticed to a non-residential side-street, the masses keeping a distance. A truck was parked to block his return to busy pedestrian areas, so he made his way to waste land by the lake.

As I returned to my lodgings, a teenager approached me.

"Ten rupees for a shoe-shine mister."

"Ah, tomorrow, I'll see ya tomorrow."

"Only ten rupees, sir. I will make them beautiful," the young lad been persistent.

"I have no time now, we can meet tomorrow," refusing politely.

"You promise."

"Yea, yea, I promise."

"O.k. I will be waiting."

Arrangements had been made to meet my Irish buddies between March 27th-29th in New Delhi. The following day I collected my train ticket at a clothing store cum travel agent cum insurance office. Strolling around, killing time until my 4:30p.m. departure.

A young shoe-shiner began pestering me and he continued for about two hundred yards. I settled on the steps of a temple and let him play his trade. But wouldn't you know it, the shoe-shiner from the previous day arrived on the scene. "No, no, no you promised," he called out.

"You promised, you broke your promise."

Throwing his box of polish equipment on the ground, close to tears, he began to argue with my current shiner.

I had to be a calming influence, a boot for each, an extra payment to keep everyone happy.

I purchased mineral water, salted biscuits and fruits for the journey. The department of ticket sales with Indian Railways normally place foreigners seated together if travelling in the same class, a German named Franz was in the opposite bunk. We exchanged stories and ideas, shared food and information.

Franz was shuffling and riffling in the middle of the night, making his exit. Also the food vendors entering at every station were not wasting an opportunity to break the night silence. Sleep is always interrupted.

The neighbouring bunks were alive and vigorous by 7a.m. If you can't beat them, join them. A group of nine post office workers were on their way to New Delhi for a training program. Once again the men overwhelming the opposite sex, Sonal representing the minority. Sanjay was the joker of the pack, ranting off about his country.

31

"We can't play sports, only Cricket, it's an English game. We all do the same things."

This guy had me laughing, Ravi unnecessarily explaining.

"Look Sean, our hairstyles are the same. Our clothes the same colour, look, look."

There certainly was a lack of variety, brown and beige were very dominant.

"The women dress beautiful," I countered.

"Hay, hay" coming from Sonal as she clapped with approval.

I hopped off the train to buy food from a platform vendor.

"Two of them please," pointing at vegetable wrapped dosas.

They're looking at me, there's a strange white guy among us.

"Oh shit," I looked round, the train was moving again. I had to make a run for it, jumping-on about four carriages down, without my food. [I always wanted to do that but it was not funny at the time] It was not a scheduled stop.

'Gee, I hope no one goes through my luggage.' Twenty minutes later the locomotive comes to a halt, I walked up the track to my carriage, the extrovert Sanjay coming to greet me.

"We were watching your bags."

"Cheers mate, I hope not too closely."

"What."

"Nothing, my friend."

Slum land communities, border the railway lines on the outskirts of the capital. Open brick huts with galvanized roofs. Rubbish strewn, malnourished kids playing among the debris. Smoke hangs in the air, steam rising from large boiling pots.

Arrival time almost two hours late, it didn't matter.

****

Back in Delhi, I walked through the station and along the dusty Paraganj district. A group carrying a long blanket were coming towards me, people were moving to the side. Then I realized, they were lepers, looking for donations. They looked sickly, skinny with bad skin. I threw money onto the blanket, as many did. Not willing to go near because of my ignorance of this disease.

I entered Ravi's guesthouse asking about vacancies, this was the nominated meeting point with my Irish buddies. The receptionist led the way to the second floor to show me a room. He knocked on the door, a voice rang-out, an exchange of words in Hindi.

'This room should be empty,' I'm thinking.

The receptionist opened the unlocked door, a man rose from the double bed.

"Who's this guy?" I quizzed sharply.

"That's New Delhi police," the receptionist answered meekly.

"Oh, O.K." not sure how to respond.

He quickly dressed and headed off down the stairs.

Napping on a hot afternoon, skiving on the job, this copper.

"The room is ready sir, here is your key."

I wasn't sure what to do, laugh or get angry.

"How many police come to this room?"

"Only onetime sir, he was feeling unwell sir."

I just smiled to myself, "can I have a room on another floor please."

"No problem sir, I will get the key."

My new room was not quite done, so I helped him change the sheets and pillow cases, an extended run with the vacuum, while he cleaned the bathroom. I thought about moving to another guesthouse, but didn't want to miss my friends.

The British created the western-style area of New Delhi. In 1911 they made it the new capital replacing Calcutta. It starts at Connaught Square, embassies, office and government buildings, tree lined residential roads. It's not without shanty towns, rural folk arriving for a better life. Setting-up home where space allows, sadly they soon become slums.

I went on a magnificent sight-seeing bus tour, every stop was vastly interesting. We visited the Humayun tomb, a sixteenth century Moghal emperor. Also the Indian Gate originally built in memory of British and Indian soldiers killed in world war one. [Similar looking to the Arc de Triomphe in Paris] Later a monument of India's Unknown Soldier was added. Nearby locals played cricket, it was the only sport I seen here.

Bahai Temple, others call it the Lotus Temple. The Lotus flower is the symbol of purity in this country. Immaculate gardens and flower beds. The roof of the buildings has two layers. Nine white marble petals that point to heaven and nine petals that conceal the entrance. It has similarities to the Opera house in Sydney.

"What do you think sir," a native asked as we stood in line waiting to enter. "It's beautiful, but how much did this cost. Look over there," I pointed to derelict buildings where washing was hanging to dry and kids played.

"I'm not sure if it was money well spent."

"I agree," a lady behind joining the conversation, "Perhaps a hospital would have been more appropriate," she added.

The native went from a proud smile to a flustered frustrated expression. Soon we were inside, observance was necessary. No religious icons, just wooden pews and copies of Holy Scriptures. One guy told me, "it is a place for all denominations to pray." Before driving to each site, the guide would take the microphone at the top of the bus and explain the next venue. After the Lotus temple I got hold of the mic and told the crew, "we are now off to the Shamrock Irish bar and we are staying there for the rest of the day." Loud applause and cheering went up, the guide give me that frowned looked.

Bangla Sahib Gurdwara was the next stop, a Sikh temple. Shoes and socks had to be removed before entering. Many of the Sikhs were refugees from Pakistan which became a country in 1947. It's a white building topped with a gold onion dome. It stands on the site where Guru Hari Krishan distributed sanctified water to the sick. Worshippers use jugs of water today.

In the afternoon the bus drove across town to 'Old Delhi,' known as the capital of Muslim India, a legacy of monuments, mosques and forts. In a constant state of decay, Lal Qila [Red Fort] stands in magnificence, a reminder of Moghal power. Inside the main gate a collection of palaces, a museum, gardens and courts. Across the street is Chandni Chowk, we walked slowly through the area and absorbed the activity in close proximity. Taxis, private cars, bicycles, rickshaws, cows, dogs, bullock carts and pedestrians trudge through.

I watched an ear cleaner, squatting, using a plastic item about the length of a pen. Pushing it into his customer's ear, poking and twisting roughly, it seems a bad idea. He finishes and motions for me to take a seat on a crate.

"That thing is dirty, it's not clean," pointing at his plastic utensil.
He rubs it on his long robe.
"Look, cleannn."
He rubs it again, "very cleannn sir."
I burst out laughing, almost apologetically, no sterilizing here.
Dentists and doctors attend patients in small offices. Shoe repairmen
ply their trade. Chai sellers, music, book, incense and clothing
vendors busily haggle with customers. Space is used, every nook and
cranny is occupied, congestion an understatement.
I'm comfortable with this but it's not for everyone. A first time
visitor can be overwhelmed by the sheer number of natives. One
English tourist on the bus was going home after one week into a two
month holiday. "I hate this place, my space is invaded all the time,"
she moaned. I tried to convince her to stay and make friends.
She was not interested, "I fly out tomorrow."
The Janu Masjid is spectacular, an Islamic mosque from the
Moghals era also, pillared corridors and domed pavilions.
"Thousands gather in the courtyard on Fridays to pray," the guide
told me. In one corner the marbled footprints of the prophet
Mohammed are installed.
For me, the most touching moment of this informative day was the
Raj Ghat, a national shrine to the father of this country, Mahatma
Gandhi. A black marble slab slightly raised depicts his cremation
point. Droves of tourists and pilgrims pay their respects, shoes must
be removed. An eternal flame, the words, Hai Ram [oh god] are
inscribed, believed to be Gandhi's last words. Killed by a Hindu
fanatic, Vinayak Nathuram Godse in 1948, just weeks before this
country's independence. Nearby are the cremation sites of two other
assassinated heads of state, Indira Gandhi and her son Rajiv, no
relation to Mahatma. All this is situated in the same park.

I returned to my lodgings, relaxed, stretched out on the bed. My day-
dreaming interrupted by a loud knock on the door. It was Joe and
Carolyn, delighted to see them again.
"Let's go Sean, I can get tickets for the train tomorrow night.
Jimmy's gone to Kathmandu with a couple of Scousers," [Liverpool
folk].
We had to play by the rules, buying rail tickets one day in advance.
It was after 5p.m., the official ticket office was closed. Joe had paid

extra baksheesh to a travel agent where I would drop off my passport.

"Everything will be ready tomorrow morning at eleven."

"Don't sell that document to a friend," I joked.

"I can get you twenty thousand rupees for this," he shot back.

"Fifty thousand and we have a deal," I tested.

"British documents are much cheaper sir," he responded. Not sure if he was serious. "Well, they would be because they have a much higher population. Besides that's like having gold-dust, think about my price," I shouted as I shut the door.

We returned to the Ravi guesthouse. Looking down from a third floor balcony, a group of locals had congregated below.

"That guy in the brown is always drunk, I know him from staying here before. Look at him, he's arguing again," Joe informing. One man was making a wooden bed frame. I counted twelve others mingling around, watching, a typical local scene. Brown shirt man was upsetting the group, overweight with a rough complexion.

"We should throw a bucket of water down on him," I lightly suggested.

"Let's do it, I saw a bucket on the roof earlier," Joe agreeing.

"No, no" protested Carolyn, who headed off to the night-market on seeing we were serious.

We had a plan; Joe went to the roof and waited for the right moment. I was on the street in close proximity to the congregation. I offered brown shirt a cigarette, as I began puffing on one myself. He came towards me and happily accepted, giving him a light. Then I offered the others a smoke, there were two takers. Then the water came gushing down, it was a direct hit. The main group jeered, laughed and clapped, I didn't show any reaction. Brown shirt was fuming, looking around, shaking his fist and mumbling. Joe was safely back in my room with the door locked. The laughter continued, neighbouring shop-owners emerged, curious about the incident. Brown shirt quietly retreated to a corner.

It was Carolyn's last night, so we went to the German Bakery, next to hotel Vishal, popular with Israelis. Noticing my Irish football shirt, a bearded guy joined us. Pat, a Dubliner had travelled south from Dharamsala.

"What's the craic Pat, how is your trip going," I asked.

"It's been brilliant, until last Monday, then some fucker robbed me."

"Oh shit, what happened?"

"An overnight train to Delhi from up north, I was sleeping on the bottom bunk, I heard some ruffling. By the time I realized it, my small bag was gone. Passport, flight tickets, travellers checks, a bit of cash, all gone"

"Are you all right for money," showing my concern.

"Yea, no bother lads. I was a bit desperate for a few days, but the Irish embassy gave me two hundred quid."

"Hay man, that's pretty good, we'll tap them ourselves" laughed Joe.

"It's not a gift, it's a loan. I was pissed-off big time when it happened, but now everything is sorted out. I'll have a new passport in a week. The travellers checks are coming through and I have made a police report. There's no hassle now, I'm over the annoyance. I'm actually celebrating, do you want some vodka? Of course you do, try this," lowering his voice.

The German bakery had no license to sell alcohol. We bought soft drinks. Quietly 'beardie Pat' topped up our plastic cups.

The following day Carolyn was heading for the airport. Not before last minute gift shopping. Joe and I dropped off stuff in a luggage storage shop.

Now our backpacks were considerably lighter. We were on our way, to Nepal. The overnight train was packed, every bunk occupied. Three Dutch women were our foreign company, tall and perfect linguistically. Two of them had just recovered from a week of 'Delhi belly.' They were planning to trek the Annapurna circuit in Nepal. I was ignorant about Nepal, had done no research and had not browsed through a guide book. My first day in India, Jimmy commented on visiting Nepal in late March, I had given it little thought.

When asked, what were my plans for this country, 'the roof of the world.'

"Oh maybe white-water-rafting, cycling, swimming, some socializing," I replied.

"So, no trekking" Nadine asked, in her national orange jersey.

"Trekking, that sounds like hard work."

"You should have gone to Ibiza," giggles all round.

"O.K. if the mountains are full of fun-loving people like you guys, I'll be a sherpa."

Indian police passed through three times, whispering to us 'watch your bags, be careful.' By 6a.m. daily commuters were entering the train. A card school had developed in our compartment. They were the happiest morning riders I have ever seen, as I eyed a game called 'Chance' from my top bunk. I could not quite follow, there was a constant exchange of jokes.

On arriving at Gorakhpur, a sea of people was on the move.

"Where's the border," I asked Joe.

"Are you stupid, we're still three hours away, we have to take a bus."

We walked for several minutes before settling at the 'Travellers café,' Joe inquired about bus tickets to Nepal.

"You can buy ticket all the way to Kathmandu," the waiter informed. We were taking no chances, sometimes when you cross the border into a new country, the new bus company will not accept your ticket. We just paid for the ride to the border, an hour to wait for the next departure. So I had curd, with vegetables wrapped in roti bread.

A rickety old vehicle would take us to the Nepalese frontier. The countryside looked dry and dusty. After one hour it was filled to capacity, several women were standing. I offered my seat to one holding a child. She refused, as others did, looking embarrassed.

"Them guys are laughing at you," Joe observed.

Was this another example of male chauvinism?

Chicken Masala

Chicken: cut into small pieces.
2 green Chillies, 5 flakes garlic, 1tsp. red Chilli powder.
1 tblsp. Chopped ginger, 2 medium size chopped onion.
1 tsp. roasted cumin seed powder, 10 black powder corns.
Salt to taste, 1 tblsp. Vinegar,
1 tblsp. Chopped coriander leaves.
Grind the green Chillies, garlic, ginger, cumin seeds, pepper corns, red chilli powder, onions with the salt and vinegar.
Apply over chicken and marinate for one hour.
Heat oil in a pan and add the chicken, fry for two minutes.
Add a little water and cook chicken until it is done and the oil floats on top.

Serve hot, garnished with chopped coriander leaves.

Nepal

'Last stop' shouted the bus porter, as he climbed onto the roof and unloaded the luggage, we tipped as expected. Parked roadside were several buses, taxis and trucks with their orange coloured cabin's decorated with Indian gods. As we walked about a half-kilometre to the Nepalese border on a bustling stretch of road with many shops and restaurants. I looked to my right, a uniformed man was shouting at us.

"Come, come" waving his arm.

"Ah, that must be immigration" says Joe.

An exit stamp was necessary, otherwise someone would kick-up a fuss later. Then we saw the sign ahead in blue and white, 'Indian border ends' in bilingual, my first time crossing a land border on foot. We stopped for a few moments and joked about the situation.

"Where is the actual borderline?" I walked ten yards ahead of Joe.

"I think I'm in Nepal now, hurry-up you're still in India."

"Stay cool, I'll be there in a couple of days," he shot back.

Up a side street was the Nepalese visa office. A payment of thirty U.S. dollars for a thirty-day visa, plus two photos, mine been a bit crumpled, reluctantly accepted for our new country.

Right, we're on the loose in a new frontier, accommodation our first priority.

"Hello, Nameste," [a Nepalese greeting with hands joined] the young lady greeted us at 'Border Guesthouse.' A one night stay was sufficient, they arranged our bus tickets for the journey to Kathmandu, the capital.

"We have two buses tomorrow morning, one at 7:30, and one at 8:30, which would you like?"

"8:30 would be good," Joe decided.

"Where's the mountains?" been sarcastic with Joe, this been a flat area. "Maybe the guide books are lying," I continued, as we went head to head in checkers.

"Shut-up Sean, I know you're trying to put-me-off my game."

Just one-hundred yards across the border and we could see that beer was more readily available.

Early morning banging on our room door had me starting the day in a foul mood. "There is only one bus today at 7:30, one bus to Kathmandu, it go 7:30," the porter was shouting. Joe, already showered and dressed was not bothered.

"To hell with them, I'm not hurrying," I snapped, barely dressed I stumbled into the dining room to order breakfast.

Joe popped his head in, "I'll tell the driver to wait for you, hurry-up."

"Get some stuff for the journey," I shouted.

Stuffing my backpack, quickly scanning the room, leaving nothing behind. Smoke was filtering through from the kitchen. A plate arrived with mangled eggs, sprinkles of ash, no toast. Gulping down the tea, I rushed off down the road to the waiting bus with it's engine running, helping the porter to load my backpack onto the roof rack.

"Sit there," the driver motioned, pointing to the front seat. There was no other choice, it was full to capacity. The first hour of the journey many more boarded, all locals, standing room only. No one accepted my offer to take my seat. The girl next to me, Kristen, is German. We chatted freely on general topics, the previous year she had visited Ireland.

"We stayed in Dundalk," she said.

"No kidding, that's where I'm from," I responded.

"Blackrock was the area, by the sea." she continued.

"Are you serious, I grew-up there, have you friends in Blackrock?"

"We didn't know anyone in Ireland. We flew into Belfast and then went straight to Dundalk. We were drinking in a pub, it was getting late, so we asked the barman where we could stay. He asked this man, who had just come into the pub, the man offered us a room at his house, Tony Sharkey." Taking out her notebook, showing me the address.

"Shit, I don't believe this, I know Tony Sharkey."

"We enjoyed ourselves, Tony took us for breakfast at the golf club looking out at the water and the mountains. He was great, so helpful," Kristen speaking fondly.

"This is unbelievable, I will send him a postcard."

A constant drizzle didn't dampen our spirits. The road twisted and turned through small towns and villages. Rice planted terraces, a healthy green, dominating the mountain hillsides. Stone wall houses, galvanized roofs. At one of our pit-stops, nature was calling, so Joe went behind a restaurant, moments later he came running out been chased by two dogs and a chef, he can move when he really wants to.

"You picked the wrong building, go behind them trees over there," I stammered through the laughter.

The porter seemed to stick to his ritual of opening the passenger door and make a deep throat noise before spitting, it was quite frequent, an unpleasant habit.

After thirteen hours we reach a dark, cold and wet Kathmandu. Helping the porter to unload the luggage from the rooftop, we hailed a taxi for Freak street, famous from the sixties, assisting Kristen locate a room before we settled for a cheap space, consisting of two single beds, a cement floor with no mats, invisible curtains, bright yellowish plastered walls. Not even a nail on the door to hang your jacket.

Seven weeks in India and I managed to avoid 'Delhi belly,' my first night in Nepal and I was in trouble. We ate in a restaurant that was clean and tidy, I ordered rice and vegetables, but the dish was served with meat mixed through. I did question the risks with Joe, but observations convinced us not to be so cautious. That night it was freezing, I awoke several times, the following morning I had dysentery.

We moved to more liveable surroundings, the Kathmandu hotel, wood panelling, carpet, thick curtains, closets, table and chairs, a balcony, television, albeit black and white, but we certainly were not intending to become couch potatoes.

We visited the General Post Office, Jimmy said he'd leave a sealed envelope of his whereabouts at the Poste Restante counter. The building was flooded, three days of rain. Stepping on sand bags and cement blocks to avoid wet feet, inadequate drainage and this was not the rainy season. We zig-zag our way through, there was lots of mail at the Poste Restante desk, but no message for us, a new meaning to sea-mail.

"I'm returning to India if this weather doesn't change," I moaned to Joe. "It's making me miserable too."

But it was almost as if the gods were listening. The following day, the temperature increased dramatically, shorts and tee-shirts again. Joe and I headed for Thamel, a tourist area of the city with bars, cafes and trekking shops. As we rode on the back of a bicycle rickshaw taxi, suddenly we noticed Jimmy, sitting on a wall with other nomads. We danced and jumped around in exhilaration, the locals must have thought we were bonkers. It was a team again, but for how long?

A night out had been arranged with other bus passengers. The 'Tom and Jerry' pub was nominated from the guide book, an added bonus was Jimmy and his new buddies. A drink-up in a real bar, the first for many weeks, an accumulation of twenty-three travellers; French, Israeli, Canadian, English, Dutch and ourselves. Jimmy and Joe were in top form, excited to see Bonnie and Jane from London. They had met earlier in Jaipur, India, sparks were definitely developing, a social night at minimal cost. The three of us were the last patrons to exit. Bicycle rickshaw taxis waited outside for customers, we squeezed aboard really made for two. As we rode across town the eerie silence broken by dogs barking, also by Jimmy's heavy laughter. As we approached Freak street, where Jimmy had a room also, he nudged me to do a runner, which we did, darting off down narrow side streets. The joke was on Joe, seated in the middle, who had to pay.

Kathmandu had many western food menus; Porridge, cereals, eggs, any style, Pizza, hamburgers, pasta, American style sandwiches. Complacency can develop, many travellers were getting stomach bugs, being less cautious with food after leaving India. But after a few days I noticed the real problem, power failures, normally in the afternoon, for about two hours. So meats turn sour in refrigerators but will still be served on your plate.

Jimmy began booking a four-day rafting trip. But when I realized that it was mainly couples, I opted out.

"What are you going to do, look we are breaking-up again," he protested.

"You don't expect me to go on a Mister And Misses trip," I responded.

"It's not really, you'll be fine."

"I know I'll be fine, because I won't be there. We can meet next week in that place," looking at a map. "Pokhara, is that where we go next?" I quizzed.

"We're apart more than we are together," Jimmy moaned.

As we strolled through Durbar Square, a young guide offered his assistance. I accepted, opposing Jimmy's reluctance.

"You can pay him," he snapped.

"Well, we don't really know what we're looking at, we might learn something."

We entered the old royal palace. A statue of the monkey god Kanumen stands covered in red paste called sindar, used for decorating idols. Inside I saw a sculpture, a Vishnu incarnation of the man-lion Narasingh, tearing apart a demon. The central courtyard was the setting for king Birendra's coronation in the1970's. Carved windows and doors with a meticulous finish. A series of portraits, Shesh kings from passed eras. This is a Tribhuwan museum, a collection of memorabilia. dedicated to the reign of more recent kings from who some people believe was responsible for opening Nepal in 1951 to the outside world after the fall of the Rama regime.

Back in the open square the guide continued talking. Now explaining about the Kumari Chowk. Entering into its courtyard, he shouted. A young girl appeared flirtingly on the second floor balcony for about five seconds. With a cosmetic complexion, but surely her handlers are creating this image.

"Please, please no camera," the guide appealed.

"This is Kathmandu's living goddess." Pouting her head like a spoiled brat. A prepubescent girl worshipped as a living incarnation of Durga, a demon slaying Hindu goddess.

Elders interview hundreds of Skakya girls of Buddhist background aged between three and five years old, who have thirty-two signs. The finalist are placed in a dark room and scared by severed Buffalo heads, also men in demon masks. If they can identify belongings of previous Kumari's and your horoscope does not clash with kings, your chances are good on winning.

The goddess is only allowed outside in festivals. Her feet must never touch the ground, retiring age comes when she menstruates as the spirit Durga leaves. A pension is awarded, but finding a husband could be difficult, for tradition has it that marrying an ex-Kumari, one can have a short life. It all sounds a bit spooky, but not to them. Many statues and stepped platforms litter Durbar square. Pagoda roofed pavilions, temples and gods, each has its own story. Locals congregate, Sadhus pray and look for offerings of money in return for a blessing.

That evening I was chatting and joking with two Israeli women. They were off trekking the next morning and invited me to join them. This is what I enjoy, spontaneous decisions, so the week ahead was planned. The lads and I were off, in different directions.

****

We met at 7a.m. and that was it, with the clothes on my back and a few duds in a bag, a taxi ride of twenty minutes to Sundarijal, the starting point. Without any preparation I was off trekking in the Himalayas, the roof of the world. The highest I've ever climbed is a Chestnut tree, with the local landowner shouting at me to "get out,' grabbing a few nuts to play conquers with my teenage buddies. This was a different league, a number of days hiking through mountains. As the taxi dropped us off, three other small groups were starting also. They certainly didn't look like seasoned mountaineers.
"But wait," I said to Tammy and Eva, "let's have a quick breakfast." Tea and pastry was the best I could muster from the local shop. I wanted to begin in a more meaningful way, trying to boost myself mentally, I noticed they had Kingfisher beer, so one each and a toast. 'NO PAIN, NO GAIN, SO WHAT THE HECK, LETS HIT THE TREK."

We were advised to travel light, drink water constantly and don't allow yourself to go hungry. One hour into the trek I was knackered. We came upon steps, hundreds of them. Counting, then losing my concentration. We passed stone wall houses with small gardens, a beautiful setting on the lower part of the mountains, but highly stressful for older folk.
A Nepalese man joined us, he looked drunk. I tried communicating but he didn't understand. We passed a number of groups of other trekkers, most were resting. They in-turn went by us as we relaxed and had lunch of rice, vegetables and curry. We later see the drunken man, asleep. I wake him, he stumbles to his feet and straddles along, then stopping at a house, the family he seems to know.
We come to a fork in the path, which way now?
"Sit down and wait for someone to come," suggests Tammy.

Germans arrive and point the way. I questioned their choice of direction. "We have maps and we are mountaineers."

Tammy was constantly falling behind, we slowed considerably for her benefit. Finally reaching the summit of this particular mountain, the signpost read: Cheng 1000 meters. The finish line was in-sight, a small cluster of buildings and a group of tents. I stumbled and fell at the first bench, clowning around.

"Is the bar open yet?" I asked four women who we had exchanged pleasantries earlier in the day, they were from Norway, Germany, Holland and America.

"My map says there is a pizza shop in this village, can I telephone an order?" The Europeans laughed, but Jennifer from Boston, "are you serious, that's awesome."

"What are you having? Pepperoni, Hawaiian." continuing to joke. The laughter continued, she didn't know how to take me.

It was a hectic first day, climbing 2500 meters. People were tired but jubilant. I ordered soup and bread, an hour later I was queasy. The village was allocated electricity from 6p.m. to 9pm. I rested in a room shared with my Israeli friends, there was no choice, each building had full occupancy. A few hours later I joined a large gang in the dining room for supper. A few senior women entered, looking properly dressed in water-proofing pants and jackets, miner's flashlight strap to their forehead. Of course they were Germans, organized. Staying quiet and listening to other conversations, I grew weaker and withdrew to my bed.

The next morning I rose early. The campers were packing-up, four teachers and twenty-two students.

"Fourteen in our group have been ill, because of this, yesterday was a rest day. It's a real challenge to keep healthy up here," one teacher told me.

Martha, from the girl group came to me.

"I looked at you last night, you were very white. I'm so sorry, I can tell, I'm a nurse," looking at me closely.

"We will go now," she hugged and wished me well.

I thanked her for the consideration, a little bit of tender loving can go a long way.

I informed my Israeli companions to continue without me. But Tammy had just returned from the toilet and collapsed in a heap.

"I didn't sleep after dinner last night, I have stomach pains. I feel sick."

I brought tea and toast to the room for the girls, then went for a walk.
I came upon a group of trekkers preparing for another day of pain.
"The worst is over, downhill from here, our last day." one said.
They looked rough and weary, aching feet and lip sores, looking like
they had not washed for months.
"Eat plenty of Tibetan bread, they have to bake it fresh," an Aussie
advised.
That evening my health had not improved. The only change in our
team, Eva had a stomach bug. We abandoned any thought of
completing this trek. One more day in Cheng and then return to the
capital was the new plan. We visited local villages in the vicinity, I
could see the poverty in the people, dirty clothes, no hot running
water. Minimum electricity, two room houses with mud floors,
sparse furniture. We played with the kids, bought them sweets and
biscuits, their feet hardened from the lack of footwear.
Light clouds floated below us. White snow peaks, purple, grey and
greens the obvious colours as we look out across these ultimate
highlands. There is beauty, and hardship in these mountains.
The next day, a three-hour decent had us back on level ground. What
we did not anticipate was the National transport strike. No buses or
taxis were running. There was literally no traffic on the roads. We
asked a group of men to drive us to Kathmandu for a fee. They all
refused.
"There is a strike," one said. "We must support this strike. It's only
one day, nobody is to drive, only in an emergency. You must
understand."
"Yes, no problem," I answered.
We continued walking, asking other locals further down the road for
a taxi. They were all defiant, "sorry, no drive today, big strike
today."
A short while later we met a large group of teenage girls, about one
hundred. We stopped to talk, they were on a school outing. The class
leader spoke with confidence. "We are from Tibet, do you know this
country? We have lost it to China, which is next door. We hope to
get it back one day. Our school is over there," pointing across the
fields.
"It was built by 'Save Our Soul' a German charity," she continued.
I wished them luck, as they posed for a couple of photos.

"Please do not forget us," she shouted.

Shortly after, I stopped at a guesthouse. This was enough walking for one day. The girls were adamant on continuing to the capital. Hugs and high-fives, then off they went. As they drifted into the distance with the misty rain, I got comfortable on the porch, sipping a beer with three kids studying me. Exhausted, it was such a relief to rest my weary limbs. A tranquil setting on the flat green fields stretching to the edge of the mountains. I admired the solidarity in this strike, all drivers sticking together, something that is missing all too often in westernized societies.

The following day, courtesy of an early morning taxi, I had one chore in Kathmandu, buying a bus ticket my only priority. Pokhara, the country's second largest town was the next 'port of call.' Cruising in a luxury coach on a six lane motorway, well, not really, that could be safe and mundane. The Prithvi highway links the two cities. Twists and snake-like in parts. Occasionally, it offers mouth watering views. But most of the journey stays in the lower valleys. It's well maintained for possibly more industrial development. A twenty-nine seated medium bus. Leg room was tight, I was lucky enough to be seated in the middle of the back row, the only person who could literally stretch out. It certainly was not designed to carry western tourists, Karl, a Bayern Munich football supporter and myself, the only folk trying to be humorous, the others dull and grim, like wet dish cloths, anchored, as if this was an incarceration transfer to maximum security. Three times we exited this nineteen century rolling contraption. Accidents, but not serious; trucks, partially blocking the road. One with a broken axel, the driver jumped on the bus for a ride to a garage, two-mile down the road. Another losing part of its scrap metal load, which Karl, the bus-driver and myself helped to move and the third occasion, a tire blow-out.

In Pokhara the bus station was an open field, a little isolated. Surely, specifically to create income for the local cabbies, a distance of about three kilometres from the tourist strip.

"Taxi, take me to the Greenpeace guest house," the nominated meeting point by Jimmy and Joe.

"It's by the lake, at the quiet side," I tell the cabbie. I had no idea, but that was the directions from our 'Scouser' friends.

Turning off the road, onto a dirt track which certainly was not for cars, I walked the last two hundred yards. Would I have to prove to be an environmentalist? It was a full house. Looking through the guest list book, the lads names were nowhere to be seen.

I checked into the 'Lakeside guest house' near-by, I was the only customer. The owner's sixteen year old daughter and her friend cooking my meals, wanting to talk to me at every opportunity.

"We hope someday to marry a tourist. Our parents will want us to get married soon," they would whisper.

"You are too young for marriage," I said.

"No, we are ready. this is the Nepalese way. But we want to go to another country, in Europe. It will be better there."

The following morning I was on the roof, soaking up the sun. I spotted familiar folk passing-by. Throwing stones but not aiming directly at them. Calling out nicknames and hiding, it was Jimmy and Joe. Jimmy been elated to see me, "Jane's doing my head-in," talking easy.

"In two days they fly to Vietnam. Joe is getting along great with Bonnie. You're my saviour, I can't take this shit anymore," he stressed. I laughed.

"Shush, they'll know we're talking about them."

The tourist area of Pokhara was basically a long street of about one kilometre with a number of short side streets. Consisting of trekking and rafting agents, guesthouses and two bars, clothing shops with a sewing machine always in action, embroidered tee-shirts were particularly impressive.

Lake Phewa Tal and the surrounding mountains made it picturesque. Lots of rowing boats for hire but not a life-jacket in sight. Cycling, swimming, short trekking trips and socializing in the bars after dark over the next few days were the criteria.

On Friday Joe was love-sick, his girlfriend hitting the beaches of south-east Asia. Jimmy was a barrel of laughs, full to the brim, a transformation. Displaying his bossy qualities again, planning the next adventure.

"The Annapurna Base Camp, it supposed to be great, this time we stick together," he insisted.

A visit to a government office was necessary for permits, for the trek. As we filled-in the appropriate forms, we chatted with Dutch and Aussies, who giggled as Jimmy and I argued.

"I'm short of cash, gimme a lend of eight hundred rupees to pay for this permit,"

"Look, you already owe me seventeen hundred," Jimmy snarled back.

"Ah, just gimme eight more and then I'll owe you two and a half grand."

"You better change them traveller's checks and pay me back soon."

We popped in for lunch, it would be a three-hour wait for the permits. I ordered rice and buffalo curry. It was not cooked, the rice was hard. I explained to the waiter, but he ignored my problem.

"Taste this," I said to the lads.

"You'll have stomach cramps with that," Joe warned.

I signalled to the waiter, he looked but ignored me. A few minutes later I had him at the table, explaining the situation. He shrugged his shoulders and walked off.

O.K. I've tried the nice way, so I entered the kitchen and planked the plate for all the cooks to see.

"Sorry, but this is not cooked guys."

They looked totally stunned by a customer entering their territory. I just turned and walked out going to the restaurant next door.

"Good man Sean, you tell em," Joe sniggering.

Between the cock crowing and the family dog barking I was normally awake much earlier than anticipated. Moving to another guesthouse didn't exactly solve the problem. At my new residence an early morning argument at the front desk had me lying awake waiting for the bloody alarm clock to go off. A loud mouthed American, virulent about his clothing.

"Look at these pants, you destroyed them in the wash. I'm not paying the room bill. You know how much I paid for these back home, much more than this bill. Now you have messed them up, this is ridiculous. What did you use? What can I do with these now? I'm not paying any money, this is unbelievable," refusing to pay the accommodation and cleaning charge.

In my opinion he was naïve, this is a third-world country. The majority of homes do not have washing machines, dry cleaning facilities are almost non-existent. The young porter probably used a bristle brush, scrubbing too vigorously. Simply hand wash your own important clothing is the safe option.

I stuffed my bag with one pair of jeans, tracksuit bottoms as pyjamas, three tee-shirts, one for sleeping, socks, underwear and a heavy sweater for the cold temperatures in early morning and late evening. Also a sleeping bag, water, salted biscuits and peel fruits of bananas and oranges. A little bit more organized this time, than the previous trip into the mountains.

I met with my Irish buddies, who stayed in a different guest house, for breakfast. We had porridge with cinnamon, then eggs, toast and tea at a small family business of three dining tables.

A Dutch couple seemed to cast a shadow over Joe's enthusiasm, warning about avalanches on the higher peaks, as the snow melted. He was adamantly refusing to join us for this trek. He had hinted the night before but I didn't take him seriously. Now, there was no changing his mind.

****

We rode on the roof-top of a bus, forty minutes to Phedi, where the trek would start. We helped Annette from Finland to climb aboard. She had a keen interest in Irish music, playing a few tunes with her tin whistle and I vocalizing a couple of Celtic numbers as we rumbled through the Nepalese countryside, at times keeping our heads low to avoid sprawling branches.

The porter gave us the signal, unceremoniously jumping down with our gear, the bus revved-on, "is it only us two?"

"I think we're starting late," responded Jimmy.

We were on our way: Annapurna Base Camp [A.B.C.] was the target, a seven to ten day challenge. The Annapurna Circuit was another option, but this is about sixteen days, depending on how your health holds up. We walked about one hundred yards along a muddy path to a cluster of huts; we entered one, which was a government office to receive a compulsory stamp. Klaus, a German friend came by, he had just finished three months charity work in nursing. "I walked for one hour in the wrong direction."

We sympathized and laughed simultaneously.

Jimbob was constantly surging ahead, the first few days I was a distant second to the pit stops. The best source of information was trekkers, coming down the mountains. We compared maps, many

51

varied, we pencilled-in specific itinerary. The general protocol was to get moving early in the morning and finish before dusk, settle into a place before day-light fades. The electricity is limited, it has to be rationed. When darkness falls, that's it, visibility is practically zero, you're in serious trouble. Even with torches it can be tremendously difficult to follow the path. One can stroll off the beaten track and get lost, sleeping rough could be a reality. Not pleasant with temperatures dropping dramatically.

We climbed to Dhampus, then Pothana at almost two thousand meters. A steep descent follows through the forest towards Bischak, which I didn't like, a steeper ascent was sure to follow.

We stopped for a quick lunch, seated next to a group of over-weigh Americans. We took comfort in the fact these guys reached the top.

"You guys sound Eye-rish,"

"You got that right," Jimmy answered.

"Our wives are visiting your Country."

"So they get the ultimate, you folk must have drawn the short straw," I bantered.

"It would appear that way. Actually, we need this, too many easy holidays," Americans not shy on conversation. It could have been a three-hour rest.

Excusing ourselves, "We have a mountain to climb."

We continued through the Khola valley and reached Tolka at eighteen hundred meters. Then a long stony staircase to Landruk, booking a room with two single beds. Day one was complete, it was 3p.m.

We were asked to limit our time taking a shower, unaware that this would be our last proper wash for several days. Cooking evening meals was in full swing. A steady stream of weary amateur hikers entered the dining room. I fetched a bucket of water from an outside pump to wash vegetables. Two Aussie acquaintances whom we first met at the permit office were passing-by. I invited them to join us later, their guide showing much displeasure which was a common reaction.

I had soup and bread, then rice with lentil and cabbage curry. We talked with fellow lodgers dominated by Israeli citizens. A Swedish girl joined us, the next table had a group of Israelis speaking Hebrew, whom we joined later to play cards. The buildings were a mix of brick and mud, some were wooden. The galvanized roofs had heavy stones on top to secure from the wind. In the mountains early nights were necessary to save on electricity.

Day two was a tough trek. After a short distance the path splits, for Poon Hill. For us it was Chromrong, twenty-two hundred meters, above sea level, the last prominent settlement in the Khola valley. There are hundreds of steps in this town, walking down into a hollow community which meant a steep climb out of it. I don't know what is worse; uphill was making me feel bollixed. Downhill, one is vulnerable to a sprained ankle, a twisted knee. In parts, the trekking area is wide enough for a game of football. Other areas, a slippery ridge, only a tight rope walker would be comfortable.

We met a group of locals; one had a chair strapped to his back. A young western man was sitting in it. A young woman walking next to them, I assumed was his girlfriend.

"What's the matter?" I asked.

"He's too ill to walk, his legs are weak," she replied worryingly. Making their way down the mountain, that's one friggin heavy awkward load for that brave tough Sherpa, but I'm sure the others helped.

The higher one goes the more expensive the day-to-day living gets. Donkeys are used to transport goods, I could hear them coming down, after making a delivery. The bells attached around their necks, ringing. In groups of six, in single file, but tied by rope so one doesn't stray. A local, guided them, flip-flops as footwear, no hiking boots with these guys. Find a safe out of the way place until they pass, otherwise you're trampled on.

As the trail enters the upper valley, accommodation is limited. We settle for a single-lodge village. They had three rooms to rent, full occupancy, two Germans in one room, the other, two females, English and Canadian. Three young men cooked for us.

"This is our grandfather, he's eighty years old," entering the room. Jimmy was trying to charm the English girl, "we'll get together back in London," but he was getting nowhere.

An early morning wash with a bucket of cold water. The toilet, a hole in the ground with planks of wood for your feet and why not, we don't need pampering.

We began to see snow, making our way to Bamboo, an appropriate name for the heavy growth. We chat with a New Zealand couple, the girl, had sprained her ankle which slowed her considerably, her partner had great patience. We reached Bamboo by lunchtime, it had three buildings, which consisted of eating and sleeping facilities. I stretched out on a bench, exhausted, just wanting to sleep, Jimmy on another. It was 1:15p.m., a group of senior Aussies from Perth sat next to us. They were on the decent, full of encouragement, which sparked the rejuvenation we needed. Another two hours before reaching Deorali.

Tired, sweaty and jubilant, collapsing in a heap on a wooden platform in a jokingly manner. Jimmy poured beer lightly on my face, a group of hikers cheering and clapping.
"What's this all about," I muttered.
"Revival medicine, knock it all down."
The perfect way to forget fatigue. As other trekkers reached this destination, each was given a beer, raising their spirits, this was an animated bunch.
With no electricity we played cards in the candlelight, the rules kept changing depending on the nationality talking. Gas heaters placed underneath long wooden tables, everyone huddled around.
"He's in there trying to cook with one candle," someone said.
A Dutch woman offered a box of candles, now that's the perfect gift. A 10p.m. curfew ensured a good night's sleep was had by all.
Day-four would be the final assault for the summit. As I sleep walked to the kitchen for a quick bite to eat, one British couple were trodden off into the morning cold. This particular day it was important to start early, the evening before we watched in awe at the sound and distant sight of an avalanche. We had to pass this threatening area by 10a.m. As the temperatures increase large chunks of snow may fall. I was in a group of ten weary souls, soon we were joined by the British couple, they didn't heed the warnings and took the lower path. But discovered steep slopes and a wide river thwarted their progress, so they had to retreat and take our route.
Because of the dangers, local guides were leading, creating a path that was temporarily lost with the snow slide. We all followed in single-file, helping to construct a safe trail. Lee from the midlands of England and Deirdre from the west of Ireland stopped for an early

lunch, Jimmy and I joined them. There was little greenery, snow and ice dominated the landscape. By now I was always ordering Tibetan bread, normally adding hot soup with rice and vegetable curry. Managing to stay healthy was a priority.

As we approached Machhapuchhare Base Camp [M.B.C.], we navigated another treacherous area. A Canadian woman had fallen, with a gash knee and bruised hip. We helped escort her about two hundred yards to a resting lodge.
"Don't go all dramatic calling for a helicopter rescue," trying to add humour.
"Rest for a while, stay overnight if necessary," Lee advising.
"Perhaps we will call the Canadian bob sleigh team to take you down the mountain. If you pass out I will give you the kiss-of-life," Jimmy tested her temperament. Alison smiled briefly through the agony. We continued to the summit wishing her and two friends good health.
The Annapurna Base Camp [A.B.C.] was in sight, the surrounding peaks got higher and whiter. The snow is two-feet deep, but I follow the track others have made, it is easier. I'm wearing a heavy sweeter, but also shorts. Yes, we're a long way from a beach but I can move my legs more swiftly. It sounds crazy, but after 10a.m. the day is warm, Winter has passed, Spring has arrived. We have climbed over four thousand meters, the final approach seemed to take forever. But why should I hurry, enjoy the scenery.
I slowed considerably, my breathing quite heavy, the air is thinner. As I crossed the finish line and entered the famous Annapurna Base Camp, a ten-foot mound of frozen snow stood between four single-story buildings. Perched on top were Jimmy and our new friends, Lee and Deirdre. So now, I could finally flash the cigars, I'd bought specifically for this moment, blowing smoke into the air. My bones ached but a felicitous feeling flowing through my veins. Do a 360 degree turn, glaciers and soaring snow white pinnacles. We were in the middle, mildly basking in our glory.
As the sun faded, it became bitter cold. Under the blankets I was fully clothed with lots of hot soup, surely enough insulation to sleep comfortably at this altitude.
We were back on the mound for the countdown to sunrise. Eye squinting purity coloured slopes becoming brighter by the second as

the world's biggest star rises above the Earth's most famous mountain range and brings a new day. The Himalayas, this picturesque reality, no one would dare miss, reluctantly throwing the smelly pack on my back. Who would not want to linger a few more seconds, an hour, another day. But the crew were moving out.

"What's the game plan," I shouted.

"Chomrong is the aim," Lee called out.

I laughed, "That's a good joke."

"It's no joke, we're going for it," Jimmy reiterated with vigour. Basically, we do a u-turn, back down the mountains. Trodden through the snow each making their own path, I was first to reach Machhapuchhare Camp. Feeling energetic, the others were not fazed, it's a long road with many turns. I left a small package with the desk person for the Canadian patient, a book 'Into thin air' which I just completed. A story on the biggest single-day tragedy on Mount Everest, signed with get-well messages.

Soon we were at a narrow ridge, a potentially dangerous black-spot section. It was rush-hour, early morning trekkers on the way up, we literally had to side-step pass them.

"Bloody foreigners," trying to make light of the tension.

Cautious slow moving for the next twenty minutes, lose your footing and you're sliding down a fifty-meter ice embankment.

The clouds began to roll-in, rain was imminent. A gap was developing, created by my conservative speed. I reached an office, for permit stamping, "We've been waiting fifteen minutes," with a pleading expression from the group to keep pace.

A thunder storm commenced, a steady downpour, I had a plastic rain cover that protected my whole body including my backpack, stretching below my knees. A perfect gift from Uri, an Israeli-Australian who departed the country three weeks earlier. A stranger becomes a pleasant friend, they pass things onto you that are necessary. Later I duplicate the process, it's the simple things that count.

I am not convinced about sleeping in Chomrong tonight, from this town we had trekked almost three days before reaching the summit. This is the return leg, yes it's downhill, a one-day time limit, it's ludicrous.

Once again I was in arrears, I greeted trekkers on the accent.

"How ya doing?"

Frail smiles are returned, others looked dejected with the miserable weather. I turned a corner meeting a couple strolling nonchalantly, chatting and laughing. I complimented their easy-going attitude, they offered a cigarette. We planked ourselves down on the wet path for a quick puff.

It's a great moment on this venture. We can't control the rain, so do not let it influence our mood. Ingrid is German, Dan from Israel. It was like a forbidden relationship, a Russian and an American, French and English, Turk and Greek. I put them in the picture of what was up-ahead. By the time I'd stud my butt, we had exchanged addresses. There are times you just get a rolling positive feeling about some folk.

A short time later I reached Bamboo and entered a restaurant, ordering lunch, with my buddies finishing after-dinner tea. Lee urged me to be the front man, as they waited for me to eat quickly. I sensed their patience was wearing thin, with me straggling behind. "O.K., I'll be the pacemaker," stepping to the front with five energetic hikers bearing down on me. This was not a time for acting the fool. A slip or trip, it could result hobbling to the main road three days later than intended.

Jimmy didn't waste the opportunity to hollow from the back, like an army drill sergeant. The speed was hectic over the next three hours. I was growing stronger, my comrades on my heels. Constant heavy rain, low clouds spoiling the viewing points.

Finally.............finally I noticed Chomrong, the valley of steps were impending. Dana from Denmark and Janet, a Finland native had faltered a little as I looked behind, but the others had disappeared, much further back. As I reached the opposite end of this energy draining valley, Jimmy and company shouted friendly obscenities, their voices echoed across the hollow landscape. I checked into a lodge and showered for the first time in days. During the evening meal Lee suggested, "let's visit hot-water springs tomorrow," checking his map. Nobody was in disagreement, we were all jaded, physical pain throughout our anatomy's.

A two-hour walk and there it was, hot springs trickled out of the ground into a man-made swimming pool. It was soothing for my physical condition. But it was no secret, others arrived, soon fifteen individuals were seeking physiotherapy relief. A Good Samaritan Israeli shared his large bottle of whiskey. A sing-song began, each native was expected to blast-out a few national lyrics. Not quite duplicating the Eurovision song contest.

'Irlande dix points' [Ireland ten points], more like nada points with me been the representative.

One more day on these mountains……………………………..that changed when I offered to assist a Japanese woman who was feeling the strains of the Himalayas. She slipped and hurt her back, so rested for three days. I carried her bag as she limped alongside. Mimi was quiet and shy, taking great care to protect herself from the sun. My friends had left earlier that morning, a quick pace would see them at their terminal by mid-afternoon. It would take an extra 24-hours for us to reach the main road, upon doing so we offered to share a taxi with a French professor and his guide.

"Your country produces great scholars," the professor enthused looking at me. We had walked the last half-mile of the trek with these guys, he had completed the Poon Hill circuit,

"It's fantas-ica. Beut-ee-full, beut-ee-full, I have a flight tonight to Kathmandu."

I paid the Frenchman our share for the Taxi, this was a big mistake. The professor was dropped off at his hotel, the driver expected us to disembark also.

"This is not our stop, where is the lake district?" I asked

"It's over there," the driver pointing aimlessly.

I sensed a problem, re-entering the car.

"One stop for everyone," shouted the driver.

"We want the tourist district please," I responded.

He drove about three-hundred meters to a junction, stopped the car and turned off the engine. I was now familiar, we were about two kilometres from our destination.

We argued, other cab drivers came to his defence. I remained steadfast, the agreed fare was paid. The driver was playing a nasty game, wanting more money, he was barking up the wrong tree. He drove to another spot and stopped again. I noticed the Police station. He roared at us, "Get out of my car."

Mimi, the Japanese woman began to cry. We were scraping, him in the front and me in the back seat. Mimi jumped out and stopped a police car, coming in the opposite direction. The cabbie became calmer and exchanged words with the man in uniform, then taking us to our appropriate destination. Not another word from either of us. A piece of trash who gives other cabbies a bad name.

Jinxed moments come in threes, this was a minor incident for what was a current problem.

As I walked to my guesthouse on the main strip in Pokhara, I met Johnny from Dublin and his girlfriend Susan.

"Hay there, what's going on," greeting them.

"Have you seen Joe?" Johnny anxiously asked.

"What do you mean, no, I'm just getting back from trekking in the mountains."

Johnny proceeded to explain a disturbing story. He had been renting a house on the edge of town. "I invited Joe to stay with us. But we had an argument and I put him out, now I can't find him."

"When was this?" I asked.

"That was five days ago."

"I know two guest houses that he stayed in before," I suggested.

The first one we checked, the desk person give us blank stares and shrugged his shoulders. I checked the guest list book, nothing.

The other residence, the owner said, "yes I know your friend in the yellow tee-shirt. He left here and did not pay the bill in full, that was last week."

Yellow tee-shirt? that's definitely not my friend Joe.

Is he trying a 'fast one' trying to squeeze dosh out of me.

As Johnny, Susan and myself were doddering on the street wondering what to do next. Along comes Jimmy on a bicycle.

"I've got Joe, I found him last night, we are booked on a flight to Kathmandu at seven."

"Let's go down and see him," I suggested.

"No, let him be, he's sleeping, he's feeling ill," Jimmy refusing.

Joe stayed in the capital a few days before flying home. Jimmy returned to India to catch his return flight back to Europe.

In Pokhara, Joe had been sleeping in a quiet room. The owner noticed him in ill-health, put the word out hoping friends would come to the rescue.

"I'm off to the Amsterdam bar to relieve the stress, you guys coming?" Johnny, Susan and myself were on a bender, chewing the fat.

Nina came into the bar for a drink, looking much younger than her early thirties. We had crossed paths on the Helembu trek a couple of weeks earlier. We were both interested in volunteering to teach. Nina had talked with a trekking shop owner in the capital who could arrange a school for us.

First I had to plan a four-day white-water rafting adventure, booked with the cheapest company in town. A number of acquaintances including Nina voiced their concerns. The general opinion was that many Israelis use this company. They have a reputation for been clannish and brash. My answer to this matter was the excursion would be the ideal opportunity to experience the true colours of the middle-east nationals. Nina and I made arrangements to meet in Kathmandu ten days later.

****

A horde of fifty-seven commoners on two jalopy coaches navigated bumps, sharp bends and steep hills for the inception of four days floating above the water. A remote vicinity on the Kali Gandaki river would be the starting point. The video camera began rolling from the moment the rafts were filled with air. Lots of chatter and hollowing, it was all foreign to me. Fifty travellers, forty-five Israelis, the other nomads with identity papers from France, Belgium, England, Australia and Eireann [Ireland].

A staff of seven, one for each boat. Our instructor Depal would voice his instructions in Hebrew, majority rules. I introduced myself as Arafat, testing the mood. Two couples from Tel Aviv, two brothers from Haifa, one a pig farmer, the other an engineer made-up our team.

"We need two strong men at the front," our instructor called.

The pig farmer Dan, and his brother Raul took up the mantle. They had a shaky start. Navigating the first group of rapids, the front men got thrown back on top of everyone else. Dan, the pig farmer, was a hefty, broad tough-looking guy. But he was sprawled across two of our team. I tried to contain my laughter, despite being in trouble. Our raft on the rocks, literally, I managed to push us into deeper water, while the others scrambled to reposition. We abruptly realized our vulnerability.

"Paddle as a team, the best way to survive," Depal shouted.

Another four rapids followed in quick succession. We avoided mishaps, keeping the dingy moving, our confidence was rising.

At the end of each day we camped by the river bank. The first instruction was to get the sleeping quarters prepared. Standing the dingy on its edge, it would serve as a wall. A canopy overhead with oars as corner posts, a large ground mat for cleanliness, job done, simple, unique and sufficient. The staff worked competently preparing the evening meal. We were busy changing into dry clothes. Spreading our wet items on the roof of our sleeping quarters, hoping they'll be dry by morning.

The bell rang, dinner was ready. Orderly queuing was not a strong point with the Israelis. I evaded the stampede, as they bustled and shoved. Many dishes of curry vegetables, potatoes and rice were displayed. I sat with Shelley and Anke, from another team. They were not impressed with their fellow citizens.

"Look at them, pushing for food."

The other members of this crew circled around. Dipendra who was the Coxswain, pointed at the all-male group.

"They're trouble, twice their guide was thrown overboard and it was no accident. I will be on that boat tomorrow, things will change. They are smoking too much. One month ago a girl drowned with another company. We want everyone to be safe."

Dipendra was a singer, entertaining his crew on the smooth areas of the river. Shelly encouraged him to belt out a few tunes, he obliged with Nepalese numbers.

As everyone settled-in for the night, "I'm off to find a hot-water bottle," they didn't understand the joke. Being to bed last in our crew meant I got the worst spot. Breakfast was cereal or porridge, with bread, eggs and chai. The rapids were a medium level by the second and third day as we moved downstream. Anchored at a river village by mid-day with stone buildings and cobbled streets. Stretch your limbs on dry land. The Kali Gandaki is one of the holiest rivers in this country. The evidence clear when in the afternoon a cremation service was in progress on a high embankment as we flowed pass. Silence simultaneously among all the rafters, a moment of reflection. An open wood pyre with a body wrapped in cloth positioned between the wood.

The third evening I washed and scrubbed by the water's edge.

Feeling fresh and vigorous, I tried to teach Irish dancing to Shelly and her crew mates. David a red-haired comical character joined-in with an Israeli dance.

"We do this at weddings," he explained.

Other areas by the river bank had crews sitting quietly talking, but one tent had high pitched laughter and joviality, red and I decided to investigate.

About twenty people in a circle passed a pipe around, jokes and stories being told. 'Red' a popular figure around the camp was not one for a quiet side entry. He barged into the heart of activity.

"Now it's time for stage entertainment," he shouted.

A duet of middle-east choreography and 'Riverdance' was put into action. The audience embraced, the party tone was raised a few notches, as we performed in the middle of the group. This was sufficient to obtain a seat at the puffers association.

We were promised that a group of dancers from a near-by village would entertain us. They arrived with flame torches, adults and children with musicians in the background. A number of us jumped-in to copy the flawless choreography. Welcome smiles, for us clowns in the night. About one hour of Nepalese Maruni, then they retreated back along the river bank.

Day-four was a short three-hour run, but the strongest rapids lay ahead. We were hanging-on, quite literally at the first group of obstacles. Two crew members were thrown overboard, picked up by another dingy. In turn we rescued Marie, the French girl. Then we braced ourselves for the next rough and tumble episode. Everyone managed to stay, despite the gallons of water that flowed on board. A frenzied reaction with buckets to scoop and prevent that sinking feeling. A roller coaster finish to rock the emotions.

Back in Pokhara we had a farewell dinner. Many Israelis were venturing to Manali in northern India. Others were travelling east to Darjeeling, the home to Indian tea plantations. I had blanked-out any pre-conditional thoughts on the people on this excursion. I reached out to the Israelis and they responded, accepting me positively. A truly fulfilling episode, absolutely no complaints. I chilled-out for a couple of days, then headed for the capital to meet Nina. She had made the arrangements for us to teach in a school in a town called

Dhading. On the bus journey to the capital, I was a lone westerner. A Nepalese guy asked about my nationality. He was home on holiday, a break from his work in England.

"I live in Kent, my job is a chef," he told me.

But I was not buying this. Later at a pit-stop, over a soda he confided that he was a member of the queen's armed forces. This was not the first Gurkha I had met. The main reason he had joined was to travel to other countries and earn a higher income.

Kathmandu is 1300 meters above sea level. It's actually in a valley surrounded by hills, a population of only five-hundred thousand in a country of 23 million inhabitants. I checked into a guest house in the heart of Thamel, a hub for tourists. A single bed, table, chair, empty dusty closet, wooden squeaky floor, low-watt light, my backpack in the corner. It was early evening, a thunder storm rolled-in, the rain bucketed down. Right now I don't know anyone in this town, no problem, being part of a gang is not always necessary. I read a little, contented myself with biscuits and bottled water. About an hour passed, the rain is still bouncing off the pavement. I dosed-off, waking in the small hours of the morning, reading a little more, nodding off again. At sunrise I helped the porter carry two large buckets of washing to the clothes line on the roof. Water storage tanks were common, satellite dishes and back-up generators. Beyond the buildings are the mountains.

The shops were busy, foreigners seeking trekking clothing. Restaurants with American style menus, Cyber cafes with vacant screens, annoyingly slow connections. Music stores with everything from U2, Rolling Stones to the latest hip-hop, all bootleg of course. One U.S. dollar breakfast, fresh bagels and croissants. The choice of essentials made it easy to settle. But dirty motor exhausts create choking fumes. 'Traffic inspectors encourage backhanders rather than enforce the pollution law,' one shopkeeper told me.

After a late breakfast with Ray and Rob, two English lads from East Anglia, who were staying in the room next to mine. We headed for Swayambhu a Buddhist temple on the outskirts of the city. On the way we passed wild pigs and goats grazing on rubbish on the banks of the Bishnumati River. Roy was mimicking pig grunts, trying to get their attention, but they were too busy stuffing themselves. A mountain of steps to climb, 365 in total, Buddhist statues on the ground floor, a second group on a higher level as we reached the top. The temple is built on a hill with spectacular views over the city. Many Tibetan Buddhists live here since the Chinese invasion of their country. Pilgrims come here, queuing to sprinkle large prayer wheels. Red robed monks, others in orange perhaps from Thailand, are meditating. At this moment they correspond with four elements: earth, air, fire and water. Also there is a fifth, space. The stupa is surrounded by many shrines and gift items donated over centuries by Lamas and kings seeking recognition. Tourists call it the 'monkey temple,' simply because it's easier to pronounce, which is actually disrespectful. This animal is a resident here, we had brought fruit to entice them for a closer look. Accepting lunch, the monkeys scurried off to higher elevation. One of them curiously grabbing Ray's camera who anxiously gave chase and whacked the defendant with an apple on the back of the neck. The poor bugger tumbled and hobbled off in shock, empty handed, fortunately for Ray.

In the afternoon we rented bicycles and took the ring road which circles the city. We visited Pashupatinath [Posh-potty-not] temple. We were adamantly stopped at the gates, non-Hindus are forbidden to enter. A local befriended us, an army sergeant. He explained this was Nepal's holiest Hindu pilgrimage site. Shiva, lord of the animals is the principle god here. Shiva also gets mentioned as a new day begins on radio stations. The sergeant pointed out the Golden Bull and a Trident, three pronged spear that are visible in Hindu temples. At the rear of the temple is the Bagmati River. People believe it's good to bathe here on full moon days and on certain Hindu holidays. A number of buildings overlook the river, available for Hindus approaching death. The dying will be laid out and given a last drink of holy river water.

We stood on the river bank opposite the Ghats where cremations were been prepared. The body wrapped in cloth and covered with wood, will be torched by the oldest son who shaved his head for the ceremony. Rest houses for pilgrims are in the area. Nearby are homes for the elderly. One is organized by the government, the other by Mother Theresa Missionaries for charity. To stand and watch in eerie silence as the cremations begin is a test of your inner feelings.

Later, as I sat on the steps of an office building in Thamel, a local youngster joined me.

"Excuse me mister, if I answer the capital of three countries will you buy me powered milk."

I smiled at the young lad, "Austria?"

"Vienna sir," he confidently answered.

"Australia?"

"Camberra."

"What about Greenland?" thinking I have him here.

"Nuuk."

I thought he just muttered something, for I didn't know the answer myself.

"The capital of Greenland," I repeated.

"Nuuk" he said louder.

"O.K. what is it you need?"

"Powered milk sir, please."

"Why powered milk?" I asked.

"Because it lasts a long time and it's good for you."

I stood up and we walked, the young lad leading the way to a supermarket, powdered milk was the purchase. Later I was informed powered milk is always the request. For they re-sell it back to the shopkeeper. Feeling slightly cheated for my small act of charity. But I guess he deserved it, for Greenland.

I met Eddie from Belgium in a local cafe. Seated at the next table, he encouraged me to visit the prison for women.

Surprised, "Why are you hanging around prisons?"

"I went there this morning to see a girl from Denmark. She got romantically involved with a local guy. She is here seven months, has over-stayed her visa. A large fine is the penalty, or you go to jail. There are women from other countries in that prison for the same reason. They need friends, try to help, man."

"Should we go there and bail them out," I quizzed.

"Sorry, I don't understand."

"If we pay the penalty fine, then they can walk free, right?"

"It could be three thousand U.S. dollars, maybe more. I think that's very difficult for you or me to pay. I asked this girl if she wanted anything. I think she was embarrassed to say something. So I went and bought her chocolate. You know women, they like chocolate. Also I give her some bananas, apples."

"Yea, yea I see what you mean. O.K. I will go."

Sometimes the girls do not have enough money to pay this fine. Not wanting to alarm their parents by calling home and requesting money. They try to find other ways to raise the finance or just do the time.

I went off on my bicycle with Eddie's written instructions. I could only find the men's prison.

'I told the security guard I wanted to visit a foreigner.'

He didn't speak English, but give a short list of names, two from African nations, one Russian, an Indian native and an Englishman, whom I opted for. There was no privacy, no visiting room. He stood behind the reception desk which had steel bars and two officers nearby. I asked him about his crime and time. The treatment and what he needed?

"Five years mate, three done. Here for drugs mate. It's o.k. here, they leave me alone."

A Chelsea supporter, from London, tough looking with tattoos. I passed him a little dosh. As I wished him well, another visitor arrived to see him.

****

On Sunday morning, I headed for the bus station, failing to track down Nina in this city, she was there, buying a ticket. We were on our way to volunteer as school teachers. One bus had just departed, so we sit and chat with a shop owner as he made porridge for us. A limited supply on the shelves of rice, canned food, cooking oil, sweets, cigarettes, bread and cleaning products.

"What was that rally in Durbar Square yesterday," I asked.

"It was the eight-year anniversary of political change. Now there is a government, before we had none. The king still holds the highest power, I do not care who the leader of my country is. I want electricity, hot water, better roads, a good school for my children. We lose electricity almost every day for two, maybe three hours," he explained.

"Is the government good," Nina asked.

He served us porridge mixed with cinnamon.

"The government does not really care. The king does not help. He should come and live here for one night. My house is small, only one bedroom for a family of five."

As we boarded the bus, we sat in the front seat behind the driver. I wanted him to play western music, giving him four cassettes; U2, Queen, the Verve and the Breakaways, my uncle Patsy's band. He smoked, so I give him a pack of cigarettes, a little bribe. We twisted and curved our way through the mountains. The bus became packed as we proceeded into the more rural areas. One young man entered with a goat, another with hens in a basket, was there an exchange market in the vicinity? I think goats are nonchalantly humorous, non-threatening but destroyers, they'll eat almost anything, quietly menacing. We arrived at a single-lane bridge, having to wait for two trucks to cross from the opposite direction. On the other side of the bridge there was no road, a dirt track; dusty, bumpy and narrow. I looked at our road map, it was a continuous thick red line, as the main roads were marked in this colour.

"Perhaps the main highway is closed for a couple of miles," looking at Nina.

"A detour you think?" she replied.

But we soon realized this is the main road. For the next two hours every bone in my body moved, almost constantly. At times we met another bus or truck, one would have to reverse to an area wide enough for both vehicles to pass. Steep drop from the hillsides, no roadside protective coloured barriers. Cautious, careful driving a necessity. We disembarked at the last stop.

"Dhading Boarding school is there, building at the top, there," the driver pointing. He liked the music cassettes, so I let him keep them.

We walked into the school grounds, through the building. Calling for attention, it was empty. A woman dressed in a long red sari passed by. We talked and made signs, but the communication wasn't happening. It was a blistering hot day, we sat in the shade. Contemplating was this, the right address.

"They know to expect us," Nina getting slightly agitated.

"I need a week on solid ground to recover from that journey. My limbs are dangling, they feel all loose," doing a wonky walk, trying to humour the situation. Suddenly a lot of mumbling and laughter. becoming more vociferous. A group of boys came running through to the backyard. Stopping in their tracks, shocked to set eyes on strange looking people from a faraway place. Then the principal, "we've been expecting you," apologizing.

"It's a holiday, we went to play volleyball."

"This is normally a school day," I quizzed.

"Oh yes, six days a week, Saturday is our free day."

We conversed amicable about our backgrounds. Ahmed, the principal was from Bihar in northern India. He was offered the job through his cousin who lives in Kathmandu and is a friend of one director. The school was two years old. A group of seven people financed the building, so they are the directors. In Nepal, government schools have many problems, the teacher salaries are in arrears, so the pupils' education suffers. The official name is Dhading Boarding school, this may sound posh, but it was no Eton. Thirty students had sleeping quarters, they're homes were a long distance for the daily commute. In total there were four hundred pupils.

The following day, being a national holiday we ventured off on a trek with Ahmed and the school caretaker, Raj leading the way. Through rice padded terraces and hillside villages. Two young women were digging weeds with stone-age tools. I offered to help. "They have never interacted with a foreigner," Ahmed whispered. Their parents offered tea and local tobacco to smoke.

"That should get you high," Ahmed laughing.

"I think the altitude has already done that," stumbling around pretentiously. We continued, approaching another village. Children in uniform came towards us, then scampered off as I reached out to shake hands.

We rested and talked with an elderly lady. She made us rice, vegetables and bread. Ahmed slipped her money, refusing my gesture. Her living room had three chairs, a table, a cupboard and a radio. The kids gathered around, on their lunch break, their uniforms were light blue and navy with lots of dirty stains. Every kid wanted to be in a photo and why not.

We moved on, strolling along a wide dusty path, two school kids in pursuit. "Look at this," Ahmed referring to the additional members. "They attend a government school where the teaching is not so good. Now they are following us and will not go back to class, I do not like this." Ahmed had a few strong words with the youngsters.

We arrived at Raj's home, where he grew-up. His father was elderly but in good health. My hunger being relieved with mangos. Orange trees were in abundance, my first sight of the vitamin C fruit, growing.

Later as we stumbled upon another school, the principal, a local farmer give us the grand tour. Long wooden seats with benches, withered blackboards barely taken the chalk, school books were minimal. No polished floors or concrete, topped with linoleum tiles, the jagged rigid earth beneath my feet. No mahogany table or adjustable cushioned seat for the teacher.

Outside, two local men were cutting lengths of wood, one each end of a long hand-saw. Ahmed and I temporarily substituting, no power tools here.

"We can only try," Baja, the principal softly spoke.

"If we educate, there is hope."

I stood there, one arm as long as the other, what can I offer?

Buy a blackboard, if I could find one. The cutting-saw too old for a museum, similar to a smaller version I seen in my grandfather's shed twenty years ago. To buy an electric saw, drills or a television with a video recorder would be fruitless, electricity was minimal.

Back at Dhading boarding school people were returning from the three-day holiday. The school had three levels, the middle floor was residential. Three dormitory rooms to accommodate the boarding residents. The principal had a room which he shared with his wife and two teenage sons. Rameesh, who did the accounts and myself shared a room, it was the school office during the day. Nina was given a tiny space, labelled the computer room as her sleeping quarters. The principal wanted all students to have a greater knowledge of the English language. He hoped by our presence there would be a positive effect.

Day one, I was allocated six classes, beginning with an excellent group of fourteen-year-olds. They inquired about Ireland, could name European capitals and had a high level of English. I talked about my life, they were not shy on asking questions. This was the general introductory theme. The following morning the principal produced a permanent schedule of five classes per day. A slight disappointment, the fourteen-year-olds were missing from the list.

So what would be my approach? A strict no nonsense disciplinarian, plenty of homework or an easy-going jokester, perhaps somewhere in-between.

A normal day began with Kanak, the cook's younger brother been my alarm clock, entering the room, awakening me to a service of chai and biscuits at 6:10a.m, followed by a brisk walk or a game of table tennis. I was no match for the teachers, kicking my butt, the students were more my league. Then breakfast is served, dhal baht, which consisted of rice, potato curry and lentil. The dining room filled with the dormitory gang, the principal on hand to keep discipline.

Assembly in the school yard at 8:50a.m., four hundred enrolled, ranging from age five to sixteen. Orderly lines formed for a maroon and white uniform inspection, always a frantic effort for the dormitory students to be ready. A prayer was cited and the National anthem was drum beat played. With the first hour free I prepared for class, teaching Mathematics, English and Science. It was basic material, read the chapter, answer the questions. Lunch was dried rice and vegetables, it had no taste and didn't relieve my hunger. At 3p.m. the juniors went home, forty-five minutes later the seniors terminate. Our evenings varied from playing football in the school yard, visiting teachers in their homes, having a meal in a restaurant or drinking with Karan, another teacher in a back street bar.

As Nina and I walked the streets, students would shout 'hello sir, hello miss.' Approaching them, "what class are you in," I'd ask. "Class five sir," the young chap would answer.

Thinking aloud 'where is this guy seated for I teach him.' Of course, out of uniform and less familiar.

One teacher Achal was very hospitable to us. Married into a family that owned a grocery store, we'd sit with her and invite kids to join us. Play games, sing songs, an audience would always gather. Curious and studying our white complexion, looking closely, some touching lightly. We were pale in comparison, what were they really thinking?

Karan had a troubled marriage, some weekends he would disappear to Kathmandu, a liaison probably. He offended Nina, barging into her room occasionally. Over a drink, I stressed to him about questionable manners, he had intentions of living in a western country. He was fishing for help, I was not offering assistance.

At 8p.m. the evening meal would be served. A humongous pot fixed with Dhal baht, forty mouths to feed. By 10p.m the whole town is sleeping. We went to bed when it was dark and rise at daylight. Dhading got electricity every second night, sharing with another town. What they received was just enough for lighting. The school generator was used for two hours every evening so the boarders could have homework help with a teacher, the minimum use was due to costs.

Friday afternoon was a social event. Each student was part of a team and everyone would at some stage get a chance to represent their group. A general quiz was held in the school yard, it was a colourful day; red, green, blue and yellow, every pupil wearing their team's colour. One part of the school had four classrooms, looking dilapidated, half built walls, no doors or windows. Three pupils squeezed into a double-desk, dusty and clay floors and ancient blackboards. Two young women were employed to supervise the boarders. Bed times, wake-up calls, washing clothes and cleaning the toilets were their daily duties.

The morning shoe polishing ritual could be entertaining, everyone was supposed to have a container of polish and a brush. As I watched the action on the second floor open patio, Ahmed the principal was available for inspection. Looking sternly, as the boys prepared vigorously. One chap was incognito among the core group, without a brush, twitching nervously. I distracted the principal by discussion of mathematic equations, allowing ample time for everyone to have shiny footwear. Then the boarders made their way to the school yard for the Morning Prayer.

Parts of the road were unpaved through the main street, the dust was horrendous caused by buses and trucks passing through. So I encouraged the senior students of class nine who had a decent level of English to write a letter to their local politician about town problems. I paid for the postage and urged the group to continue with this procedure once a month until a positive response was received.

Now, let me ask the reader, do you believe in ghosts?

It's not a trick question.

I certainly do.

Out for an early morning stroll, I bumped into Ahmed.

"Ah the very man I need to talk with," greeting me.

"O.K. I'm listening."

"Ehh, I have to give you some background first. The caretaker of the school, you know his house next to the playground."

"Yea, I know."

"A family lived in that house before him, it was a family of three. All were electrocuted by falling wires in their garden, where the school is now built.

The father got it first while he worked in the garden. It was quite a big area, his wife found him and then she came into contact with the electric cables. The young daughter came looking for her mother and so she died also."

"My goodness, that's a sad sorry," rubbing sweat off my brow from the morning heat.

"In the Hindu religion, one month after passing-away a special ritual is performed by a priest to send the spirits on their final journey. I think it was not done for this family," Ahmed continued to talk quietly.

"Sean, have you heard any strange noises at night?"

I shrugged, "I'm not sure."

"The kids say they have seen movements by the window, some are scared, struggling to sleep. Rattling sounds are heard at night around the building." Ahmed was planning to go to the roof and pray intently asking the spirits to go on their final journey.

"This happened two years ago when we had a volunteer, Manuel from Spain. My wife and I, along with Manuel went to the roof and prayed for a number of nights, asking the spirit to take that final journey. It seemed to work, but now it appears something has come back."

My feeling was I'm not spiritually strong enough to tackle this issue. But in hindsight, who is. Later I was thinking, I did hear laughter as I lay in bed one night, doors banging at late hours. Subconsciously pondering it was unusual.

It was mid-May, noon-time temperatures soared, influencing the locals to stay indoors. Umbrellas been used, as sun protection by the few who ventured outside. The patio on the second floor was a spectacular viewing point. Hills and low peaks, rice terraces, valleys, Dhading town in the middle. One evening I experienced a lightning storm; no thunder, not a drop of rain. In the distance, beyond a mountain, the sheet lightning flashed constantly. Slowly it came across the hills and gradually edging towards us, inching over our heads and beyond the next mountain. Brightening the darkness of the night sky, flash after flash after flash. No thunder, no rain, a surreal moment.

I was enjoying my time in Dhading, the teaching giving me a sense of inner satisfaction. In the classroom I was determined not to have favourites. Bring the quiet pupils out of their shell, if possible. I didn't want the extroverts to dominate. The general level of English was exceptional, but there was a minority who were struggling. Some of them had initially attended a government school where their education suffered. Sometimes, towards the end of class, I would get the best student to explain in their native language, what the lesson was about. Remembering when I was at secondary school, our Irish language teacher insisted on speaking Irish only, leaving some of the class in the dark on the poetry we had just covered.

Phurba, a wise guy of class eight and also in the dormitory, I quietly warned him about his behaviour. Nothing changed. Play acting and annoying the chap next to him, also tantalizing the younger boarders, after class, he was bloody testing me. I put Phurba standing on one leg facing the wall, the following day I did the same, this time for the entire class. It did the trick, he became more obedient, slowly becoming my friend.

Nina and I were a novelty to the students, a break from the routine everyday teachers. I wanted them to talk as much as possible, practice their English. I encouraged them to come to me in the school yard or on the street. Many did, we played football or had racing games. The girls, a little shy for obvious reasons, Nina worked with them.

The teachers dressed respectively, shirt and tie for the men, sari for the women. Almost everyone looked older than their age suggested, was this because of the general poverty? They couldn't walk into their homes and flick-on cable television and relax in the comfort of air-condition. Do the weekly shopping and purchase groceries that enable you to cook a different meal each evening. To visit a relative, maybe no roads, the only access, by walking, perhaps a long distance and what if you are elderly. The health care system is almost non-existent. We had the same food every day, I was always feeling a little hungry, buying fruits and biscuits to relieve this, a good place to lose weight for oversized westerners. The hospital was opened but there was no surgeon, a single-story building of half-a-dozen rooms. "It's in god's hands if it's anything serious," Ahmed explaining. Richie from Chicago was living in the area, a volunteer with the American peace corp. He became ill in the first month of his arrival in Dhading. He was flown to Thailand for treatment, lucky enough to have the U.S. government pick up the tab. Richie had two basic assignments.

Cooking could be a problem in the home, no proper ventilation or escape route for the smoke. Chest and lung infections were common. So after three months training he would visit small towns and villages, requesting to see leaders in the area. He would teach them how to build chimney stacks for the smoke to distract. In turn, these leaders would educate others in the village, on this task. Also he would build more suitable toilets for improved sanitary.

"I walked for miles every week, putting these projects into action," Richie explained. A brilliant idea to send young people to developing countries and help improve the personal lives of people in need. This program was started by the Kennedy administration in the 1960's.

I invited the older boarders to chill-out downtown one evening.
"We are not allowed to leave the school grounds, a teacher must be with us."
"Let's go, I'm a teacher."
"We must get special permission from the principal, he is downstairs meeting parents."
"The principal is the king," the lads joked. "He is the big boss, he is the super high-king."
I just stood and laughed.

Ahmed was encouraging us to stay until harvest.
"The whole community will be working in the fields."
But my flight ticket was for June 6th, it was non-changeable.
It was our last week and Nina suggested a party for the boarders. We decided not tell them in advance, otherwise lots of other students might show-up. So we bought biscuits, chocolate, cake and soft drinks, batteries for the Ghetto-blaster. The older boys duplicating

my dance moves trying to impress an attractive Scandinavian. I boogied with Depak, an eight year old girl, the only female boarder. Light brown skin, huge dark eyes, her personality would melt your heart. Afterwards Ahmed invited us to his living quarters to knock back some Whiskey. Karan was in attendance also, hinting about his personnel life, the alcohol was talking. We chatted about the upcoming football world cup. Ahmed dwelled on the simple pleasures of life. "Many will be watching, but some can only dream about watching. Remember us when a goal is scored."

Earlier in the day we bid farewell to the students and teachers. A special presentation was organized in the school yard. Class terminated early, a pupil from each year presented us with a flower. We took centre stage and publicly thanked and advised the congregation. Later a number of individuals quietly came to us with handmade cards, simple words of well-wishing, it was brilliant. For a couple of weeks we lived exactly like the locals. Mingled with the masses and tried to entertain. I guess the easy part was, this is new, so we can tolerate this lifestyle for a while. It's not a major struggle for us because we can walk away anytime.

Nina and I had to go through that bumpy dust track again, but this is part of the experience. Another four hours, I had time to reflect; to buy a football for one group, but I couldn't find one. Perhaps skipping ropes for the girls. Make a cement pavement, so they could mark-out hopscotch. Weekly cinema tickets for six months to one class. Buy new blackboards. Build extra toilets, so there is less queuing at lunchtime. Just a little help, practical and social. How can I really make a difference. I'm returning to the western world, where people have plenty, but still want more. A place that selfish individuals dominate, it too often appears. Periodically, I will think about these energetic but somewhat isolated young folk. I should return one day with some form of help. I should,................right?............. But will I?
Dhading town is near the epicentre of the 2015 Nepal earthquake, loss of life has been heavy.

Back in Kathmandu the receptionist of my guesthouse assured me I'd have a ticket for the bus to the border the following day. We knocked back San Miguel in 'Tom and Gerry's' bar in Thamel. Benny was there, an Irish guy from Tyrone, we had crossed paths numerously.

"I'm going to Darjeeling [India] tomorra, my visa was up three weeks ago. I don't give a damn what they say at the border, they're getting no money in fines from me," laughing as he downed a whiskey, with a drop of water. "I'm off to the Underground, ah yas coming."

We joined him, but when we went outside there was an early taste of the monsoons. It had just rained for about two hours, the water was knee deep on the street. Bicycle rickshaws queued, an obstacle course to get seated, a short taxi ride to a street with decent drainage. Benny did not know the real name of the bar, he called it the underground because it was in a basement. But the only action were the pumps, the heavy rain flooded the place. We returned to 'Tom & Gerry's,' a second floor bar, now I realized why.

One night's accommodation at the border, then I walked briskly to the Nepalese immigration office for the exit stamp. The officer testing my mood by suggesting, I was a day late. I make mistakes but I'm not gullible. If he was hoping for a backhander, to start his day, he was pushing his luck at the wrong stall.

****

Re-entering India, I boarded a mid-size bus for the three-hour journey to Gorkapur. Five minutes into our trip, the driver swayed to one side of the road, then the other. There was an "ooooh" from the packed vehicle, emotions were been blurted out. We could have toppled over, he managed to regain control.

"That was lucky," the passenger next to me looking worried.

"Too many bus crashes in this country, life is cheap."

"What do you mean?" I asked.

"Sir, we nearly crashed and if we did, nothing would change, the dangers will always be there. The bus is overcrowded as you can see. Too much luggage on top, the weight, the roads are narrow. We are over populated and under serviced. This bus driver probably gets paid by the amount of passengers he carries, that's why most buses have so many people."

Gorkapur is a lively town, at least the part I seen is, I booked into a hotel opposite the train station. They charged by the hour, per room, because of the train times. I enquired at the reception desk about tickets to Varanasi, they sent me to a travel agent.

"Yes no problem, I can get you ticket. 7oo rupees only sir."

I laughed, only to contain my anger.

"It's a gud price for you sir."

"I think the right price is less than 200 rupees," I shot back.

"If you want a cheap ticket sir, you must wait five days. It's very busy sir, people are travelling sir."

He was not wrong, was there a vicious rumour that a Chinese invasion was imminent. I strolled around the station observing, the queues were endless to buy tickets. Three cows were perched in everyone's way, two sitting, one standing. To chase them out would be logical, but this is India, which could be bad karma.

At the building entrance, one young man was cutting pieces of wood from small tree branches. Each about eight inches in length. Business was brisk at one rupee, customers; all men were buying and putting them in their mouths. Brushing like a tooth brush, I was assured it was perfectly healthy.

At 7a.m. the next day I was checking-out the ticket counters again. The sign reading: 9a.m. opening time. Push carts were parked outside the hotel, their owners sleeping on them. Dogs underneath, sheltered from the morning heat. Returning after breakfast, ticket sales had started, I looked for the shortest line. Then another window shutter opened, I moved quickly, now there were about ten people ahead of me. This was acceptable, but nothing seemed orderly. Within thirty minutes it was a duplicate of yesterday, vastly crowded. No comparison to anywhere else in the world. The people behind me in-line, over-shot their proximity. I twisted and turned, to create a little room. They seemed determined about invading my space, their spicy breadth doubled the irritation.

"Please do not stand so close," I asked.

"O.K," the tall one acknowledged, with a head shake that is common in this country. But nothing changed as the line inched towards the sales window. Were they trying intimidation methods in the hope I'd run off to another queue. Then he coughed, the tall one, right into my ear, no attempt to block his germs with his hand. I twitched slightly and sighed, furiously rubbing my ear, looking at this guy. He showed no emotion, no apology. I waited a few minutes, then pretending to turn, I stood on his foot, with reasonable pressure. I had caterpillar boots, he had sandals. He yelled "ahhhh."

"Oh, I'm sorry," I gestured.

He hobbled to one side. It did the trick, keeping a measurable distance from me.

Finally reaching the window, "One ticket for tomorrow to Varanasi, please." The sales clerk played around on the computer.

"I can put you on stand-by, you can check later."

I played innocent, "I do not understand, what does that mean. I must go to Varanasi tomorrow."

Two people tried to nudge me away.

"Excuse me," brushing them back with my arm.

"Stand-by, the train maybe full," the clerk muttered.

"I do not know what this is, I need a ticket please, just one ticket." I was not retreating, standing my ground.

After a long pause, "O.K. 170 rupees," he said.

Persistence paid-off. Sometimes a station clerk will test you, hoping you will offer a bribe to receive a train ticket. If one is on stand-by, then you must go and check the name-list of passengers travelling, it's posted on the entrance of each train carriage.

The next evening as the train thundered in, an infinite number of carriages. A huge long train, many young men were congregated on the roof. I exchanged pleasantries with an English couple, Becky had a ticket but Gary didn't. They ordered two tickets at the hotel, only one was delivered. We checked the list as we entered the appropriate carriage. Becky's name was there and mine, but no Gary.

"What should I do?" he asked worryingly.

"Try again tomorrow," I said.

He looked totally pissed-off.

"Only joking, come on, let's go, you can hide in the toilets," I said laughing. Becky's seat number was next to mine. Two hours into the journey I noticed the ticket conductor was on his rounds.

"All right Gary mate, spread yourself on that seat and I'll throw these sleeping bags over you." We put the rucksacks on top and sprawled ourselves a little. Becky and I played cards disguising the third party. So no drama as our tickets were checked.

My flight was in four days, so with the early morning arrival in Varanasi, my first priority was to buy another ticket for the journey to Delhi. I queued before the clerks clocked-in, a hassle free purchase. After some authentic slumber in a quiet back street guesthouse, I plunged into the urban chaos of traders and consumers. Religious souvenirs, colourful fabrics, I passed a large image of a Hindu god, Garnesh. Then I see a mosque cordoned off with steel bars to prevent a group of Hindus changing the building into a temple, one local explained. A funeral possession passes by, I follow from a distance. Soon another in quick pursuit, the body is on a stretcher, covered by a sheet with flowers sprinkled on top. Four men are carrying the remains, a small crowd is following. I step into a café to give respect. But also feel nervous tension, as one does in such a situation. A tout offers a tour of the Vishvanath temple, I politely refuse.

"Which way to the Ganges?"

"Go straight," as the other guides jostled for my business. Some houses have spiritual decorated entrances, others with Indian style verandas or balconies. A culmination of shrines, minarets, temples, domes and towers. Derelict palaces from passed eras dominate as I approach the river, dedicated to Shiva, lord of destruction. One person points me in the direction of the busiest cremation area, there is a steady flow of possessions. The body placed on a concrete slab, known as a ghat. Wrapped in cloth, wood placed all around and on top. The oldest male in the family of the deceased begins the cremation.

Millions of pilgrims come here to cleanse their body and soul. It is believed by Hindus that this river holds the power of salvation. Many visit the river at other areas, but Varanasi is the holiest site. Some devout Hindus would like to live their last days here, in old age. At different parts of the river I noticed elderly folk praying. The steps by the water's edge is clogged with people washing themselves. Others are observing, paying respects to a loved one. Further down there is an open laundry, men and women beating wet clothes on the stone slabs. Boats are shuttling as overcrowded taxis. I notice the remains of a cow floating aimlessly. The Ganges rises in the Himalayas and enters the Bay of Bengal in Bangladesh. Horrendous fumes in the evening rush-hour from rickshaws, cows munching as always on rubbish. The living are active, the dead are laid to rest, the Hindu way. For a few short hours I gawked, open mouthed from the sidelines.

Another night, another train journey, the ceiling fans at full speed, the temperature rising, as I struggled to sleep. By now it was June, forty plus, Celsius on the thermometers. Under my sleeping bag, I stayed clear of conversations.

The following day, back in the capital, the avenues and alleyways in the Pahraganj in New Delhi were quiet because of the draining heat. By 5:30p.m., the locals are off to the night markets, too hot to shop during the day. Four times I jumped in the shower, the sweat oozing out of me, the power continuously cutting out for short periods. Luggage had to be retrieved from a storage company, the desk person motioned me to help carry the bags from the basement. Gingerly watching my footing on a creaky wooden stairs. One bag belonging to me, two were Joe's, who by now was in Ireland recovering from his mystery illness. As I gazed along the stacked metal shelves, each item had a number, some luggage was covered in dust.

"How long are these bags here?"

"Maybe one year sir."

"What about these red ones?"

"1.5 years, maybe longer, I check my book, sir."

"Surely it's owner would not suddenly decide to jump on a plane and fly half-way across the world to fetch a few pieces of clothing.

"My friend, why do you keep this luggage? this label is old."

"Maybe the owner come back sir."

"Listen my friend, they will never come to collect these bags. Give them to a charity organization."

Four hundred and eighty rupees was the low cost for two months storage. So extra weight to lug but personally I had lost about fifteen kilograms with less meat consumed.

Later in the evening I headed to an obscure mini-budget movie, 'Titanic.'

Of course, you all seen it, well, most of you. But this was no ordinary viewing of sitting quietly and swallowing popcorn while sipping a cold soda.

From the early scenes the audience was out of their seats, chanting and cheering. In the romantic moments, lots of young men jumping and shouting in the aisles. It seemed there were certain moments they were waiting for and then letting rip. It's a long movie and this crowd had their own rules.

With two days remaining I couldn't leave without visiting India's most famous landmark, known to foreigners. A two hundred kilometre bus ride to Agra. I shared the back seat with Lenny, an English gentleman, Jennifer from Denmark, Peter and Christine from Hamburg, gracious and informative. Four Bombay pageants periodically mingled, Talikha the most amicable. After I departed her country we continued to correspond. Feeling parental pressure to marry, she sought advice on working in a western nation. She certainly had the qualifications to be accepted overseas. Unfortunately as in many cases with this desire, the process requires patience which wears thin, even with the most eager.

Agra, the capital headquarters under the Moghuls in the sixteenth century. We entered the grounds through a large sandstone gateway with an arching koranic inscription. Facing a long reflecting pool, there it was; the majestic Taj Mahal. Manicured lush gardens leading up to this magical historical structure. A marble minaret on each of the four corners, built at a tilt in case of an earthquake, they would fall outwardly. Standing on two bases, one of sandstone and above it a marble platform three-hundred and thirteen square feet, worked into a chessboard style design. Facing the Taj from beneath, two mosques proudly situated on the left and right. The Yamuna river flows at the rear. The onion dome is spectacular with another dome inside it, the main dome rising above the minarets. Inside the mausoleum the light changes through chiselled marble screens. Shine a torch closely, one can see the flower work, petals and leaves, translucence also, which is quite amazing. The tiny breaks are not visible because of the delicate brilliance of craftsmanship. This marble monument has a haunting tale of love, lust and sadness. Muntaz Mahal, the second wife of emperor Shah Juhan bared him fourteen Children. She died at birth accompanying her husband on a military campaign in 1632. Two years later the project began, the tomb took seventeen years to construct. Shah Jahan became ill and spent his last years locked in the Agra fort, a short distance downstream on the Yamuna River viewing his wife's resting place. Built to honour their love, an estimated twenty thousand labourers were used on this project. Shah Jahan was laid to rest next to his beloved Muntaz, of Persian origin. The tombs are in the basement, above them are false tombs, a common practice of mausoleums of this type. Buried in a crypt in an enclosure in deference to Muslim tradition that no one should walk upon their graves. Looking at this magnificent building, just how much power did these Moghuls yield.

Earlier I had purchased a turban, amazingly this head gear is fifteen feet in length. The bus driver helping to wrap this material back and forth around my noggin, add a sarong which resulted in multiple requests for photo shots from the natives.

A short drive and we would doddle around Agra fort. Built by Akbar, his son Jahangir and the grandson Shah Jahan of the Moghul empire. The complex contains apartments, mosques, halls and dungeons. A wall surrounds the fort covering over one mile. The Yamuna River is on one side. It was also protected by a moat and another wall to stop access to treasures. Elements of Hindu arches and the Asian influences imported by the Moghuls. Rich remnants of gilded decoration that has deteriorated from the palace centre court are visible. Jahangir had a love for wine. Nur Jahan, his strong willed Persian wife helped her husband run his empire. But after he passed away she was to hold power and live out her days in Lahore, now the capital of Pakistan.

Shah Jahan also took over the reins, implicating new ideas. Arched roofs on pavilions, housing his daughters. Cool underground rooms, probably for summer. A private mosque is visible, built for the women of his harem. The empire's citizens and European emissaries came to visit the powerful monarchs, special areas built for such audiences. All explained by our driver.

The street hawkers and vendors in Agra are the most aggressive I have encountered in any country, literally in your face selling memorabilia amongst other things. Confrontation is inevitable, as one middle-aged tourist had a boxing stance wanting to retaliate for his daughter been jostled. Before I travelled to India I received immunizations for a number of diseases.

The administering nurse informed me that the Taj Mahal area was notorious for bacterial problems. Western health authorities would acquire this information from insurance companies. In reality this was 'scam city.'

A local man, acting as an agent would approach a tourist, offering an opportunity to make a claim on their travel insurance. The tourist allowing themselves to be hospitalized complaining of stomach pains. A certain doctor would handle this case, completing the appropriate paperwork. The only obstacle is the insurance representative, he would normally visit the patient within three days to check the authenticity of the claimant. So a three-way split on the financial claim between the agent, patient and doctor. I met four different travellers who took part in this swindle, three were women. I would have preferred to stay in Agra a few more days, to absorb the history at these sites. Unfortunately my time was up.

A taxi pick-up at 3:30a.m. for my flight out of Delhi. Another bargaining episode was necessary. This time it was low key, perhaps too many passengers checking-in to cause a scene. With Joe's excess baggage the clerk established the overweight price at two thousand, two hundred and forty rupees. I dug deep, twitched and searched. Eight hundred and fifty-two rupees was my limit. The airline steward accepted without a fuss.

Vegetable   Curry

3 onions [sliced thin], 3 cloves garlic [minced]
1 tsp. ground coriander, 1tsp. ground turmeric.
Half-tsp. ground cumin, quarter-tsp. dry mustard.

Add 6 cups potatoes [unpeeled, scrubbed and diced].
Dash of peanut oil for flavour

When almost tender add:
4 cups: broccoli, cauliflower or cabbage [chopped].
Salt and pepper to taste, 2 tomatoes, 1 tsp. curry powder.

Russia

A visit to the Russian embassy was worse than a trip to the dentist. At least when you lay back on that chair and hear the drill, you know what to expect. An inner preparedness has been built-up, and when you walk out, a bit disgruntled, the job is done.

It was Monday morning, I had just returned to London from a holiday weekend with friends. I rushed home, dumped my bags and headed off to the western area of the city, an A-Z guide book stuffed in my pocket. I found the Russian federation complex without any problems, a huge wall with an equal size solid steel gate. Just how much scrutiny did this place attract in the past?

Two people were entering, I followed. On reading the sign, last visitors:11:30a.m. we were fifteen minutes late. Inside there were three lines of people, two for visa requests, the other for payment. I looked around in search of the appropriate forms, then joined a queue. Eavesdropping on the people in front, one explaining to another the visa route, one story, then a second.

I was confused, intervening, "what I had to do?"

A well dressed guy explained, "book a hotel in Russia for the first three nights of you stay. Ask them to send a confirmation fax which is necessary proof that the embassy will seek. But it's not cheap, the regular charge is thirty U.S. dollars for that fax."

Also, I discovered a recommended hotel to complete this transaction are normally expensive. I was planning on a six-week stay and to rent an apartment. On the stroke of twelve noon one window shutter was hastily pulled down.

A customer raised his arms in disgust, "all I want is information," he yelled. I noticed anxiety expressions on other customers.

Two women walked outside, I followed, asking them about the visa rules.

"We are Russian, but we do not work for the embassy, if they get aggressive with you, then get aggressive back."

I suddenly felt a lot better, 'I will not leave until I receive answers.' A wasted trip only adds more stress. On re-entering I noticed one woman slouched against a wall looking annoyed.

"It's difficult," I said.

"Yes" she answered.

Then in an arrogant forceful voice, an embassy worker was saying to a young man, "tomorrow, come back tomorrow." The customer looked sheepishly, he probably had taken the day off work at his own expense to organise a visa. So this is what the two women outside meant about getting aggressive. 'Stand your ground, fight your corner' I wanted to prompt. Soon after, a second shutter went down. It seemed the employees were sticking to a time schedule, if the application was not stamped and approved, well tough.
Suddenly the room was almost empty. I went to the payment window.
"What exactly should I do for a holiday visa," I asked.
"I do not know, I only take money," the girl answered.
"I need to know, can you help me," holding the eye contact.
"Knock on window number three."
Proceeding and following suit. After a long silence, the shutter was pulled back. I was given several pieces of information. A visa service agency would be my best route. Yes I can certainly see Russia leaping ahead of Espana for the number one European holiday destination.
Twenty minutes later I was walking through Piccadilly and down Regent street. I got a shock, someone actually looked at me for more than two seconds, must have been a tourist. Most people as they walked were looking at the ground, like they had lost something. With the digital age, not much has changed, people are hiding behind their iPhones.'
Look down and you look ten years older, hold your head up and you appear five years younger. Gravity, this is a message for all those conservative, shy, lacking-in-confidence folk in London. It might be a good idea to read that last part again. Release that free-spirit and your peers should also, c'mon London, it's not too much to ask. I guarantee life will be more fun, interesting and successful.
I arrived at the service agency to find their prices were not low, one hundred pounds sterling for a business visa which would be necessary for my stay of six weeks.
"Holiday visas expire after one month, extensions are complicated," the clerk informs me. "I bet they are," I shot back.
The most expensive visa I've ever applied for.

Three weeks later I was off to the once forbidden lands. The flight was surprisingly full. Next to me were an English couple on their way to a friend's wedding. A western European and his Russian bride, a growing trend since communism had fallen.

The arrivals area in Saint Petersburg airport was very dull. No frills, no cheerful interior, no smiles from uniformed officials.

Denis, one friend I was corresponding with was waiting as promised, a heavy-set guy in his mid-thirties. His attire was old-fashion, brown pants with a matching chequered jacket and a flat cap. A half-grin that showed a mixture of gold and decaying teeth, his English slow and deliberate but understanding.

The surrounding area of the airport was derelict, unkempt. We drove to the city in an old beat-up Lada, a common vehicle in this part of the world. Dennis had organized a flat for me, about a forty minute ride. On the way we passed magnificent military memorials.

Buildings looked frail, parks untidy. I'm the other side of the 'Iron Curtain' there's no turning back now, beyond the frontier of secrecy and espionage. I'm a little pensive, not wanting to say too much. But the conversation is holding, on the light side.

Upon arriving at my residence, we climbed three flights, the edges of the concrete steps broken-away. The walls were a faded green, it was dark. "People steal the hallway lamps," Denis explained.

Inside the flat, two women were waiting, one elderly, who was the owner, the other, a well dressed thirty-something real estate agent. Greetings were exchanged. A living-room, kitchen and bathroom, I sat on the couch which turned into a bed, 'reasonable comfortable,' I thought. Everything was brown; the arm-chair, table, wardrobe, floor, cabinets, mats. Even the wallpaper, which was probably a nice beige at one time, black and white television. The kitchen sink was big, steep white enamel, iron cast type, one could bathe a small child in it and a large black vintage-style kettle. The toilet did not flush properly, the shower had no curtain, but at least the water pressure was good. I asked questions about the area. Denis sensed I was not convinced, "oh, we drove in the back way, let's take a walk and show you the main street," he suggested.

There were lots of neighbouring residential buildings. Large trees blossomed everywhere. Muddy paths, puddles of water were aplenty.

My initial felling was, 'I'm sorry, I'll just get a hotel room for the first couple of days.' But I did not want to panic. It seemed I was on a busy bus route. Small family owned shops and a large supermarket were a short distance.

"The metro trains are just ten minutes walk," encouraged Denis.

The agent was pushing me to sign the rent lease for one month. Denis was certainly not giving me any support. Still having doubts about the area.

Naturally I'm feeling lost, the first day in a new country.

"Can I pay for one week as a trial?" They agreed.

Later I walked to the metro, clocking thirty-one minutes. To hell with that, it's a bit of a hike, coming out of the train station late in the evening, trying to figure out the bus routes or negotiating a taxi. Paying for just one week, I was feeling justified.

I contacted two other locals I had been corresponding with. Three new friends, we covered many miles the first week, visiting the usual tourist spots of museums, churches, palaces of the czars. Boat rides on the Neva River, it's tributaries and canals.

No longer Leningrad, Saint Petersburg has character, delightfully coloured buildings: yellows, greens, blues and some reds. Nevsky prospeckt is the main avenue. With one friend Luka, we stumbled upon an Irish bar, one evening. An Irish couple sat next to us, in town for a few days, on their way to the Baltic States. The other side, three locals were soon conversing with us. Luka, been the interpreter whenever necessary. Later they took us to a nite-club which was free to enter for foreigners. Dutch folk joined our group and of course the up-coming vital World-cup qualifier clash between their country and Ireland dominated the friendly exchanges. The Amsterdam lads acknowledging the amicable relationship that had developed over the years between the two countries in football circles.

Famous for its theatre, Saint Petersburg has many shows. Admittance for foreigners is a much higher price, so get a local to buy the ticket and do not talk when entering. Swan Lake cost ninety rubbles [about $4], such elegance and panache. Another show I went to had ten different acts of music, acrobatics, dance and singing, ticket price thirty rubbles. I paid more for a beer at the interval. Inna, had bought the tickets, a neighbour to Denis, a professor of history, in her mid-thirties, with a fourteen-year-old son who spoke perfect English. One of her friends, Natasha had a large personality, heavy laughter. She was married and living in Germany, had just returned to her native city for a short holiday. People were keen to give me a taste of Russian culture. A hectic first week of infinite walking left my feet worn-out. Literally knackered, I had a day-off, venturing every couple of hours from my bed to the fridge.

An early morning phone call had me scrambling around. It was decision day, pay another week or move.

"I have got a flat for you," it was Denis.

"Write this on paper, Sean. Meet me at Bolshevikov metro station at 10:30 a.m. [Spelling the name slowly], by the escalator. Pay the taxi no more than one hundred rubbles. I think you will be o.k. Just put your hand up and someone will stop."

It's a popular place to meet in ex-soviet countries, in metro stations at the top of the escalator.

One can flag down any car and ask them to take you to your destination. A taxi license is not necessary, everyone is entitled to make money. Now, I've hailed cabs in western cities, but this is an entirely different ballgame. No local to lead the way, just me in my rawness. I don't speak the language, but at least there will be no meter running.

Sure enough, a beat-up old Lada stopped, within the first minute.

"Bol-shev-i-kov met-tro," I said loud and clear, twice, then showing him the name written.

"Da, da" [yes, yes], he nodded.

"One hundred rubbles," I flashed clearly.

"Da, da."

Making myself comfortable in the front seat with my backpack in the back. Faded leather seating, partly ripped with the sponge cushion peaking through. The driver looked pension age, receding grey hair with matching rugged beard. For sure I was a little nervous, but right now it's him and me, and I'm not scared of this chauffeur. We drove through many apartment block areas, on narrow driveways with lots of potholes, like he was taking short-cuts. Upon reaching my destination, I spotted Denis, so no anxiety.

The new area had many facilities, a large supermarket, side street bars, restaurants and mini-shops. Five minutes to the metro, been vigilant as we made the short walk. The same agent was involved, looking smartly attractive with white trench coat and spectacles. The owner was present also, a middle-aged lady with a heavy polo-neck. This flat was more modern, certainly a better location.

Three hundred and fifty U.S. dollars per month, plus one hundred and fifty dollars for the agent, was the asking price. Quotes were always in U.S. dollars. I smiled to myself, trying to hold my composure. $500 they want, hard-necks these folks have. The agent was probably visualizing an easy payout. This was the second time in eight days that I had to pay her a fee.

I browsed around, opening cupboards, turning on taps to test the water pressure, all eyes are on me. I pointed out a few things; looking at the cooker, I certainly could do a breakfast fry-up, but it would be lunchtime when it's ready. The stove-top rings took forever to heat-up. The shower hose was all leaky and the toilet tank took ages to refill.

"Yes, but this is Russian style," said the agent, laughing along with Denis.

"It's Russian style, but not a Russian price," I responded, walking back into the kitchen. Denis conferred with his agent friend, in Russian of course. Then came to me, "What do you want Sean?"

"I will pay three hundred dollars in rent and forty commissions." She agreed without hesitation.

****

There were blocks of flats stretching to the horizon. Flats, flats and more flats. Turn off the main street, a maze of narrow drive-ways, winding and twisting through the residential areas. The playgrounds were in a mess, long grass, abandoned cars and over-flowing dumpsters. It seemed no one cared, enough. Potholes everywhere, 'filled in November by snow and ice, one good thing about the harsh Russian winter,' a local joke.

Unwanted furniture, construction debris, broken footpaths, tattered fencing. A closer look, many buildings were shabby; dirty windows, worn cement floors in the lobby. A lick of paint was well overdue. A heavy stench was evident when I rode the elevator which was squeaky and shaky, with so much trash rodents were part of the community.

The keys the landlord had given me, could barely fit in my pocket. Seven inches in length, quite literally. One for the hallway door, I had to twist four times to unlock. It was inevitable this would cause me grief at the worst possible times. Twice in the first week I struggled with my dangly keys in the small-hours. Each time I had to ring a neighbour's bell to rescue me. Clever enough to alternate who I called, apologizing sincerely, saving me from an ear bashing.

An early impression was people do not smile a lot in this country. A stern look, concerned about something. But as you get to know them the sense of humour becomes more evident. Some may say, they do not have much to smile about. Many would feel they were restricted, not allowed to fill their potential, they did not know anything better.

I asked Dimi, the manager of one Irish bar, about foreigners living in Saint Petersburg.

"Before '98 there were many," he said. "This bar was busy with Europeans, Americans and Canadians. But after the financial crises they left. Russia was in trouble, the rubble had crashed. Citizens queued at their local bank to withdraw their money. Six rubbles were equal to one U.S. dollar. Suddenly it dropped, twenty-eight rubbles to a dollar."

"That's a real crises, Dimi," shaking my head.

Dimi was helpful, giving me advice on local issues. His bar had a steady crowd, Thursday to Sunday, live music was an attraction.

"Our customers earn a good salary. Lots of young and middle-aged people come here. I'll introduce you to some of the locals."

On the street, men had dress pants, wool jumpers and shoes, jeans and sneakers were not common. I visited one shopping centre in midtown. Lots of boutiques, western styles and western prices, but women customers were in short supply. So been fashionable was an expensive problem for both genders.

I met with Andrei, a correspondent, his level of English was minimal, but his girlfriend Anna was fluent. Andrei, originally from Siberia, asked me about the history of Ireland, he knew about the problems the British occupation created. I would counter on the changing times during the 1980's in the Soviet Union.

Andrei spoke and Anna interpreted. "There is suspicion that Andropov, a Soviet leader in the early 1980's was bumped-off. Formerly he was a K.G.B. front man. As a result he had secret information on many. At the time poverty was becoming a major problem. Lots of money was spent on countries in Africa and Asia, trying to keep them friendly with the Moscow regime. The Afghanistan war was current, disabled veterans were increasing. The Soviet people were becoming dissatisfied. So Andropov tried to make changes. Cutting back on expenses and increasing labour productivity. But he had forces against him. During the Brezhnev era special structures had formed, a type of mafia. They were happy not to 'rock the boat.' They would have access and ability to put Andropov out of the game. But of course it remains a mystery. People involved are still living."

Another round of beers, the conversation flowing, as smoke hangs in the air with many lighting-up especially women.

"There is mixed feelings about perestroika and Gorbachov. Russians have a joke, one day the master said let me bark, but moved the plate away."

"Sorry, I'm confused," looking across the table.

"It means that people are given more freedom. They can read books that were prohibited, watch Hollywood movies. Later they can travel abroad, live as they wish. Pop and rock music became popular, concerts of non-official musicians were allowed. In mass media they wrote the truth about what was happening, then and now from 1917 to 1985, now you could speak freely about the Kremlin leadership and their policies without the fear of been imprisoned. Before, only state companies existed. Now private enterprise was developing. Foreign cars became evident, so a new era of freedom. But on the other hand, there was a lack of consumer goods, food, clothing and cosmetics. Food could be bought only in exchange for special cards. It was limited, one kilogram of sugar, one kilogram of rice. Milk, bread and cheese could be bought in small quantities. One may have to run around many shops looking for groceries, there were no supermarkets."

I listened intently as my friends explained, Andrei gesturing as I tried to interrupt with a follow-up comment.

"As changes continued during the 1990's with Yelsin, as our leader some soviet groups had well-paid jobs with no financial worries, economic recession, they could handle. Relieved, that strict control from the central government had diminished.

Then there were the poor, fighting for their lives. To earn an honest living was difficult. They had freedom, but also poverty. People joined the criminal world. Protection rackets, illegal trade, drugs, thieves, killers. It was dangerous to walk the streets late at night."

Anna and Andrei were great company. Both had a strong interest in politics and current affairs.

On a Friday I could pick-up a local English newspaper which advertised the action around town. Stunned to read about what happened in New York on September 11th 2001 that airplanes had crashed into the twin towers of the world trade centre and hundreds were killed. A city, that I have enjoyed living in and have many friends. I did not know until four days later while browsing through this weekly publication. It is something I'm not proud to say, that I had predicted, not in this way of course. As my sister emphasized weeks later from the many discussions we had over time on world issues. Now over a decade later the whole truth probably has not come out.

I met with Luka, one evening. We walked through parks, just enough light coming through the trees. In the distance we could see a small fire burning. As we approached, it was simply a group of students having a party, playing music. We quickly left, Luka asking me for money.
"How much?"
"Anything," he shrugged.
"Three hundred rubbles, is that enough. Where are we going?"
"You will see." We entered a local supermarket and bought two cases of beer for five hundred rubbles. "We will make this a better party." The students were stunned, but all smiles as we made the delivery. They asked me questions.
"We do not meet many foreigners, we want to talk with people from other countries."
So we chilled, knocked back the local brew and shared a few laughs. Suddenly a gang of army guys appeared. They were wearing long heavy green overcoats. Everyone went quiet. I offered them a beer, "the war is over lads." Luka nudging me, to say nothing.
They accepted cigarettes, warmed themselves next to the fire for a few minutes and headed off.

In comparison to us in western countries, the locals didn't plan in advance. If I called someone on Wednesday and said, 'can we meet Friday?' They would say, 'call me Friday afternoon.' Was this because of economics or perhaps the communist way? Where everything was organized and controlled by the state.

A few days later I went to Moscow train station in the mid-town area. I was planning to visit Petrozavodsk, a town ten hours north. There were many ticket counters, all slow moving, which is normal for this country. It came my turn, the sales person did not speak English, but was helpful. Writing prices for each class and train times. She was patient and polite, unlike some customers behind me in the queue. One middle-aged man began yelling. I smiled at him, giving a hand signal to calm down. I turned to the counter but he came alongside. He's angry, and it looks like he wants to rip my head off. Taller and broader than me, I could smell the alcohol, giving him a friendly nod. What else could I do? Is he an ex-Gestapo guard, wanting to dump me in the Gulag. His contour became sterner and starts ranting at the desk person. Another man came forward, and pulled him away.

Many times I noticed natives did not like to queue, in shops, restaurants and in the metro stations especially. They would try and nudge in-front of you, by going to the top of the line to ask a question, then, buy their tokens.

"I guess you see we can be aggressive," one friend said.

"But it's not malicious, it's part of our personality. Do not take this seriously, simply hold your spot, do not give way," she advised.

I was packing a few things for my overnight trip north. Suddenly I heard a loud bang. 'What the hell is that?' goes through my mind. Water was gushing from a pipe underneath the kitchen sink. I searched frantically for a switch-off valve. Then I went rushing down the hallway banging on the neighbouring doors, getting an answer from the fourth apartment. Over-coming the language barrier by bringing the lady to my apartment to show her the problem. A few more people arrived, moving some ceiling tiles to locate the valve. It was too-tight to twist by hand. Then a plumber came to the rescue with a large adjustable wrench. As I moped-up the mess, some of the neighbours helped. But one guy was insistent that I give him money to buy plumbing parts. He didn't speak English but I knew what he wanted. He kept asking, over and over. Then I saw him take chocolate from the living room. I shooed him away, putting him out. If I give him money, I'd never see him again.

About an hour later I answered a knock on my door. A lady began complaining in angry tones, but quickly calmed down when she realized I was a foreigner. We went to her apartment, directly underneath mine. It had two feet of water in the kitchen. "Two time in six months, two time," struggling with her English. I apologized, as the stress and annoyance was visible. She had a half-size flood door that stopped the water spreading to other rooms. I changed into shorts and a pair of extended wellingtons that we borrowed from the reception area and got busy scooping out the water. She would probably need a new ceiling. I called Denis and explained the situation so he could relay it to my landlady. Then I headed to the Moscow train station, arriving thirty minutes before departure. The station was busy, lots of passengers mingling. I saw a few western backpackers, probably on their way to the capital for the Trans-Siberian Railway. My train, the 10:20p.m., to Petrozavodsk was delayed. I strolled around, for sure there were undesirables but this is normal for a big city-centre train station. Stylist suitcases were not part of the local's itinerary. Plastic cotton bags were most common, unconventional.

At 11:15p.m. it came up on the notice board. My departure time was 11:40p.m., platform five. I bought a beer and made my way to the train. Each carriage had a conductor, checking the tickets, serving tea or coffee upon request. Also, giving wake-up calls before reaching your destination.

As I boarded, a young woman checked my ticket. I walked to my birth noticing this was a first-class carriage. I thought that I bought a second-class ticket. Cyrillic alphabet on my ticket, I could not read, like double-dutch to me. But sub-consciously thinking, 'oh maybe I purchased the more expensive option.' I entered my cabin, it was organized for two passengers. It was super clean, pillows with white covers and sheets to match. A dark blue cover rug, brown blankets and lots of towels on the rack above. I stashed my backpack neatly under my bunk. Hung-up my jacket, took-off my boots, got my book and made myself comfortable. About ten minutes later the conductor came-by, asking for my ticket. In her best English she said, "nu, nu, Mus-koow."

I looked at her bewildered, trying to figure-out what she is saying. "Mus-koow, Mus-koow, " she repeated more loudly as she waved her arm. I jumped up, getting my stuff together.

"Fas, fas'" she urged.

I hurried to the exit door. I tried to explain what the notice board said, "Platform five for Petro-za-vodsk."

A passenger boarding intervened, he looked at my ticket, "that train go one hour ago, go information, maybe buy new ticket. This train for Moscow."

Definitely confused, something is not right here, who do I turn to now for help? The Moscow train began pulling out. I moved to the opposite side of the platform. I asked one conductor, "Do you speak English?"

"A little," she answered, gesturing with her hand.

"This train go where?" I asked

She looked blankly at me. I showed her my ticket.

She nodded, "yes, yes Petrozavodsk."

I breathed a sigh of relief.

In western countries there will be platform five. The opposite platform is platform six. But the Russian system is platform five right-side, platform five left-side. Being illiterate in Cyrillic, I misunderstood the notice board. My friend Tamara in Petrozavodsk, been a school teacher would have a story to tell her students. The western European clown who could not figure-out the correct train to board. Thank goodness there was no embarrassing phone call to be made from the capital.

An overnight train disembarking at 7:30a.m. Tamara had booked a room for me in the local hotel Severnaya. It was ten minutes walk from the station, arriving in time for breakfast. A large red brick building with little glitz, but clean and presentable, my single room costing all of $5. Tamara became interested in Ireland after reading a magazine story. She had many books on the emerald isle, making attempts to study Gaeilge, the Irish language. So I became a short-term teacher, helping her pronounce words properly. Breaking new ground with SLAINTE, [cheers] CEAD MILE FAILTE, [one hundred thousand welcomes] POG MO THOIN [Kiss my ....]. Also, AN BHFUIL CAD AGAM DULL AMACH GO DTI AN LEITHREAS [may I please go out to the toilet]. Every student at my local Blackrock primary school would not forget that one. When nature called you had to ask in Irish. I should be better at speaking my native language.

That evening I went to check-out the local scene with Tamara. A larger in each bar, perfect for chasing the shots of Stolichnaya. A local nightclub was the finishing line. It was like an old theatre with high ceilings and balconies. House-music pumping, stage dancers adding extra entertainment, language barriers being overcome with dance floor action.

On the menu for the following day was a birthday party for a friend of Tamara. A chocolate cake and a case of Baltika was my contribution.

"Too much alcohol," Tamara politely protested.

A fire been topped-up with loose branches, pre-cooked food wrapped in foil. Old clothing was the popular choice as we arrived in a secluded area of a forest. The group was dominated by well educated married couples; engineers, teachers, doctors and medical personnel. Their low salaries made life a struggle.

No gathering is complete without the local brew. Every half-hour the Russian vodka was raised or rather downed from plastic cups, these people are pros. at handling this liquor. In communist times there wasn't much else available to drink, it's a domestic product and inexpensive.

One teacher Varinka, had good knowledge of music. Her father taught at musical institutes. In the past he was occasionally allowed a special visa to perform in Russian orchestras in western Europe. He had friends in London, where Varinka stayed for a summer and studied music. Varinka explained, "it was a challenge to make friends, people were nice but not friendly. Everything changed when I met Pat Murphy from Ireland in a jazz bar." I interrupted with a cheer.

"He could play the guitar and the banjo, a rugged looking guy, always drinking that black beer, oh yea, Guinness. I liked his character and humour. We both had a love for music, I have good memories of this guy. We always met in the pub."

"Did you invite him to visit?" I quizzed.

"He promised to write but that's all it was, a broken promise."

Later as dusk grew, the laughter became louder. Husband's and wife's seemed to poke fun at each other.

"They're all drunk," Tamara whispered.

"That's a relief, so am I," I replied.

A Russian sauna was repeatedly mentioned. "You must try it," everyone would say. We cleaned-up the picnic area and shared a taxi to the town centre.

Next day, Saturday, I was off to experience the infamous sauna. A forty kilometre drive to a dasha, the name for a small country home. A number of natives are lucky enough to own this special countryside dwelling and seven were willing to hang with me. They are generally small bungalows, normally with vegetable gardens and an orchard. Potatoes are commonly grown, also carrots, cabbage, onions and turnips. This is northern Russia, nothing flash here. This piece of land is of great importance, in the past in communist times when food was in short supply. Today also with the capitalist economy, shops are well stocked but the cost of living is expensive. The countryside was a dull green, the harsh winters do not help, wooded areas in abundance. This dasha had the perfect location, one kilometre off a main road at the end of an unpaved laneway. On the edge of Lake Onega, the largest body of water in the province of Karelia. There was one bedroom with two double beds, a large living room with lots of furniture. Five couches actually, which enabled everyone to have a comfortable sleep. Food contributions were collected, once again I had a case of beer on my shoulder, and a bottle of vodka.

The sauna was prepared, burning short logs on a stove that created intense heat. Pouring cold water on the furnace resulted in instant higher temperatures. I received the body cleansing. Stretched-out on a wooden frame, a continuous sprinkling of water for several minutes on my body with tree branches resulting in temperatures of an unbearable eighty degrees............. Celsius. Finally relief comes as I escape to the outdoors, but a shock to the system, as I soak in the chilly waters of the lake. It's suppose to drain the bacteria from your system. Meanwhile next to the sauna was a changing room, a break from activities. Where we were sculling beers, were we defeating the purpose? Each person had to go through the cleansing treatment, otherwise you were the target of jokes.

Next morning, while most were still sleeping, I noticed Zhanna, whose parents owned the house, digging in the potato drills. I went to help. She explained that her parents love the dasha, "there is enough food here to see us through the winter. We can have fried potato and salad for breakfast."

I asked about life in communist times.

"You know Sean it was hard before and it's hard today. We had to queue for food in the shops in the old Soviet system. The government tried to take care of the big cities first, making sure there was enough food so the people would not demonstrate. The shops were always bare, then there would be a delivery and everyone would go at the same time to buy what was been delivered. The delivery vans were not consistent."

We climbed across a fence into a neighbouring field to pick Mushrooms. They were everywhere, some as big as my hand.
In two minutes we had enough to feed everyone.

"We did not know how life was in other countries, we had nothing to compare. Now we know. The shops and markets have everything today, but it's still a struggle. Our salaries are low. We can get a good college education and earn degrees, but the right job with a decent wage is difficult. Civil-service jobs do not pay."

Later at the breakfast table I asked my new friends if life has improved with communism now gone. I wanted to hear collective views. I listened as Dimtri explained, "registration is a major issue, proof of where you live. One just cannot pack their bags and move to another part of the country. To change your residence you need a new registration, this is done at a government office. They do not like to help, a bribe will get the job done, $300 is what they want."

"What chance have I with a salary of $50 a month," Victor jumping in. "Students can receive a new registration if they attend a university in another town, many go to the big cities like Moscow and St. Petersburg to study. When their legality expires they still continue living in the city. Later they will get jobs and hope that their new company will not check the documents specifically. Also people in this situation will not want a policeman checking their identification. It goes back to communist times, when the government wanted to track your movements."

"Do not be surprise if a policeman stops you on our streets. Natives from the south are a target, countries like Georgia, Azerbaijan and Armenia. It is suspected there are drug elements from these areas," Milvana's voice, coming from the end of the table.

I interrupted to tell about a police incident I encountered.

"Late one night I came out of a club called Havana, in Saint Petersburg. I walked about one hundred yards, finding a good spot to stop a taxi. I had about four drinks, I was fine. Suddenly a police

Lada stopped next me.

Three policemen came from the car.

"Dock-u-mints, Dock-u-mints."

I had no passport with me. Showing other photo identification, bank cards also. They looked really close with a flashlight, examining. Keeping calm, but nervous on the inside, my eyes fixed on their movements.

"Pas-port, pas-port" they repeated.

"In hoo-tell," one questioned.

I nodded in agreement, "da, da."

Then one of them was putting his torch on me, shinning it from head to toe, slowly up and down about five times. Was he trying to provoke me? I just ignored and looked away. Everything was handed back. "Goo-hoome Shau-awne, Goo-hoome Shau-awne," the tall one spluttered.

"O.K. no problem."

"So what do you think of our policemen? they even have to stop a visitor to our country. We feel some of them we cannot trust," Milvana speaking up again.

"We have a national passport that's necessary for travelling around our country," the gorgeous Ivana with turquoise eyes and blonde hair informed me. "We also have an international passport for overseas."

"What about Russian and Soviet leaders?" I asked.

They were all optimistic about Putin. "We want him, we need him to be a good leader," offered Viktor.

"He has come through the ranks and is trying to make progress."

"Yeltsin, was he good?" I queried.

"He was embarrassing, drinking too much," Ivana answered.

Some were familiar with the Shannon airport incident when he was too pissed to disembark to meet waiting Irish officials.

"He prevented a coup by the old guard," I tested.

That's the only thing he did,' Alex shot back.

Later we went for a walk. "I can see the owners take good care of their dasha gardens."

"There is a hint of pride, that it yours, enjoy the benefits," Dimitri responded.

Eventually Gorbachov was mentioned, with older folk against the changes and the younger generation more optimistic.

Alex took the initiative, "I think it happened too fast, we were not ready.

Today there are many homeless on the streets. Pensioners have to beg, their allowance is too small. Some get financial help from their families, but others are in trouble. It's not good to see our elderly singing on the street or selling goods from their homes, trying to make money.

I explained, "You know Gorbachov was a popular man in the west. He met with European leaders and negotiated with America. He was a fresh-face and willing to do business, unlike his predecessors. In the United States, Reagan receives a lot of credit for ending the Cold War. For sure he increased military spending and that put pressure on the Kremlin in a financial way to match them. In my opinion nothing really happened until Gorby came into power."

Yury, who was a drummer with a local band, "I agree with the Irishman. Gorbachov let the people be heard. He allowed democracy take it's course in Eastern Europe. These things led to the ending of the arms race and the threat of a nuclear war, this is why they liked him in the western world. He put an end to the cold-war."

Dimitri adding, "The U.S. will always claim victory, but the change had to come from within. Russia and Eastern Europe changed and there was no war, no killing."

"What about living conditions, before and now?"

"I just bought a flat," said Tamara. "It cost fifteen thousand dollars, but my salary is only forty dollars per month. It's like this Sean, in the past during communist times all city dwellings were municipal, built by municipal companies. The waiting list was horrendous, twenty years for some people. Living quarters may have been a mouse hole. They wanted a bigger flat. It was tragedy for many generations of Soviets, they may die waiting. If one was in good terms with anybody from the municipal government, then the waiting time could be much shorter. Not to mention corruption, like bribes or gifts. There was one exception from the general order. There were cooperative building societies in towns and cities where people could hire-purchase an apartment. Paying a solid sum of money as an entrance fee. About twelve hundred rubbles, when the average salary was eighty rubbles. Very few could afford such an option, only those who worked in the north, in the polar regions, in the gold fields or if they held a profitable post. The only property that one could inherit was a country house. But these may not have proper heating systems or running water.

Today the system has completely changed. Buying and selling is normal, but property is so expensive."

I advised Tamara to apply for teaching jobs in Western Europe. She could save enough money in two years to pay for her new flat.

"I did not correspond with you so I could move to another country," she humorously replied.

"Take advantage of our friendship if you wish, when the chance is there," I advised.

A fantastic group willing to extend the hand-of-friendship.

****

The following night at 11p.m. I boarded a train heading south to the city known as 'Venice of the north.' Not to disturb my fellow passengers, who were sleeping, I quietly settled into my compartment.

As morning dawned the carriage conductor knocked and entered, offering coffee, we gladly accepted. The other occupants were Olga from a small village in the Arctic Circle and Mikhail from Murmansk, a military town on the Arctic Ocean. They offered me bread, a cold boiled egg and biscuits, I countered with juice and bananas. We talked sports and the cold war. Mikhail did his military service in Cuba.

"Ooh, Castro country. It sounds exotic and you get the chance to spy on the Americans," me been a little sarcastic.

Mikhail explained, "there were tears from my family as I prepared for the flight to Havana. In Cuba we did not take it too seriously. We would write letters to American children, we want peace not war. I did not see the U.S. as an enemy. It was exciting to be there, but our free time was short." Overhearing a conversation in the next cabin, Olga warned me to be careful, pointing next door, "don't let them cheat you."

I nodded understandingly. Strangers know a foreigner is on board, they may target you.

At our destination the platform was crowded. "As you can see someone is always here to meet you," my wife will be here, joked

Mikhail.

Yelena, who I met in Pertozavodsk, had returned to St. Petersburg and called to offer to be my tour guide for the weekend. Delighted for her company, I was ready to explore. She lived on Vasilevsky Island, in the western part of the city, near the gulf of Finland, a scenic area, popular in the long summer evenings. Walking distance from her residence, there is a beach which is stony with scattered debris. I guess there is little other choice for swimmers.

We moved around town taking trams, buses and the underground metro. Buses are electric connected to a cable system, how is that for clean energy, even though the vehicles looked decayed. The train stations were decked in marble, elegant arches and pillars adorn the hallways and platforms, almost free of commercialism. Vendors would walk through carriages selling newspapers, toiletries and candy. The escalators, my goodness, those escalators, down to the platforms are massively long. Three minutes was the average riding time, very deep under the ground, think about that for a moment. Built this way for safety against enemy attack, a cold-war tactic. In the London underground tube system an average escalator ride would be less than one minute.

First point of visit with Yelena was Piskaryovka cemetery. At the entrance there is an exhibit of photos that needs no explanation, the nine-hundred-day siege in this city by the Germans in World War Two. Almost half-a-million buried in mass graves. This was the biggest designated area where fatalities were taken. Raised mounds marked by each year during this war. Each mound was about fifteen meters wide, by forty-five meters, I measured it, music coming from speakers that fit your emotions. To stand, stare and wonder just how many are buried here, it's a moment to reflect. Certainly more heart wrenching for the natives. History books inform us of twenty-six million Russians killed fighting the Germans, twenty-six million. It took a crazy like Stalin to stop another crazy like Hitler.

We moved to other parts of the city. Saint Isaacs cathedral, which we climbed to it's tower for an aerial view. Buildings of various colours visible, grey's dotted the city concrete, but the bright colours added a unique character. Then onto the Kazen cathedral on Nevsky prospeckt, inside this sacred church is the tomb of field marshal

Kutuzov, who led the Russians against Napoleon in 1812. In communist times this building was a museum of atheism.

Finland station, on the Neva River, where Vladimir Lenin arrived in 1917 from Switzerland and later a second time from the country of Finland, a statue of Lenin is out front. Downstream, Kresty prison, a holding place until your court appearance. The Peter and Paul Fortress, which was built to defeat the Swedes, later it became a prison but now a museum. The Hermitage, is the most visited attraction, a combination of old and new Hermitages within the Winter Palace. Home to the Tsars until the communist revolution in 1917. It has a spectacular display of art including works by Picasso, Rembrandt, Monet, Renoir, Matisse and Rubens. Gold and silver displays of Greek and Scythians that date back to BC times. Material from the bronze age. Murals on walls and ceilings, a creek in your neck admiring the majestic meticulous finish product. A second visit was necessary getting lost in my audio. Suddenly, many hours later receiving a tap on my shoulder that it was closing time. It's surely a top ten museum on our planet.

Later in the evening as Yelena and I strolled through an old part of the city, I could hear someone shouting. Looking around and then up. On the fourth level of a red brick building, a man waved. An empty cigarette box was dangling above our heads attached to a string. "What the hell is this?" I asked.

Yelena laughing, "you can see he wants to have a smoke."

"O.K., tell him we'll come back in five minutes."

Returning with two packs of cigarettes, tying the string tightly around his request. Rejoicing loudly as he collected his addiction. Yelena explained, "this is a military hospital, some servicemen fake their illness. It's a way to avoid been posted to war areas like Chechnya."

A hectic schedule the following day with visits out of the city. Petrodvorets; Peter's Palace [Peter the great] is here. Refreshing gardens and numerous water fountains. Near-by is a hydrofoil for a fast return to the city. Unable to enter the palace because of renovations.

In the afternoon we made our way to Catherine's Palace in Puskin, a breadth taking bright blue exterior with golden domes, restored after world war two. Inside amazing light and glitter from mirrors,

windows and gilded wood-carvings. Patterned silk wall coverings, a state dining room, amber room, Chinese blue dressing room and so on. Certainly the Germans would have stolen a number of treasures during the war years, others were stored away for safety.
Catherine the second, the infamous 'Catherine the great,' it's rumoured she had many lovers, and planned the death of her husband, she was in power from 1762-96.

Talking about lovers, Rasputin has been labelled as 'Russia's greatest love machine.' He prayed a lot, but was not a monk as some people think. Working in the fields he experienced a vision of the 'virgin Mary.' He left his western Siberian village to seek enlightenment. His compassion, generosity and comforting talks along with his teachings that promiscuity could bring redemption, by asking forgiveness later. It made him popular with some aristocracy women. He managed to cure the haemophiliac son Tsarina Alexandria, a member of the royal family. His influence in this family made him an enemy among ministers and generals. They blamed him for disasters in World War one, this inevitably led to his death.

Back at my base which was a little less luxurious than the suburban retreats of the czars, the plumbing was still not mended. Denis once again would be my interpreter.
"Please tell the landlady if the pipe is not fixed, then I'm getting extra keys made and giving them to homeless people with the address attached."
"No, no that is crazy idea."
"Denis for ten days, the pipe is broken, I cannot use the kitchen sink."
He also obliged by writing a note for me requesting an overnight ticket at Moscow train station, avoiding frowns from the public and language barriers with the clerks.
My days were numbered in Rasputin's country. I could not leave without seeing the headquarters of the twentieth century communist Soviet Union. Many newspaper articles, television stories and documentaries I had absorbed through the years. The Russians were portrayed as a dangerous, distrusting enemy by western nations. But I could not hear or feel any animosity by the general public towards

the west. If it did exist, no one was admitting it.

I Arrived at Leningrad station in Moscow, a quick wash in the men's room, after the overnight ride. Not quite congested as daylight developed. But I did queue and pay fifty kopecks, less than one rubble for a few flimsy sheets of toilet roll.

'They won't go too far,' came to mind. I put my hand out for more, but the heavily dressed lady seemed to be dismissing me. I give her ten rubbles and received a handful in return, using them for cleaning the toilet seat even if I did not intend to make myself comfortable. The cubicle door was, well quite literally two feet in length, twenty-four inches, in the middle of the door frame with a big gap at the top and bottom. The toilet bowl on a raised platform, so when the deed is done, one must step back down onto the floor level to avoid exposure, then fix your clothing. To answer nature's call, this was no place for the pampered. Public toilets, just a bit too public, but you got to laugh. I guess it goes back to Communist times when one could not be given enough cover behind a public toilet door to do something secretive, the citizens cannot be trusted.

Taking the underground train to metro station Komsomotskaya, destination, the Kremlin and Red square. My faith was in my guide book, exiting at what I hoped was the appropriate station. The Cyrillic alphabet signs of the station names were a maze to me. The streets had a typical subdued quietness. I walked towards a causeway, my map showed the Moscow River, next to the central government buildings. A large red wall came into view, this had to be it. I strolled across bol kamenney most[bridge].The kremlin, the edifice mainly a yellow colour with a green roof, surrounded by a spectacular garrison type red wall, the biggest wall I have ever seen, On the outside, flower beds bloomed, the watered grass, lush, trimmed and neat. Traffic trickled by, 8:05 a.m. on a distant church clock. I stood there and gazed for long periods, the elevation from the bridge made the view panoramic. A local came walking with his bicycle, finally someone, to take a photo of me with this unique fortress in the background. On the opposite side of the river Japanese tourists exited a bus, no shortage of clicking. Walking parallel with the river viewing the Kremlin from the rear, I reached bol moskvorstsay most [bridge] at the other end.

Ninety minutes had passed, the Basil cathedral was in my sights, I had wondered exactly where it was situated. This was the one building which makes me think 'Russia.' Ironically, with it's oriental turban domes, it is the ultimate symbol of Russia, unique colours and shapes. It has nine chapels built in the sixteenth century to celebrate 'Ivan the Terrible' successfully taking the territory of Kazan. Basil cathedral named after 'Basil the blessed' who is buried on the grounds. Unfortunately someone knew I was visiting, it was off limits surrounded by scaffold for renovating.

Following my guide book, near the Basil is a round wall where 'Ivan the Terrible' made a public confession about his executions on his perceived enemies. Also the place where 'Peter the Great' had two thousand Streltsy members killed because of mutiny. "Yea that's just great, Peter."

I stopped at a souvenir stall, K.G.B. joke tee-shirts, miniature comic images of former communist leaders, which I bought after a bargain challenge, a decade earlier this type of purchase would not have been possible. The noose had been loosened from around the nation's neck, one can talk freely now. I asked a vendor about life today.

"It is difficult, I am not rich. I need to help my parents, they are pensioners, too old to have jobs. They receive a small income from a pension, but it's not enough. I have a wife and one son, we survive but I need to work many hours."

He liked Putin, "he is our best chance for stability."

One part of the square has a GUM, Gosudarstvenmy Universalny Magazin [state department store]. In the past these shops had empty shelves. A middle-aged teacher explained to me,

"Not much to sell, long lines were normal, it all changed with Gorbachov."

Today it's a bright elegant shopping area, with western designer names like, Christian Dior and Hugo Boss. A history museum is nearby, also a small cathedral, the original building was demolished by Stalin because it impeded the flow of the special celebrations of the Soviets. Twice a year these celebrations were displayed to the world. A military parade, on 'May Day' and 'Revolutionary Day' in November, a message of strength to the west [Western Europe and America]. Perhaps in reality the Kremlin was serving a notice to the natives and it's bordering nations;

'Don't mess with us or we'll crush you.'

Lenin's granite tomb stands at the foot of the Kremlin. I had to queue in a specific area, meticulously searched by guards. Strictly no cameras or backpacks, a storage room available for personnel belongings.

As I approached the mausoleum, a verbal message from security, "No stop, keep walking."

Upon entering, military on either side with stern expressions. I walked slowly down a stairs, given my eyes time to adjust to the darkness. I turn right, strolling through, looking to my left. A glass cage in which Lenin rests inside, a reasonably small figure, in a suit, shirt and tie. He looked exactly what I had imagined, from the many photos and statues I had encountered.

A number of armed soldiers standing in green uniform as I emerged from the mausoleum at the foot of the Kremlin wall. Here are many of the Soviet luminaries, special busts above the graves of Stalin, Brezhnev, Andropov and Chernenko, all leaders of the Soviet empire, for me they were easily recognized. Luckily a student with his parents could explain others who were given the honour of a Kremlin burial:

Dzerzhinsky, founder of the K.G.B.

Sverdlov, the first official Soviet head of state.

Zhdanov, second in command to Stalin after World War Two.

Frunze, a military leader in the 1920's, who conquered central Asia for the Soviet Union. Inessa Armand, Lenin's lover.

A plaque marks the spot where the ashes remain of Yury Gagarin, first man in space. Zkukov, military leader in World War Two. Hydrogen bomb team leader, Kurchatov.

As I roamed casually in Red square reflecting, men who appear in the history pages of the twentieth century. How many fatalities were created by some of these people.

Perhaps Lenin died too soon, Stalin, who succeeded him, ruthless in his pursuit to remain in power. Why did they feel the need to keep expanding control?

What was Stalin's theory?.............. Keep the masses down, install poverty, makes rebellion more difficult. I'm guessing. Sixty years ago, who had television, newspapers? Lack of communications, live reporting. The world is a smaller place today, now with the internet, more opportunity to inform of wrong doings. But also propaganda exists, certainly with many of today's media companies owned and controlled by wealthy people who stamp their opinion. So freedom of the press, does it really exist, perhaps, in small doses.

Back in Saint Petersburg I visited Yelena and her friend Zoya on Vasilevsky Island. Zoya, originally from Almaty, the capital of Kazakhstan. They had organized a group for a Russian sauna, city-style. As I sipped tea in their apartment, feeling sorry for the girls, they were washing their clothes in a miniature washing machine. It didn't hold much of a load, then they had to hand-squeeze the water out of each item of clothing, try that with bed sheets. The kitchen was soon clogged with clothing racks, with no other place to dry their washing, for it was raining outside. I wanted to just grab all the clothing and bring it to a Laundromat and throw everything into a dryer, but such services were nowhere to be seen. To buy a washer and dryer for these new friends would make such a difference to their lives. I'll never moan again about doing my laundry.

We headed off for the sauna, meeting other people on the way. Six from each gender changed without hesitation in a room that consisted of two sofas, a table with chairs and lockers, each person displays a sheet, it's their territory, they make the rules.

The procedure only Russians know, first we sweat beyond our limits, well certainly I did as they periodically poured water on the hot furnace. After exiting the sauna, you threw-off your covering and dip yourself in a small pool, individually and privately, this is the shock treatment from hot to cold. Next was a game of water polo in a hundred square-meter pool, which is a tough game that zaps your energy. Then a shower, grab your sheet and wrap it in your own unique, ancient Roman-style. Returning to the changing room to drink beer and socialize. The room soon became smoke-filled, the locals love a fag. These folks were all friends, uninhibited with the situation, repeating the sequence three times.

Now, I wonder if I could round-up a group of friends for a similar evening's entertainment. Highly unlikely, and we in western society are supposed to be hip and unfazed.

I was about to leave the country. An accumulation of cheap compact discs and Soviet souvenirs prompted a trip to the post office. No space in my backpack, so send them home. This would be no casual errand. The CD's would have to be checked for their authenticity in a building across town, the clerk insisted. That necessity was scraped.

"I don't believe this, it's a load of baloney. This is only music, do they think it's a secret plan to assemble a bomb," I fumed.
"It's not my fault," Yelena, my friend snapped back. We argued about filling the forms correctly. My boxed package, minus the CD's was sealed in cotton cloth, sowed, glued and tied with cord, no fancy trimmings here. Two hours and twenty minutes to complete the transaction at three different desks.

Zharkoe

2 lbs of boneless beef
One onion
One glove of garlic
Black pepper, salt
Carrots
Tomato pasta
Oil
Potatoes

Cut meat to little cubes. Fry with oil. Add chopped onion and garlic. When it's almost ready, add tomato pasta and half-a-glass of boiling water. Peel potatoes, cut to big slices. When meat is ready, add carrots, then potatoes to the pan, with a cover, add salt and pepper [to your taste]. Serve hot.

Belarus → Ukraine

I was eager to visit Tatyana, a school teacher from Minsk, the capital of Belarus. We were corresponding for five years. First there was the small issue of a holiday visa, but that involves government departments, which inevitably will have obstacles in this part of Europe.

An invitation from a citizen of Belarus was one option. Tatyana would have to send the appropriate paperwork, stamped and approved by a local government office. Proof of our friendship and many other queries would need to be provided.

An invitation from the Belarus tourist board would be an easier route to take. Money was wired for the cost of this invitation to the appropriate office in Minsk. Express overnight delivery of the invitation was promised. A stressful move, seven days later the package arrived, on Friday afternoon, August 18th. My Russian visa expired on Monday August 21st.

Extensions on Russian visas are problematic, to say the least. Yelena, my good friend was my assistant. Making the necessary phone calls, chasing the paperwork and enquiring about the exact procedures, a native language speaker was imperative.

Now I know by this point the reader is probably confused, well just read the last part again and you'll be even more confused.

Early Monday morning, August 21st. I hurried off to the Belarus consulate with my express delivery package. Yelena leading. I had the invitation, but I still needed a visa. Anxious moments as we struggled to find the appropriate office. Eventually on doing so, down a side street, up a narrow stairway. There was a queue of three, but of course it was slow moving. Visa approvals must be completed by twelve noon. It was after 11a.m. when we were welcomed in. Naturally, there would have to be one more problem, payment must be made in U.S. dollars. I stayed to fill-in the appropriate forms, Yelena dashed off to a Bureau de Change, returning as closing time approached. Yelena interpreting as the consulate employee talked.

"How many days would I stay in Belarus?"

"About ten," I shrugged, not taking the question seriously. A ten-day visa was what I got. My guide book advised that thirty-day-visas are the norm. I was not smiling. Late in the afternoon, I hugged and kissed good-bye to Yelena and Zoya, we had become good buddies. The deep blue train slowly pulled out of Petrograd station, which was getting a facelift, like many parts of this 'White Nights' northern city. I shared a cabin with a woman of about forty and her nine year old daughter, Natalie. English was one of her school subjects, so I helped her put sentences together. They were friendly and accommodating, ordering tea for three, sharing their biscuits and cake. I slept well, got dressed at sunrise and viewed the Belarusian countryside from the carriage hallway, allowing privacy for my compartment companions. Lots of small cottages with galvanized roofs, vegetable gardens and orchards, the locals were already in the fields working on their plots. We passed through industrial areas, most looked derelict now. During the Soviet era this state was a major producer through it's many factories. With the collapse of communism so did the local economy.

On arriving in Minsk I was pleasantly surprised by the modern central station. It had all the facilities one could ask for. I sat with my backpack in the main concourse. It was 8:10a.m. on a sunny August morning. I was studying the map of the downtown area in my guidebook, marking places of importance. I would shack-up at the Hotel Jubileynaya. Reservations had been made, part of the enforced visa rule. The station was busy, people on the move, arrival passengers been greeted by loved-ones. I glanced at the vast timetable, destinations in Cyrillic: St. Petersburg, Brest, Moscow, Odessa, Kiev. I was in no hurry, an hour had passed, an automatic teller machine [a.t.m.] near-by did not get a single customer. I wondered how many locals had bank accounts. Unsure the value of the Belarus rubble, I withdrew one hundred thousand rubbles. I watched carefully with my map as the taxi driver made his way to the hotel. Been a stranger, I'm wary of been ripped-off with a detour drive. Checking with the receptionist, 1,865 rubbles to one U.S. dollar. That's great, a huge bundle stuffed in my pocket worth damn all, about sixty U.S. dollars. I telephoned Tatyana, who dropped-by that evening.
"I think this is the most expensive hotel in this city," she blurted out through laughter as I greeted her.
"There wasn't much choice," as I explained the visa route.
A straight talker, who took her teaching job serious, friendly and

helpful, escorting me around the city centre, pointing out landmarks. Huge statues of Lenin, significantly one outside government buildings.

Minsk is the cleanest city I had ever visited. Opposite my hotel was a large park, flowers and trees blooming, lawns perfectly mowed. I did not see a single person on the green areas because the public were prohibited. In this city there are a number of areas that are off limits. The police were highly visible. Sitting on a wall, by a museum, a young uniformed officer was quickly onto me. "Huh, huh," grunting. 'Move on' was the message. One may find the heavy law and order presence a little intimidating.

Lukashenko, the president has a tight grip on this country. He keeps moving the goalposts to ensure he stays in power. Traffic is stopped every morning so his motorcade has a hassle free passage to his office, how vain is that. He makes himself stronger, but his country weaker. It's not an attraction for overseas companies because of the president's personality and ideas.

Communism is gone but many laws remain, the general population does not feel free. Many have Russian background, independence for these citizens has not brought prosperity.

In my hotel room on the second evening, the phone rang.

"Do you like sex massage for money," coming from a woman's voice.

I'm thinking how she got my room number, the front desk must receive commission, all hush, hush I'm sure.

"No, no I'm sorry, I do not pay for this," I politely said.

"I give you gud time, you like very much," the lady replied.

"Did you ever have massage with an Irishman?" I asked.

"I like Iishmann, I give you gud price," she answered.

"My friend, you should pay me," I shot back.

"Cheap price, I take gud care of you," she responded.

"My friend you have to pay one-hundred-thousand rubbles if you want to meet me," I'm telling her.

"I give you gud time, I go your room." She says.

"One-hundred-thousand rubbles only, one-hundred-thousand, you pay," I repeat.

"You crazy, you crazy," she shouted and hung-up.

She probably called my room the first evening also, while I was out strolling around town with Tatyana. The ladies of the night' had enough clients, no shortage of businessmen and a group of Greek-Cypriot tourists showing lots of interest in the hotel bar.

I was paying $70 per night for a hotel room, plus daily living was accumulating to over $100 per day, too much for me if I'm to travel for many months. With the help of Tatyana, I checked other hotels that were mentioned in my guide book. One was being reconstructed, another was a total dump, no proper running water and dirty rooms.

My health was actually deteriorating a little more each day. I had developed a dry cough, niggling and annoying and flu was setting-in. I bought 'over the counter medicine' but it was like eating sweets, no potency. So I decided to leave after four days, the visa was only for ten days anyway.

The following day I purchased a train ticket for Lviv, a town in western Ukraine. I met with Oleg for a coffee, two days earlier he went very much out of his way so I could find an internet shop, which had a lousy connection but managed to send a few important messages. At the station it was Bon-voyage to Tatyana. She explained to the carriage conductor to 'pencil me in for a wake-up call at Lviv.'

The journey was slow, very slow. A cabin shared with a conservatively dressed middle-aged lady. I coughed almost continuously, apologizing periodically. No sympathy was shown, she departed after an hour. I was feeling crap and probably looked crap, dozing-off periodically.

The train stopped, my head was resting against the panel next to the window, thinking about nothing, a long silence. Then the cabin door squeaked, as it swung open. Three men in Soviet-style uniforms with stern expressions appeared. I straightened myself up. One stared down at me as he drew closer; he was trying to say something. I pulled my passport from the inside pocket of my bomber jacket and handed it over. He looked through the pages, making comments to his associates, every previous stamp was studied. Then he began to browse through his official notebook and comparing something. My mind started racing, have I got anything illegal. My heartbeat increased, is he looking for a way to poach dosh out of me. It was just past midnight, a heavy darkness with few lights outside, a real feeling of isolation. Would this be one of those dreaded border crossings that we hear stories about, I'm not sure we are even at the border.

How much money is allowed to be carried. I have local currency and Russian rubbles. U.S. dollars are hidden in my backpack. Quite a large sum of travellers checks also. The rules are different here and frankly, I don't know them. But let's not panic, I can handle this.

A much older officer came by, words were exchanged between them. A long pause and then the page was stamped.

Off they went, maybe there was bigger fish to fry.

Fifteen minutes later the train came to another screeching halt. I could hear the noisy entrance into our carriage, heavy stomping footsteps grew louder.

'Oh shit, here we go again.' Was this the contemporary K.G.B. They stopped at my cabin, a large pair of black boots, then a second pair. I looked-up, a broad rugged face in heavy military style overcoat gazed at me.

"Ello" in a deep voice, then a wry smile.

I guess this was Ukrainian immigration.

"Pass-purtt," with his hand out.

Relaying it to his assistant, who examined it thoroughly.

"They say you fom Olland,"

I half-smiled "Ire-land."

The senior officer took off.

The younger one having decent English, asking "how much mon-nee u ave."

The question caught me by surprise, fidgeting and pulling currency from my pocket.

"50 dollars, U.S., Russian rubbles," quickly checking, "623. Belarusian money not much," shrugging my shoulders.

"Not for me" he responded, "customs," pointing at the heavy lady that suddenly appeared at the cabin door.

I returned her smiled and nodded.

They both disappeared returning five minutes later with the appropriate stamp.

"Enjoy your oliday."

At least they had courtesy.

The train pulled into Lviv station, 5:40a.m. on a large clock. The taxi drivers were there in droves, one greeting me as I disembarked the train. "Taxi sir, taxi sir."
'Too early to check-in at hotel Lviv, I'll hang-out a little at the station,' I'm thinking.

****

A new town, new country, the second largest inside Europe. I had friends here, Svetlana and her family who I had visited on a previous trip. I rested on the steps outside, with a coffee and a sandwich, I didn't know what it was, some kind of meat. I was hungry and I will eat anything when my stomach is rumbling. Watching the action as a new day began. Commuters were arriving, many were elderly women with headscarf, long skirt, apron and long overcoat. They seemed to be heading for the local market. Pushing small trolleys packed with sacks of potatoes, onions, carrots, apples, leeks and cabbage, probably grown on their family plots.
Many struggled with their loads as they negotiated the steps, coming out of the station. A simple ramp would be the answer.
In the waiting room, people were sleeping, large bags were plentiful, no stylist luggage here. A heavy fusty stench hung in the air.
I bought local currency, the hryvnia [pronounced greev-na].Russian rubbles were accepted. Belarussian greenbacks, I had hundreds but couldn't get rid of them.
That evening I met with Svetlana, who spoke good English, her sister Kalynia, a little less and their mum. I had contacted them a week earlier to announce my arrival. They were well dressed but all looked concerned. We shared a few beers and soft drinks in a mid-town restaurant.
"Come stay with us," she offered.
I accepted without hesitation.

Next day I knocked on their seventh floor apartment at twelve noon. A stranger answered, she was not sure how to react. As I stood there wearing a big black seventies-style-Afro-wig and sunglasses, in a hunch stance, my backpack strapped-up.
"Hello, you speak...... English."

No answer, but a little smirk.

"Maybe Russian…….French,………o.k. Spanish,……………...
German, oh no……..Ukrainian, yea, da, da."

She nodded in agreement, laughing a little more now. I was just acting the clown, having a laugh. They were expecting me but sent their friend to answer the door. I stepped into the apartment, three women emerged from different rooms, lots of giggles to loud chuckles. Svetlana, Kalynia and their cousin. It was like, they were playing a trick on me, by hiding and I was playing one on them. Everyone wanted to do a party piece with the wig, the girls shaping it differently with head bands and ribbons.

Their apartment was spacious with three bedrooms, a kitchen, bathroom and living room.

Later, I suggested privately to my hosts that we tip-over to the local shops, "let's have dinner ready when you mum arrives home from work."

We bought the usual items of meat, vegetables, fruit, milk and bread. Svetlana was slightly embarrassed, but her sister was less bashful. Total cost of $22 [U.S.].

Her mum had a job, bartending. Seven days on, seven days off, for a salary of $25[U.S.] per month. Their father had somehow managed to get a visa for Greece and was gone there to work.

Svetlana explained that, "things went good for eight months. He had a job in construction. Money was sent home each month. We were not rich, it was just enough for our weekly needs. He had an accident at work and injured his back. His boss is not interested in helping him. So he is trying to recover his health. If he comes home there are no jobs here."

"Yes, I am so sorry, I can imagine his boss, not caring about safety issues. He is probably arrogant and disrespectful," as I tried to offer some comfort.

The following day, Oleg, a neighbour came by and offered a walking tour. So off we went with Svetlana as our translator. The Ivan Franko theatre dominates the town centre at prospeck Svobody.

"Oleg has performed in this building many times," Svetlana explained.

"He has travelled to Italy and France to sing in Opera concerts."

He managed to persuade the custodian to allow us a quick look around. The interior is dominated by a massive central staircase. Icons of passed eras and a picture gallery are located on the upper level. The stage was been prepared for an evening show with lighting and sound been tested.

Back on the street Oleg belching out his operatic voice in a humorous way, gaining attention from Saturday afternoon shoppers. A large recessed flower bed out front of the theatre where once stood a statue of Lenin.

"We are Ukrainians, there will be no Russian leaders in this town." The translation continued in the middle of this tree lined prospeckt. "Taras Shevchenko, this is our country's leading poet. He fought to keep the Ukrainian language. Look at these beautiful flowers that people lay at his feet every day. This is a special area for national gatherings," Svetlana continued.

With seats and tables, pensioners congregated to play checkers and chess. I was invited to a challenge in checkers, becoming victorious to the surprise of everyone. I declined my winnings from the elderly local, a ten hryvnia bet.

We entered the Ivan Franko Park, another famous poet, located near the Western university. A middle aged man was performing hand stands and then deep stares on his knees with the usual whiff of alcohol. Speaking of which was part of our itinerary. Slavutych beer was the order at each café, with vodka shots thrown in periodically. Svetlana opting for soft drinks to keep some sanity in the group. Museums and churches were plentiful, many restored by the catholic Community. Cobbled streets give it a historical feel, this area ruled by Poland at one time, but Stalin changed that after world war two. In western Ukraine people are nationalist, strong belief in their own country. They speak their native language and don't like Russia, who could blame them. Unable to control their destiny, ruled from Moscow for many years. Oleg, always breaking into verse to shock others around.

The next day I went to see a doctor, as my illness was sustaining. Svetlana, doing the talking as I kept quiet. For sure the previous day of drinking didn't help. But I wanted to entertain my new friends, they needed a break from reality. An attractive lady-doctor examined me. She never cracked even a hint of a smile in the ten minute visit. Women in this part of the world have natural beauty, but they always seemed to be worried about something.

Later I asked Svetlana, about making a payment.

"I told her you are my cousin from Poland, she thinks you are poor like us." More medicine, but with little effect.

I bought chocolate for my hosts, this would be a massive mistake. Upon eating it, Svetlana, elegant and graceful, Kalynia, a slightly wilder touch, developed food poison.

At 3a.m. a doctor was called, they receive injections for their stomach pains. I had slept through the drama, shamefully offering an apology the following morning. What would they really think of me, just a few days as their guest and I tried to vanish them.

It was a common problem in the former Soviet countries. Food items did not have expiry dates marked correctly. With the girls resting I went off to enjoy the sunshine. I took a bus to one park, strolled around in the shade of tall fully bloomed trees, but no open area to stretch-out. With the help of mothers wheeling their infants, I seek two other parks. Lots of trees but no central lawns to sunbathe in this city of one million inhabitants.

Trying a native dish, I had Golubtsy, which is cabbage rolls stuffed with meat and potatoes, tasty and filling.

Returning to the seventh floor apartment where events had taken a turn for the worst. My eviction papers were waiting for me. At least with the 'Big brother television show,' the warning signs are visible and your housemates have a say in the matter.

The girls were in the living room, I decided not to disturb them. Reading my guide book in the kitchen where their mother made me a sandwich and tea. Later the three women seemed to be having a serious talk, loud verbal exchanges, periodically. Then the mother came to the kitchen, looking dejected, handing me a note, written was "that I must not stay in the apartment. Their relatives do not want a foreign man under the same roof as three women, I must leave today."

The family did not want me to go, but their uncle was adamant. He lived near-by and would make trouble if I stayed. Svetlana, was in no mood to tell me, writing the note for her mum.

I responded, "this is your house, not your uncle's. I can pay you for accommodation instead of a local hotel."

Their response was that I would be gone in a week, but they had to live with their relative. The mother was visibly annoyed as she walked me to the elevator.

A taxi brought me to hotel Lviv, where I didn't stray too far for the next three days, trying to get healthy.
Svetlana is so humble, bumping into her on the street one afternoon.
"Haaaay, what's going on, let's have a burger," I offered.
"I cannot stay long, I must cut my friend's hair," she said.
"Ah it's o.k. you can do that tomorrow night."
"Sean, she will pay me two hryvnia. I can give this to my mum so she can have the bus fare for work tomorrow."
I literally had to force Svetlana to accept crumpled local currency I pulled from my pocket, that moment has never left me.
'I can help now, for a few days, perhaps a few weeks, but what happens then,' I was thinking as I prepared to leave.

The weather was becoming cooler rather quickly, so I boarded a train to travel south for Odessa on the Black sea. Jumping on a locomotive is my favourite way of distant journeys. Lviv to Odessa, 16 hours, from the west to the south, through miles of flatlands. The former bread basket of the Soviet Union, perfect for farming crops, vegetables and potatoes. Also the front lines in world-war-two, for a time. When the Germans eyed Russia, Belarus and Ukraine were occupied first. These two countries had enormous loss of life and structure.
I shared with a school teacher and her daughter who had just completed a nursing degree, excellent company, a vivacious family. We discussed life in Europe, east and west.
The former 'Iron Curtain' today is a rust bucket. Relics of a past industrial era are visible. Factories that once flourished are now empty shells.
In the smaller towns on long station platforms women with rugged complexions sold homemade food; salads, sandwiches and fruits. Many wore traditional aprons and headscarfs. We contributed to this local economy and shared our purchases, the items passed through a window.

****

We finally reached Odessa, coming to a halt shortly after 8a.m., a popular holiday destination for the natives and Russians. Large square box trunks, cotton sacks, bulging plastic bags tied with rope littered the platform. Porters scurrying with vintage wooden trolleys offering their services. I strolled through the main concourse with my backpack tied firmly.

One elderly woman approached me, holding a sign, KOMNATI, KOMNATI, advertising for lodgers. I asked how much, giving her a pen. $15[U.S.] she wrote.

"No, no" shaking my head with a smile.

I sat down for a moment, contemplating about a place to stay. It was Friday morning, the weekend. Surely all the budget hotel rooms would be full in the downtown area. I walked through the main front doors, down the steps, about four people approached me with offers of accommodation. I listened and looked at their signs, $15-$25 was the price range. Lodging in a private house for a couple of nights was probably the best option.

Soon I was surrounded by middle-aged to elderly folk, most were women, all offering rooms. One tall elegant-looking lady suddenly appeared at the back of the group.

"Most of them are not good places to stay," she said in near perfect English. "How much," I asked.

"25 dollars," she replied.

I smiled and shook my head, no, 'a bit too slick' I'm thinking.

I had a local street map, I wanted to stay near the waterfront, walking distance from downtown.

Then the elderly lady, who made the initial approach, slapped a sign inches from my face. Forty hryvnia in large writing.

I showed her my map, explaining a couple of landmarks.

"Where is your house?"

She pointed to an area on the map.

"O.K. let's go," I said.

We hopped into a taxi and off we went. Checking my map, we certainly were not going in the direction of the waterfront.

My lodgings were in a six-story residential building. I was served breakfast of boiled eggs, toast and black tea. Milk is not commonly used, a luxury item for many. I was given a large room with an uncomfortable bed. I wrote down the phone number and address of my host, went to the nearest bus stop and headed off downtown.

Odessa has a population of one million. The city centre with a grid system is easy to navigate. The Opera house, it's most famous building with circular shape architecture was receiving a face-lift. Near-by the Potemkin steps, 192 in total, they lead down to the second biggest lake in the world, the Black Sea. The port was busy, the clinking of cranes is evident from a distance. Many cargo boats dot the horizon, waiting for a space at the docks. The Black Sea is of strategic military importance for the Soviets during communists times and today, surrounded by a number of countries: Russia, Ukraine, Bulgaria, Georgia, Romania and Turkey.

Derybosiskia Street is the main artery in midtown, named after a Frenchman, de Ruby who lead the capture of the area from the Turks. Market stalls were active selling art, antiques, pottery and native souvenirs. Artists dotted the sidewalk, portraits their specialty. Later as dusk came upon us, I asked a guy who was doing a questionnaire survey, for directions. We chatted for a few minutes, he invited me to his English speaking group.

"We meet every Friday to practice our English. Please come, just give me ten minutes, two more customers."

As we walked, moving further from the busy pedestrian area into dimly light streets, I had a slight suspicion. 'Is this a trap? Right now it's one against one. 'What can I lose, about sixty hryvnia in my pocket. That'll not break the bank,' I was thinking.

It was a pleasant surprise, a wide range of young to middle aged locals in a brightly furnished room. My companion Vladimir, introduced me. I was put in the spotlight, seated in the centre. Many questions were thrown at me about my personnel life and Western Europe. Also on Ireland: Molly Malone, [Fictional character] Oscar Wilde and James Joyce [Irish writers, the latter some students were studying his work. He is actually the second most studied writer in the world after Shakespeare]. There was education in this room and I had to dig deep to keep-up. My first day in this a mix of industrial, commercial and holiday port town, I had made a new group of friends. It was a good feeling. I asked Vlad for help with finding an apartment. I showed him my current address.

"Oh no, this is the wrong part of town. It's not suitable for a tourist, meet me tomorrow and we will find something."

He helped me get a taxi back to my lodgings at the right price, refusing the initial asking fee from the driver.

Next morning I departed from my elderly landlady and checked-in downtown to a $9 room. This hotel was drab, creaky stairways, jaded wooden floors and walls that didn't see paint for twenty years. But what do I care, it's temporary.

I met with Vlad, "Come I will show you something."

We walked along Pyrmorsky Bulvar, buildings renovated with a touch of grandeur. Leading to the Potemkin steps, where I was the previous day. Now twenty-four hours later, the scenery had added glamour.

It was Saturday, 'Brides Day.' Every twenty minutes a wedding party passed through the Opera house gardens and along the cobble stones leading to the steps. It's high altitude with heavy growth in the backdrop down to the sea. Skilled looking photographers directing and clicking, the guest list normally limited for economic reasons.

In the afternoon we tipped into a bookie, a few friendly bets on The European football championship games. Ireland were playing Russia in Moscow. We won enough for a few nights entertainment, picking Holland, Slovenia, Portugal, Spain and Belgium for victories.

Vlad was joyous that the Russians won.

I questioned this, "you are Ukrainian?"

He explained, "I don't feel Ukrainian. Life has not changed much since independence. Many people I know have Russian background, I speak Russian, let's be Russian again."

We checked the newspaper for rental adverts. Vlad made the telephone calls, making sure not to mention that I was a foreigner. Certainly the price would be jacked-up. Arkadia was the recommended area.

"This sounds too far from the city centre," I protested.

"Trust me" he replied, "it's near the beach, with shops and some night-life." Appointments were made for the following morning.

The first flat, the owner was present. She was like a gramophone, loud and repeating herself. It looked like a storage warehouse, too much furniture. The next flat had an old-fashion interior look, but spacious. The price was right at $45 per week, a deal was signed with the real estate agent and I would move-in the next day.

The owner was there to meet me, a chemist, showing me her identification. Accompanied by her daughter, Katharina who was a college student. They were keen to make me feel welcomed and comfortable, insisting on a weekly visit with clean bed linen and towels. Katharina, invited me to meet her fellow students at the local university.

"We could do talks," she suggested.

"On what," I asked.

"On your life, Europe, economics, politics, your family, general things. Come today if you wish, it's just about one mile from here."

"Sure, why not, I'll drop by at lunch-time."

Katharina, wrote the address and directions. We met at 1p.m. at the campus coffee shop. My scepticism soon subsided when Katharina brought me to the teachers staff room. I was introduced to a number of teachers, the English lecturer Tamara, introducing herself, took charge.

"We need permission to do talks in the classroom. I like this idea, it's an opportunity for us all to talk with a foreigner on a casual bases."

I was thinking, a few sodas and a bit of banter in the student canteen, but they had planned and wanted much more.

Administrators kept 'passing the buck.' We had to visit three offices before a decision was made, Tamara, translating proceedings.

"This is the top man," she whispered, as we entered yet another office.

After a short conversation, "I think he is not a spy" the top man said.

I laughed, "the cold-war is over, but my country was not involved."

"Who knows the real players," he responded with a wry smile.

Tamara confided, "we'll do this during the English class, but keep it a secret, I don't want everyone to know."

The following week was pencilled in for three talks.

Friday night had rolled around, I could hear the sound in the distance as I walked towards Arkadia beach. Coloured lights flashing, a full house, the music pumping. No standing on the sidelines, that's monotonous, hit the dance floor.

One girl returned my smile, with a beautiful grin. Soon we were chatting, Irina was her name. Speaking pigeon English, but at least it was better than my Russian. She had dark hair and dark eyes, that'll get my heart-rate up. In a group of six, conversing with the others didn't go much further than smiling and clinking our glasses. Sadly, she was leaving in a couple of hours, "my train go at seven." She was returning to Minsk, in Belarus, this was a work-related trip.

A few days later I was playing football on the beach, Vlad and two of his buddies making it two against two. The ball accidentally hit a sunbather and knocked her soft drink. I apologized and bought her another. Galina was her name, on holiday from Minsk. This city I had visited three weeks earlier, finding it a tough job to make friends, now within a couple of days I was meeting friendly vibrant folk from that town. Galina and I became buddies, we communicated in Spanish. Studying this language in my secondary school days was not a total loss.

In my neighbourhood I was becoming familiar with the local traders in the fruit and vegetable market, also the shopkeepers where I bought meat, bread, milk and beer. I could buy food to cook dinner at the cost of $1, very economical. In the building I shared beer with neighbours on the next floor. The conversation stuttered, but the hospitality flowed.

The local electric buses and privatized mini-buses were inexpensive and frequent, six kilometres to the town centre. Taxis were plentiful, if I was running late, just put my arm up and within one minute someone would stop, normally a Lada car driver. Anyone can use their car as a taxi. If they are heading in your direction, they will take you. The price I always negotiated before making myself comfortable in the front passenger seat, moments later getting the driver slightly agitated by clicking-on my seat belt.

"Noh, noh" they would grunt in protest. The car radio would be changed to one with English songs.

I borrowed a bicycle from Rona, who was director of a private English school across the street from my flat. Seeking her assistance with trivial issues, using pay phones, getting directions. Rona and her teachers, Yury and Oleg liked to chat with me. I would cycle on the narrow beach road that was off-limits to traffic, fresh air and exercise.

Other foreign visitors were floating around Odessa. Craig, an Aussie, had a questionable attitude, probably never bought a drink for anyone in his life. Also Dave from California, we became friends but not too close.

Then there was Remi and Edger, the Dutch lads, typically amicable, on their way to Australia on motorbikes. An e-mail came through days later. A sixteen hour ferry ride across the Black Sea to Istanbul took ten hours longer. Their bikes badly damaged from the rough seas.

Bob, another Aussie was looking to marry a local.

"I was here last year, I was seeing a girl, but then discovered she is engaged. I'm meeting someone tomorrow who I have been writing to."

An Irish bar was an attraction for the foreigners. It had the usual interior memorabilia, beers and spirits from the 'ol country,' but not always the right clientele.

It was here I met Irish guys, two from county Kerry and another from Limerick. They were on a contract to install a floating crane at the docks. Every evening the Kerry lads would hit the high stool. John, in his mid-twenties would talk about football; Kerry and Liverpool. Flirting with the waitresses, they didn't understand his jokes.

Pat, much older would say, "we have problems on this site. I think they don't trust us westerners. They're always stopping the progress of the job, especially the older ones. That Igor is a 'pain in the butt,' he gives you that suspicious look. I'm not going to him anymore."

I explained, "yea lads, through my correspondence I learned some of the teachings in the old Soviet block was that the west is weak. Communism was better, the west could not be trusted."

"Maybe he's ex-K.G..B." [Soviet secret police] I jibed.

"He's got a chip on his shoulder about something," John chipping-in.

"Win them over lads, take them out for a few pints."

When life is moving smoothly it's inevitable for a sudden change. One evening I was resting, stretched on the couch, wearing shorts and a tee-shirt, reading a book about Russian history. I heard a door bell ring.

'Is that mine, or next door,' I was thinking.

About twenty seconds later I heard a door opening. I went to see, in the hallway were three men, probably in their late-twenties.

"Oh you here," said one looking startled.

"Yes, who are you?" I said aggressively.

They began to laugh, "my father live here," the bulky one said.

"I live here," I shot back.

"One moment, one moment" he responded, expressing a calming gesture. "Two more weeks on lease, now he in Kiev."
I went to pick-up the phone in the kitchen. Calling Vlad, there was no answer. Searching out Rona's number, explaining the situation, putting one of these guys on the line.
I nonchalantly strolled to the bedroom, fetching my trainers, feeling vulnerable in my bare feet. They were watching me.
Suddenly they rushed out the door. I give chase, struggling with the laces untied as I stumbled down three flights of stairs. They disappeared out of sight. I ran to the main road, in the distance they were jumping into a cab. Wise-guys, scumbags, away with keys to the apartment. Relaying the incident to my landlady, through Rona as a translator. The locks were changed the following day, the locksmith dressed in combat gear.
"It's the workman's style around here," laughed Vlad who had come over to visit. "I guess their friends had rented this flat before and they got extra keys cut. They are probably from Kiev and are down here on business. They were taking a chance, hoping the flat was empty," he explained.
A few days later I was going off cycling when I noticed the outside handle of the door was broken, lying on the floor, had these idiots returned.

At the Friday night English language meeting, one guy was talking about cultural differences, he had just returned from a business trip in Italy. Most were drawing a conclusion that Ukraine had too many administration obstacles. I chatted with Olena who had great humour, Vlad, pushing for me to take her for a drink.
We met the next night and after one Scotch n' soda on the rocks,' she left. Said she had to attend church the next morning.
I thought we were on a date but forty minutes in, Olena didn't just call for a 'time-out,' the game was abandoned. Somewhere along the way I made a positive comment on America and sensed that slightly scorned glance coming back at me. She jumped into the opposite track. Was I been used and abused, well........................ she did have smelly breadth, which is worst than a fart, because it's there all the time.

****

The talks with the university students were refreshing, politely asking many questions about my life. Then I turned the tables, pointing out that their country had gained independence just twelve years ago. A whole new process has started, this new system will take many years to grow into something positive. Everyone has a role to play.

"This is your country now, so try to make a difference. It will not happen overnight, but it will happen," I encouraged. Some talked about emigrating. "Our future will be much better if we live in a western country," one guy at the back shouted.

"O.K. students, please understand that wherever you live, one must need an income. In the west of Europe life is not easy. People buy houses and cars with money borrowed from banks. These loans must be paid back. A person may lose their job, then they can have trouble paying a loan. So there is pressure to keep things right," I explained. Complaints about the government were most common.

"They show no leadership, Kuchma our president is no good," one girl voiced.

"O.K. when the next election comes around make sure you vote against him. Get all your family and friends to vote against the government," I encouraged.

"We cannot trust them, they will probably cheat in the election," coming from the back again.

"Don't lose hope, if something is not right, then go to the government buildings and protest."

"Sir, we need a leader, will you help us," with a pleading expression. I started laughing at his frankness.

"Young man, that's three times you have talked. You are strong, you have courage, I think you could be a leader."

In 2005 the Kuchma government won the general election. Thousands of Ukrainian citizens took to the streets in their capital, Kiev to protest vote rigging. Weeks later a second election was called, which brought a new leader. This was the 'Orange Revolution.'

In 2013, sadly, Ukrainians are protesting again because of bad government and war could breakout.

The night clubs at Arkadia beach were very interesting. Certainly not as busy or flashy as the dance venues in the popular holiday areas of Western Europe. One had an Egyptian style arena, another shaped like an igloo. A third, my favourite had a Greek fortress theme. Semi-circular terracing facing a multi pillared stage with the Black sea in the background. Disc-Jockeys spinning a mixture of western pop and rock with local hits, also techno thrown in. At intervals donned in ancient Greek attire, dancers performed, later a solo act by one individual, shrouded in female fabric.
"That's a man," I predicted as my companions expressed doubt. "The shoulders are too broad, the body is a little stiff. Surely a woman would glide across the stage more smoothly," I challenged. As the act terminated the clothing became undone to reveal my suspicions.

These clubs were vacated in October and left to an eerie silence until another summer would roll around. Alternatively, other venues were opening up in the city centre for the winter. For me, Odessa, on the Black Sea was a welcome change from the masses that flock to the Mediterranean. No contending with the British larger louts, or the punctual Germans who take all the beach umbrellas and get the best spots, the Scandinavians who are so good-looking but too disciplined. With few westerners it was a greater opportunity to mix with the natives from the former 'Red territory.'

Ten Hrynvia was the agreed price, expressing ten with my hands. "Da, da," said the driver, a short ride to Odessa train station. As I hopped out with my backpack, paying the fare, the driver stared and asked for more money. I think he was saying eighteen, I give him ten which was enough.
"Fucking Irish."
"Fucking Ukraine," as I closed the car door.
The waiting area was like a furniture showroom, long large couches, coffee tables, reclining armchairs. I relaxed with a bottle of Obolon beer for company. A station worker greeted me with a smile, "ticket please" in perfect English. She informed me that my train was already in platform four, observing that I was a foreigner, offering a little help.
An overnight train ride to Kiev sharing a cabin with a tough-looking

fat native who I had to nudge several times for his snoring. The other passengers were Syrian, surprisingly.

"It's much cheaper to study in this country," they informed.

Having trouble sleeping, one of them kept yapping. I hushed to her a number of times, always in vain. Until about 3a.m., eventually in my best Arabic with a dash of Gaelic I told her, "Salam, le do thoill, dhun dha ghob." The silence became deafening.

Before reaching Kiev my cabin companions had departed. I was now joined by Anna who lived in a small town, a couple of hours from the capital. She was on her way to the German Embassy.

Local women were mingling outside the main train station in Kiev advertising rooms. Anna fluent in English, German and of course Ukrainian, helped me clinch a deal in accommodation. A small flat, five minutes walk from the station. I offered to buy Anna breakfast for her goodwill gesture. "Come with me to the embassy, we can eat later," she insisted.

She explained it would take three trips to Kiev to receive a visa. "Germany is the easiest country in the European Union for us to enter. I have lived there before and have friends in Hamburg. I speak the language so a job is not a real problem."

It was 8:30a.m., the German consulate was probably the busiest place in the whole city at this time. Long lines had already been formed. Travel agents were displaying flyers on bus prices to Berlin. Others offered reduced airline fares. One security guard asked me if I was German. "Yes, I um fum Berrlinn," in my awkward German mimic.

Ushering me into a much shorter queue, Anna following, the paperwork was completed in twenty minutes.

"This normally takes about three hours," she giggled.

My blarney worked this time.

At a local café I wasn't sure what to eat, no specific breakfast on the menu. Everything gets served almost together, they had no sense of timing. Anna continued her friendly banter, "my family have friends in America, Germany, Canada and Israel. Many people want to leave my country. A good job is hard to find, money is a problem for us. My brother is a good basketball player, he will try and get a college basketball scholarship in Canada or America."

I wished her well as I walked her to the platform for the return journey.

****

So why did I come to this country?

Many of us have a soft spot for some far-away place. There is not always a transparent reason. The Black Sea was one of mine. A flight to Turkey could be the choice, but that's too obvious. Let's take another route.

Why not go behind the 'Iron Curtain,' communism has collapsed, the 'Cold War' has vanished. Eastern Europe and beyond has become a whole different status.

Today with many new independent nations, the time had come to taste the secretive off-limit lands, so Ukraine was the pick.

On my maiden trip, eighteen months earlier as we taxied towards Boryspil International airport terminal in Kiev, there was a feeling of isolation. I counted seven other planes on the tarmac, all had the Cyrillic alphabet logo. The area looked aged with little glamour.

At the immigration desks the entry forms had awkward questions, the process slow. A sense that I am a long way from home, thinking, 'there is nothing here, what am I getting myself into.'

In the arrivals hall I tried for a bus but could not read the signs. The information desk gave me blank stares and shrugs.

"Can anyone speak English?" I asked.

The taxi counter was communicative, simply because they were out to rob me. I produced my guide book and showed them my intended destination, the Saint Petersburg hotel written in Cyrillic also.

Sixty U.S. dollars was the asking price. I point blankly refused. Then he came down to forty, eventually we settled for twenty-five.

A dual carriageway from the airport, mass residential blocks were visible as we drew closer to the urban streets. Also many three-storey office buildings with shops on the ground level, an east European feeling of structure duplicates, small windows and lots of concrete.

Upon arriving at the hotel, I questioned, "is this the Saint Petersburg hotel?"

"Da, da," the taxi driver nodding and pointing.

Comparing the sign over the door to the Cyrillic in my book, I could see no resemblance.

The front desk lady was most helpful speaking fluent English. I paid one hundred U.S. dollars for three nights. Each day she asked for my opinion, questions on service, food, people and the city.

"Please be frank, tell me what you think."

"Well at breakfast the coffee was too strong and the bread was stale."

There was a definite improvement the following morning.

I met with two of my correspondents, lunch with Kate, a primary school teacher who had a shy personality.

"My English has improved so much with our letter exchanges," she beamed. "No charge for this," I joked.

"I am studying English, three months left in the course, then I will try to teach private lessons."

"That's brilliant Kate, try to target businessmen as clients. You can charge them a high price," I advised.

Kate told me that teachers help students pass their test exams.

"We give them the answers when it's necessary. Life is financially hard for many families, so we feel sorry for the students."

"Does anyone fail?" I quizzed.

"We do not want anyone to fail, we try to help everyone."

"At university, some teachers accept a bribe from students, to receive a good grade."

"Some chance of that happening in Ireland," I responded.

In the afternoon Akalena came by, "how much you pay for this room?" was the first thing she said. Stating the price, she looked at me in a shock expression. "We will have to get you out of here. Do you know my salary for one month is $50."

"O.K. lets buy a local newspaper and check the accommodation section."

On my flight, one English guy told me, "go to Kreschatyk street, it's downtown. Get to know the people, the women are beautiful."

Looking at Akalena, he was not wrong, tall, slim, blonde hair, hazel-green eyes, very attractive.

We met a real estate agent at Independent Square, which was in the process of a major reconstructive development. As I looked through the security hoarding a massive crater with hundreds of workers busy laying foundations, health and safety didn't look too good.

We entered the Metro underground, a very long escalator took us deep below ground onto the platform. Arch formations everywhere, brown and beige been the dominant colour, the lighting kept to a minimum. Exiting three station stops later, we walked quite a distance before the agent asked for directions. The area was dilapidated, broken footpaths full of weeds, grass growing on the road, shabby buildings.

I voiced an objection, the agent insisted on keeping the appointment. We passed a military barracks, young women were shouting through the high metal gates to their fancy uniform men. Finally after walking thirty-five minutes we reached the address.

A three-story building, elderly people seated in the backyard on rocking chairs, the men smoking pipes, the women knitting. The agent communicated with one lady who summoned us inside. Everything looked seventeen century, the cupboards, furniture, pottery and utensils. The fridge door was heavily taped to keep closed. The stairs was narrow with linoleum of an undistinguished colour. A low ceiling in the bedroom, certainly the bed was Napoleonic, metal framed headboard and base raised on a platform, a ceramic piss-pot underneath. Only a man of five-feet-nothing could stretch-out on the mattress. Did a local museum close and they bought the contents.

"I will take it," testing Akalena.

Who responded with a fearful stare. The agent and Akelena laughed all the way back to the metro station, conversing on our mission.

I was invited to stay with Akalena's family until I found a suitable place. Apartment blocks littered the Kiev suburbs, my new temporary home on the ninth floor of a fifteen-story tower block. Shots of vodka were the opening course for the family dinner, continuing through the evening. Not a sober head, by desert time. The neighbourhood was similar to Saint Petersburg, rugged dusty paths through the housing blocks. Shaky elevators and discoloured brickwork, the playgrounds in need of repair. Local markets with women vendors, traditionally dressed, selling home-grown produce.

Metro stations were a hive of activity, people selling old-house wares, toys and clothing. Flowers were always a common commodity. We continued to look for an apartment and three days later the search ceased. I moved into a modern building with eighteen floors, fully furnished with wall to wall carpet, cable television, a domestic luxury. A walk-out balcony, twenty-four hour security, gardeners. Many diplomats resided in the building, $400 for one month. I had a view of possibly one of the world's largest statues, upon visiting the metallic image, a woman brandishing a sword and shield, officially known as the 'Defence of the motherland' monument. Visible from many parts of the city as it overlooks the Dnipro River. The message seems to be, 'don't mess with the Soviets, you will lose.' Nearby, are World-War-Two army tanks and planes. At the base of the statue a museum dedicated to both world wars.

The Afghanistan museum and monument is a short distance away with the names of many who perished. Of course this is one war the Soviets lost. So the structure is small and subtle, possibly one of the reasons for the fall of communism.

A fifteen minute walk from my residence is the Caves monastery. Kate, my school teacher pen friend been my escort. Making friends with Dan at this the city's most visited tourist site. He was now living in New York, back in his native homeland to see his family. My friends translating as the group guide led the historical tour. A huge bell tower which offered us panoramic views, gold domed churches, cobbled courtyards. Underground labyrinths lined with mummified monks, their remains wrapped in cloth and stored in glass cages. Monasteries turned into museums, historical structures in immaculate condition.

The most charming street in Kiev is Andriyivsky Uzviz. Angelina and Jaroslava, local friends walked me through on a Sunday afternoon. We started at Sophia's cathedral, at one entrance to the grounds of the cathedral are the remains of Kiev Patriarch Volodymyr Romaniuk, which are actually outside this estate.

The Ukraine Orthodox church paid allegiance to the Russian Orthodox church for many years. In the 1990's it broke ranks from the Russians. This created hostilities and in 1995 tensions erupted into violence. The Ukraine government in fear of retaliation from Moscow refused the Kiev Patriarch to be buried inside the grounds of Saint Sophia's cathedral. His resting place is at the gates, outside the grounds, where you would park your car. It looks a bit strange but I guess his followers were adamant, doing the next best thing. Many protesters were injured with police, religious men behaving in an unsavoury manner. I guess we are all sinners in different ways. Angelina explained her brother is an orthodox priest, married with two children. Because of his status, he is not allowed a high position within the church. Only single people will be in the hierarchy, which I think is a good idea, perhaps the Catholic Church could follow suit. Looking across the open square, opposite Saint Sophia's, a magnificent monastery is visible. Saint Michael's, with seven golden cupolas and a bell tower built in a vertical axis.

It was torn down by the communist regime in the 1930's to make way for a central building, but nothing ever got erected. In 1996 the foundations began for this current building. It's blue and white in colour, simply beautiful. As we approach Andriyivsky Uzviz, another breath-taking structure comes into view. Blue, white and gold, this is Saint Andrew's, with five crossed shaped domes. The purposed site, it is believed the apostle Saint Andrew erected a cross. It's elevation creating a more spectacular effect. With views of the Dnipro River and the vast residential concrete jungle beyond, this street is high with a downward spiral. An artist's headquarters with galleries, gift shops and cafes. Street vendors sternly reluctant to drop their prices as I attempt to haggle. Humorous postcards depicting Khrushchev and Kennedy, the Soviet and U.S. leaders in the early 1960's who almost went into battle over Cuba, the Cold-War era. Only a decade earlier this stationary would not be tolerated. Reaching Podil, which is the historic mercantile district. More tourists' attractions, the most infamous, the Chernobyl museum, a fascinating exhibition on the World's worst nuclear disaster. Numerous photos of the clean-up crews who were exposed to high levels of radiation. Many other pictures which did not need any linguistic guide. In 1986 during testing of a nuclear generator, a reactor blew-up, supposedly ninety times more radioactive material than Hiroshima. Some reports say thirty-one people died in the initial explosion. Perhaps thousands perished later due to radiation sickness. The Ukraine health organization issued 4,600 fatalities, but who knows the official figures. Prypyat is the official town which was evacuated and remains at high risk today. Thousands worked in the clean-up which stretched to a 30 kilometre zone. About five million people in northern Ukraine, southern Belarus and south-east Russia were in immediate danger. Chernobyl is about 100 kilometres north of Kiev and 10 kilometres from Belarus. I'm sure many of the readers know this,.................right, maybe not. Some folk have returned to their contaminated lands, producing milk, meat and vegetables. Belarus was the most affected country.

Angie and Jaro [as I called them] were good company, explaining what they could. They had a fruit and veg. stall at Bessarnabsky market, just off Khreschatyk street. I was impressed by the cleanliness and quality foods, but I stayed clear of the butcher counters, chicken and red meat, openly displayed regardless of the high daily temperatures. I also avoided dried fish sold on many street corners.

There is a saying 'Brandy makes you randy,' but that's boloney, it makes you drunk. For my new friends it was Stolichnaya vodka, that's a safer bet, have a few, be merry and lose your inhibitions, just a little. A couple of shots and they would raise the level of vigor, great company on a weekend night with the ability to see the funny side of life.

Khreshchatyk, is Kiev's commercial boulevard, wide pavements, Soviet style building blocks in architecture. A constant thriving of locals, appropriately dressed for the weather. In summer brightly coloured clothing is the norm, but in winter keeping warm is a priority. Fashion statements especially with older folk is non-existent. Top heavy overcoat, headscarf and boots. The underground pedestrian paths were littered with vendors. Sadly one does not have to walk too far to notice a pensioner with their handout. Because of a paltry government salary, some will receive financial assistance from their families. But others have little choice but to take to the streets selling trivial items or singing. Many vantage points are occupied by these seniors, imagine your grandmother having to do this.

I invited Akalena for a night out, socializing in bars and night clubs were not exactly part of her itinerary, her salary did not allow it. We met in a downtown area, she was in the mood for dancing, looking more glamorous than a nominated actress on Oscar night. Arriving at the Cave nightclub, taxi drivers milling around outside waiting for a fare. As we entered through the main door, there was a loud bang, then darkness.

"Sorry, sorry, we have problem," said the doorman, locking us out.
"Surely it's only something small, they'll have the power back-on

soon," trying to reassure my friend. Minutes later the doors opened, the crowd was filing out. Then an announcement, "we will have power back-on in ten minutes."

I spoke to one guy wearing a Glasgow Celtic football jersey.

"It happens sometimes," shrugging his shoulders.

His female companion, a Dutch scientist was working on a European project, testing the soil for contamination because of the Chernobyl disaster.

"How is it," I quizzed.

"Well the plant is situated just ninety minutes drive from here."

Interrupting, "is it safe to eat fruits and vegetables."

"For you it is, been here for a short time, the food will pass through your system. Many have returned to their homes which are not far away from the plant. In my opinion that's a bad choice. This tragedy is such a stigma for this country," the Dutch woman informed.

A second announcement was made, "Sorry we have big problem, the power will not come back on tonight."

"We are off to do some drinking in the park, come with us," offered the Celtic-jersey man. But Akalena was annoyed, all dressed-up. We found an elegant restaurant still opened, a good atmosphere with a pleasant crowd. But the damage was done, dancing is what she wanted, but could not get.

****

Now on my second visit to this country, Independent square was completed. A new monument erected to celebrate Ukraine been a country. Fountains, shrubs and flower beds, seating and decorative pavements. An underground shopping centre, fast food emporiums, a delightful place to relax. Designer clothing stores were a mystery to me, how they survive.

"Only top corrupt government officials and their families can afford to buy there," one local put it. Purchasing customers were in short supply in these shops. What must the middle-aged and elderly be thinking? Reared in the communist system, now everything is changing before their eyes. Ben, a Canadian enlightened me over a few bottles of Obolon.

"There was nothing here ten years ago, Khreschatyk was a dimly lighted street. There was little variety in the shops, basic food and products. No bars, not a trendy restaurant. The locals bought cheap vodka and visited their friends. Dress code was monotonous, a limited choice. Russian Lada cars were everywhere.

Now look around, khreschatyk is like a Christmas tree, it glitters. So many new things have sprung-up. There is an abundance of goods in the shops. Bar and restaurant scene is growing, it's a dramatic change for anyone over thirty, for they would have been educated and worked in the old system," Ben continuing as I listen intently. "Before people hadn't got much, but it seemed enough. The majority were on the same level, invites to a neighbour's home were common. Now it's a free-for-all, it's about financial survival. Individualism, greed creeps-in, life becomes more impersonal. Invites to a neighbour's home are less frequent because of financial problems. Food and beverages cost money. I've been around these parts for about twelve years at the Canadian embassy here in Kiev, sometimes I'm sent up to Moscow. I know the terrain.

I was paying ninety dollars per week for my current accommodation. Five minutes walk to the Central train station which has an adjoining metro underground. Plenty of taxis and mini-buses for transport, I could not complain about getting around.

I headed off to O'Brien's Irish pub, one Friday evening. There was a mixed crowd of locals and foreigners. A number of the ex-patriots have started a business here, many have married a native.

I met a guy called Tom from the midlands in the U.K. His father English, his mother Irish, a sprightly character, married to a woman from southern Ukraine.

"Met her through a dating agency, it's three years since I tied the knot, it's going well." Tom would analyze the local women in the bar.

"Look at this one in the red, she is sitting there waiting for a guy. Sometimes he doesn't arrive, he's probably a businessman, it's an arrangement.

Some women have to find an alternative way of making money to put food on the table."

"That's very sad, I guess you can't always see it."

"Yea, that's right. But for me, I know what is going on, it's a growing problem here."

I asked about nightclubs, everyone said the 'Cave.' "Come along with us," Tom encouraged. "I'm going just for a laugh, my wife is gone to see her parents."

Two Germans and two Canadians making it a group of six. A queue had developed when we arrived. We were welcomed into the venue by the doorman bypassing the line. My new friends joked with the club staff. "Foreigners get priority, they normally spend more money," Tom informed. "It's not disrespectful, it's just a fact."

A full house, there was no space at the rotating bar. Tom was in my ear all night, explaining the possibilities of business opportunities but also the corruption of local government officials.

Outside the club, taxis were lined-up looking for business. I was reluctant to pay the taxi driver for the ride home, I thought he was at the wrong address. I did not recognize any landmarks that I memorized. But on closer scrutiny he had driven to the rear of the building. My apology was accepted.

The following evening, Saturday, I returned to O'Brien's, as Tom had insisted. "What are you drinking," he greeted me.

"The same as you," I answered. It was early evening and he was already half-tanked with Baltika. He introduced me to Tony, soft-spoken from southern England. Politics would dominate our conversation. I asked about the welfare of the country.

"The Ukraine government is very corrupt, it's highly evident. They get money from western nations to complete a project. But the hierarchy make sure a slice of the financial pie goes into their back pockets," Tony doing most of the talking, as I listened.

"Look at Independent Square, that was built with foreign aid. The president and his cronies probably slipped a couple of million into secret bank accounts."

Tony stopped for a moment to hear a news story on the television about Yugoslavia. "You know I lost my wife in that war, she was in the Polish army. I went to the war zone to try and find her, but I could not get the right kind of help. I ran around like an idiot, I could not get any official information. They would just pass me on to another organization. It was very dangerous, too many snipers who were trigger happy," almost in tears as he talked.

"So after that you came here," I asked.

"I have lived in Eastern Europe for the last eight years. I studied eastern European languages at Uni, I am now married to a Ukrainian woman. Lots of guys are coming here to find a wife, I guess it's like new pastures."

Of course I offered my sympathy.

Then Tom jumped-in with his forceful comments about football as the sports news came on.

"Leeds United that's my team. They're back again, history will repeat itself, Leeds will lead the way," Tom raising his arm in jubilation.

"Sorry mate, they haven't won anything yet. Their spending power will collapse, millions in the red. Buying too many players, something will crack."

"Leeds are on the brink, we are here to stay. I'll buy shares at that club."

"Bankruptcy is coming for them, we'll see how many shares you'll buy then," I replied.

Tony ordering more drinks enjoying the exchanges. A year later Leeds football club had major money problems. Today, they are in a lower division, struggling with their finances.

Dynamo Kiev is well known in European football circles. In recent years their best players moved overseas for the lure of higher salaries. Involved in the European Champions league, the biggest club show in football. Feynoord from Holland would come to town. In this tournament Dynamo play their home games in the national stadium. Eighty thousand capacity, a big open arena, not much cover if it rains. Nobody had warned me about the itinerary. Which if you arrive prepared will include; a newspaper or small towel because the seats are wet from the frost, a horn to blow, ear-plugs to soften the noise and be in good voice to cheer and sing, 'Dee-na-moo, Dee-na-moo.'

One guy kindly offered me part of his 'Kiev Times,' just enough to keep my ass dry.

"Sing, sing, sing" he encouraged.

The home team winning 2-0 with second-half goals. I had ear ache for three days, because from the folks next to me to the fans in the top row on the opposite side, there was one dominant sound, the blue and yellow [the national colours] blow horns.

I would attend an English speaking group who practiced their language skills, led by an American Christian. Making a new acquaintance, Natalie, a local dentist, whom I used, because of her inexpensive treatment. She had done three months training in Ireland, enjoyed football and invited me to Kiev's next home league game. Offering her money for the ticket, she adamantly refused. Total cost for four tickets was three U.S. dollars. I could not understand why so many military were inside the small stadium. Security of course, I guess they need something to do. Perhaps hanging around the barracks breeds boredom.

We have all heard about the severity of Russian winters, a heavy snowfall give me a taste of the weather that spreads across the former Soviet states. A prompt message, that it's time to leave. But I would wait for the mighty Italians, Juventus would visit for the next champions league game. In attendance with Natalie and her friend Eddie, who was a bank employee. His one piece of financial advice was, 'not to invest in Ukrainian banks that offer high interest rates. These banks disappear overnight with your money and somehow can never be found.'
These games kick-off at 10p.m. to coincide with the western European game times of 8p.m. I had higher elevation in the stadium this time. The police were everywhere, I was searched several times before reaching my seat. The beer drinkers were been snuffed-out by the law all through the game. Of course this was creating a hostile feeling among the vast crowd. A tumultuous roar greeted the opening goal. The blue and yellow horns were out in-force, We were armed with one each. Certainly less annoying when you are committed. Juventus carved out a 2-1 victory, 'you know the lucky Italians.'
It was after midnight when we exited the stadium, temperature minus seven Celsius. A warm bar was the option, Natalie leading the way to 'Eric's,' owned by a well known German. Seated next to us at the bar was a New Zealander. No incognito here, with his All-Black rugby jersey. On a mission for his government, involved in promoting emigration to his home country, just a small matter of having one hundred thousand dollars in your current account. Poland would be his next stop, a smart way to travel.

Next day I had a dental appointment at 4:30p.m. Having lunch in a

cafeteria style restaurant downtown, it's low prices attracted many.
A familiar accent ahead of me in the queue.
"Are you Scottish" I asked.
"I am, trying to start a business. Come join us, we'll be over here,"
he motioned.
Ray, a Celtic supporter, well travelled, warm and amicable,
introducing me to Renee, his girlfriend. Before I could wet my lips
with the first beer, Ray returned with more cutlery and another round
of drinks.
"Hurry-up Sean there, you're drinking like a girl."
He was planning to open a small casino, black-jack tables and poker
machines.
"Is there gamblers in this town?" I asked.
"There is, it's growing. At one time there was no gambling in the
communist system. Now with capitalism, everything is changing. I
worked for ten years in casinos in the Bahamas, so I know a thing or
two. I have just started working in a local casino, here. My employer
is a potential partner, I know he's testing me at the moment. They
don't understand, you must take a loss at first. Let the customer win,
let them get ahead."
"I seen you in the Golden Gate Irish bar, one night," I said.
"Yea, it's ridiculous, you walk in there and the waitress follows you
around with a menu, it's like a life folder. The bartender pours you a
drink and he thinks he has done you a favour. Too many staff, I
know they are trying to create jobs. But the employees need to
loosen-up, you know what I mean.
It's not a real Irish bar, they sell Irish beer and spirits, but the
atmosphere is missing."
"What's missing," asked Renee.
"A hundred Irishmen, this man's country is great. They'll laugh and
joke with you, no one is a stranger."
"Where are you living now?" Renee asked.
"London at the moment, it's a bit impersonal."
"Damn right it is, you could be dying on the street and nobody
would care," Ray bluntly adding.
"Let's go to the sports bar, I start work at six," he suggested.
He had lots of knowledge on world geography, but the conversation
kept coming back to sport.
I called Natalie, my dentist to reschedule my appointment, she give

me a 7:30p.m. slot. There were two surgery rooms at the dental clinic. Four dentists shared two treatment chairs. Alternating shifts, first patient could arrive at 6a.m. The last leaving after 9p.m. Try getting an evening appointment in Ireland, they would think you were high-on-drugs for suggesting it.

Two days later I was on an early morning bus ride to the airport. One big difference from western airports is I had to go through passport control before checking in my luggage, so one must say goodbye to friends and relatives much earlier. There was an Irish bar in the duty-free area, owned by Aer Rianta. [The Irish airport authority]. All these Irish bars across the Communist landscape, you'd never feel homesick.

The departure lounges were clean and tidy but not exactly overrun with frequent-flyers. I was on my way to Helsinki, Finland for a connecting flight to Hong Kong. Nine passengers boarded the plane, that's right, nine.

We were not dissidents receiving immunity and a safe exit passage. Nor were we the off-spring of oligarchs, chartering a flight for a few days skiing in an exclusive resort in Scandinavia.

"I am sure we can have free beer today," I joked with the flight attendant. At thirty thousand feet a group photo was an obvious request.

Ukrainian 'Borsch'

One middle size beet
Half of small white cabbage
One small onion
One average red pepper
Tomato pasta [8oz.]
1 lb beef with little bone
Two potatoes
Bay leaves

Boil about 2.5 litres of water with meat for 1.5 hrs.
Sauté chopped onion and chopped beet [peeled], chopped red sweet
pepper on the vegetable oil for 15-20 mins. Then add tomato pasta
and a few spoons of broth from the boiling meat. Leave it on small
heat for another 10 mins. Then turn off the heat.
Peel potatoes, cut each into 6 pcs. Then add to the boiling broth
when meat is almost ready [after 1.5 hrs.] Add salt. Cut cabbage to
little pcs. Then add to the boiling water.
When it's ready [approx. 20 mins later] add sautéed vegetables to the
boiling water with meat, potato and cabbage. Add 2 bay leaves and
let it stay on small heat, 10-15 mins.
When serving, add sour cream or chopped dill.

Finland → Hong Kong

As the pilot began to make his approach, down below the serene snow-white landscape extending to the Baltic Sea. A European Union member state, so no complicated visa entry here. A twelve-hour wait for my departure flight, a one-day taste of the Finnish capital. At minus fourteen degrees Celsius, there would be no Polaroid shots of ducks in the local ponds. No urban slickers having their lunch break at the city centre water fountains, or no seagulls lurking for the food scraps. I exposed myself to the elements of Helsinki for fifteen minute stints. To prevent frost bite I'd shoot into a building. Whatever was there, a shopping centre, an Art Museum, a restaurant, a Lutheran church, a bar, a tourist office.
The streets were heavily sprinkled with grit. December 25th was five weeks away, the store fronts typically dressed. Darkness came by 4p.m. At seven Euros for a pint of beer, this was no place for an overseas stag weekend.

The 747 flight was full, a temporary migration for the warm shores of south-east Asia. Our journey was via Bangkok, in which ninety percent of the passengers exited. I took advantage of the one-hour stop in Thailand, grabbing a few bottles of Bailey's Irish Cream in the duty-free. Two hours later we touched down in Hong Kong. I was looking forward to meeting Ruby, whom I had an on-off correspondence for about three years.
At passport control, the queue was long but moving briskly. As I got through to pick-up my luggage, scanning the appropriate bay, I noticed a backpack opened on the conveyor belt with its contents falling out. Closer scrutiny revealed it was mine. A plastic bag with toiletries spilled-out. Further down the conveyor, black jeans. Then a few minutes later a sweater and tee-shirts came along. People watched bewildered, others in amusement as I scampered around a little flustered collecting my belongings.
In the arrivals hall I noticed my 'plain Jane name' on a cardboard sign, held by two guys whom Ruby had asked to meet me. A quick photo, before signalling to them, I'd never had my name held-up. Jorge and Rob, were both Philippine, now living in this city. Feeling guilty as I realized they had been waiting three hours, the lads were

quiet spoken and shy. We boarded a double-decker bus which would be a phenomenal ride crossing the new bridge that links Lantau island with Kowloon, it was sparkling like a festive tree. In fact most areas we passed through had a seasonal look. I had the ultimate viewing point, the front seat upstairs. Road signs in two languages always look more interesting, in this case English and Mandarin. Every three weeks Jorge and Rob cross the border into mainland China to collect a small cargo of merchandise for Jorge's family clothing shop, so they have a busy lifestyle.

We exited at the last stop, Hung Hom bus and railway station. Jorge making a mobile phone call, "they will come in ten minutes."

It was almost 11p.m., two women arrived to greet us, Clare and Gina. As we made our way to their flat we passed a number of Florist's with employees preparing arrangements.

"There is a morgue over there, that's why we have all these shops," said Clare laughing. We climbed a narrow stairway to the fourth floor.

"Lucky we're not staying at the top," Clare, a constant giggle when she spoke. The two women, also Philippine shared the flat with a third fellow native. I was served tea and cake, an immediate comfortable feeling in my temporary residence.

The following morning Ruby came round before nine, a light-hearted embrace, meeting in the flesh. Visitors were arriving at the apartment, 'why so early' I was thinking, I did not understand.

But later Ruby explained, "many from the Philippines are domestic workers and Sunday is our day off, everyone has meeting points, you will see today."

Ruby led and I followed, taking a yellow double-decker bus through a tunnel underneath Victoria harbour and into an area called Central. We decided to have breakfast, climbing three flights of escalators, all the time battling our way through crowds, mostly women. Why, so many people and so many women. Was there a fashion event or perhaps some local heart-throb appearing?

The restaurant was full, we shared a table with strangers. I went to order at the counter. Looking around, I just realized that I was the only male customer. Pancakes and scrambled egg for both of us.

We strolled off to meet a group of Ruby's friends, first to a Metro underground station, then to a shopping centre. We had the afternoon in an apartment, food dishes were shared followed by karaoke.

Everyone present, were, surprise, surprise from the Philippines, Jorge and Rob were there. Later in the evening we returned to the Central district, this area was littered with Philippine folk. Groups sitting on blankets playing cards or board games.
Ruby and her buddies met with their dance instructor who put them through their paces. An animated team of eight, practiced for up-coming social events attended mainly by their fellow citizens.

Hong Kong has over two hundred thousand Philippine domestic workers. Many live-in with their respective employers, Sunday is their day-off. Multitudes congregate in 'Central,' others meet at a friend's flat, just like the people who were arriving at my hosts dwelling that morning.
By 8:30p.m the streets were almost deserted, many had a curfew, 9p.m. the most common time. So there it was, a hectic first day in a city where east meets west.
Monday morning and I was on my own, time to discover the city for myself. Hong Kong is a shopper's paradise. Never ending malls, getting lost is a certainty. As I ventured around a new district each day. Hung Hom, Tsim Sha Tsui [T.S.T], [pronounced chom cha choi], Central, Causeway Bay, Wan Chai. I was surprised by how few ex-patriots I seen, the population is ninety-eight percent Chinese. Was there a mass exodus in 1997 with the handover of power, the British would not dare attempt to renege on this deal. Handing the territories back to its rightful owner, the Chinese. The Anglo-Saxons would be no match for Beijing who would simply take it by force.
This city is a hive of activity, markets packed with vegetables, fruits, meats and poultry sometimes alive in the form of chickens in cages. All under one roof, but there were problems, every week bacteria alerts on the news. Municipal authorities would close a market for inspection, the live chickens been the usual suspects.
That view at Tsim Sha Tsui [chom cha choi] looking across Victoria harbour with the Central district on the opposite side. Sky-scrappers with Christmas designs of Reindeers, stars and Santa Claus covering the whole profile of these buildings. Two massive white cruise ships docked inches apart, passenger ferries darting back and forth.

I became more comfortable navigating, maps and guide books no longer needed. Frequenting Irish, British and Australian bars for a bit of lunch. It became clear that many foreigners still reside in this harbour city. The English football game between Arsenal-Manchester United attracted a full house in Delaney's pub in Kowloon. Many bars advertise 'happy hour' until 9p.m. But of course this deal mysteriously disappeared with the match starting at 8p.m. local time.

Five minutes after the final whistle ninety percent of the customers had made an exit. An English trait, old habits die hard. Who could blame them at double the price for a pint than you pay back home. One would need the salary of a CEO not to have an empty wallet after a night out.

Later I met with Clare and her friends at the Holiday Inn. A stylish bar, after a few hours drinking, the dreaded bill came plus an expectant tip. Kenny, from Newcastle, England was part of the group.

"Let's go to Smokie's, it's less pretentious." He was a resident for six years, so he would know.

It lived-up to its name, crowded and fumigated, two rock bands rotating. My vocal chords were wet, 'feeling loose and full of juice.' Kenny was mingling, introducing me. He had a job with an import-export company, making sure the orders were shipped-out on time. Drinks were coming my way, not sure who was buying. Last orders were called by the bar staff, so I skipped off to hail a familiar red and white vehicle that has a license to pick-up idiots like me in the small hours of the morning. I noticed Kenny in a takeaway cafe, checking to see he was alright. He had a tank-full, and wasn't sure how he was getting home. So I invited him to kip with me. I was dropped off at Hung Hom station, forgetting my exact address, the driver had no English. "I'll walk from here, thank you,"

It was not a jumble maze from the Chinese alphabet, quite simply Baker street, where I was residing.

Kenny was half-asleep, it was a struggle to wrestle him from the back seat.

He would stop every block and sit down. Bigger and heavier than me, it was taking ages to get home, not to mention the four flights of stairs we had to climb to reach 4A. He disappeared into the bathroom and didn't come out. He passed-out in the bath, I managed to pick the lock early next morning. Not wanting Bella to know, who was the senior figure of my hosts. The auntie, they called her.

Because of a morgue two blocks away, the Baker street florists were doing a thriving business, the only shops opened after midnight. Casket stores were also plentiful, no discretion here. Openly displayed, stacked like surf boards as I strolled to a 'Seven-Eleven' shop for my breakfast milk. Trying not to look, this will take time to be comfortable with. As the days went by I feckin regretfully noticed the ground floor of our building was more storage for caskets. 'Damn, that's just great, I'll sleep better now,' moaning to myself. Sunday's were always eventful, watching Ruby and the gang, play in a local volleyball league. Afterwards attending a talent contest, with members of the Philippine consulate in attendance. Someone thought it was a good idea to stick me in as a judge. There were three categories, dress code, performing and been artistic. Reciting poetry, singing, cultural dancing. Individual designers in dress ware. Pastries and cakes with clever trimmings, one could not fault the effort, they were all winners.

Gina, a flatmate and her friend Beth had a midweek day off, so they took me sight-seeing. "You must see the peak," they enthusiastically encouraged. Aberdeen was our first pit stop with its massive floating restaurants. The sanpan women selling tours for a closer look at the lifestyle. We accepted a free ride to the Jumbo boat, a massive decoration of a red and gold dragon. Hundreds of paper lanterns hanging from the ceiling. Yachts, park in orderly fashion. A cluster of residential towers rising to the clouds, mountains with rough growth in the background.
We moved on to the peak, a very steep tram ride to the observation deck. It's not for the faint-hearted, a fifty-five degree angle climb through barren rock, which probably makes for good foundations, hence the skyscrapers. Eighteen hundred feet about the streets, I gazed for ages at the manoeuvring of harbour traffic below, the busiest water-way on this planet. The Central district is at the forefront, Kowloon and the New Territories beyond. Even at this height, there is a shopping mall. But wait, there is more, quickly rushing for the ferry to Lantau island.
Then a bus which took us through roads that were undergoing

maintenance to prevent landslides. Po Lin monastery, the largest outdoor bronze Buddha in the world, twenty-two meters high, sitting on a pedestal. Made in mainland China and shipped in 1993, taking ten years to construct. Of course there is the small matter of clamouring 268 steps to the base. The Buddha is seated in a lotus position on a Lotus flower, the right hand calmly raised. Underneath is an exhibition hall. Souvenir stands, a mural stating events in the Buddha's life. Plaques on the wall, naming large donators.
Relics: some teeth and bone fragments said to be that of the real Buddha. "Next month there will be thousands here, it's the anniversary," one security guard informed us.

The next day I took a solo trip to see the boat community. Cheung Chau island, a traditional old-fashion village. Sanpans and junks in abundance. The waterfront was busy with pirate and seafarer folk with a lively market. Nearby a beautiful white sand beach, too cold for a deck chair. Blue and pink buildings with romantic balconies. Delving into the local cuisine of wonton and noodles. This is home, fishing from the front porch, fresh cod for your tea, who can argue with that. It was a step back in time, perhaps the Hong Kong before foreign occupation. The British claimed Hong Kong island after defeating the Chinese, in the first opium war in the 1840's. Later extending their claim on Kowloon which is part of mainland China. Surprisingly cold weather warnings on the television news. Twelve degrees Celsius, fine by me, but my far-eastern friends were bundled-up.

Friday evening, bar-hopping in Lan Kawi Fong with Clare and her friend Victoria who seemed to know everyone.
A local man, Mister Lei joined our company, telling me he employed a Philippine domestic worker.
I asked Mr. Lei 'how much time-off does his employee have.'
"Every Sunday she off."
His employee had the usual twelve hours free-time on a Sunday, from 9a.m. to 9p.m. "She get her birthday off also," said Mr. Lei.
"How many hours does she work each day?" I asked..
"Every day she makes breakfast for my family, start at seven and finish after nine, maybe ten," replied Mr. Lei.
I pressed this man about the long hours his employee worked and the

little free-time she was given.

"It's the law," he responded.

"But the law says they are entitled to twenty-four hours, one full day off," I pointed out

"Noo, noo I am responsible for her."

"What if she would like to go out at night for a few hours, to see a movie, meet some friends."

"Noo, she not allowed," Mr. Lei replied.

"This is not fair," I shrugged.

"It's the law, it's the law, she happy in my house," he intervened, his voice growing more agitated.

"O.K. listen for a minute, people need time-off. How would you like if your wife stopped you going out at night. Give your domestic helper more time off and she will feel better, she will enjoy been part of your family."

"Noo, noo, noo it's the law, if something happen I am responsible." Shaking his head with contempt for my suggestion.

"She is an adult, show some kindness," then I tipped off to the toilet as he shouted after me.

I had listened to the constant stories from many domestic workers. Some of the Hong Kong Chinese were difficult employers. Phone calls by some employers' everyday to check on their home helper, in some cases numerous calls. Time limits on grocery shopping and playground activity.

'I am the boss, you are the maid' was the message I was visioning. A domestic worker, their contract normally lasted two years. When it expires many return to their homeland to visit their families. It's compulsory for the employer to pay the air-fare, but some refuse creating more problems. So an employee can suffer in silence for fear of losing their job.

Gina was involved in an organization that helps workers to fight back. She was also committed to a broader battle. The Chinese government was planning to introduce an income tax on domestic workers. The household folk are at the lower end of the wage scale. Many of their families at home in the Philippines are financially dependent on this salary. I had seen the mass demonstrations by the domestic workers against the new tax system.

The word was European and North American families were more liberal employers, offering more free-time, so allowing privacy for the family. To be fair I also met a number of domestic workers that had no problems with their Chinese employers.

O.K. let's talk about something else, what is it with the Chinese and neon lights. Visit any 'Chinatown' in an overseas city and there will inevitable be a cluster of signs. The 'Golden Mile' is a joyous walk. Glittering in the evening, Nathan road, the official name, the commercial heart of Kowloon. Many side streets littered with flashing lights. A mixture of eastern and western cultures clashing, Oriental restaurants, European designer clothing, Chinese made watches, prices at a snip, western pubs. Most travellers have a few days in this city, accommodation prices can be exorbitant. I was lucky to have lodgings in a city district for less than the price of a pint of beer.

Vacating my current lodgings to make way for new a permanent tenant, this was arranged before my arrival. The final ten days of my stay would be in Kennedy town on Hong Kong Island. Two minutes walk to the harbour, fifteen minutes to Central, by bus. Dominated by shops selling dried fish products and oriental medicine. Incense smelling temples sandwiched between residential high-risers.
My new flatmates all over the age of fifty, worked long days. It was almost too quiet in contrast to Hung Hom; the humorous laughter of Clare, the political astuteness of Gina and the generosity of Bella.
I frequently used the local restaurants, the staff looking pleasantly surprised having a Caucasian amongst the customers. Good conversation did develop, "Are you Scottish," one man asked as I ordered rice, chicken and chow mein. He talked about the economy, "It's bad, now we are part of China, I cannot find a job. I am fifty-seven, what hope is there at my age. There are people who kill themselves because of no work, all the jobs go to China."
'Maybe sell your house and live in mainland China, the money will stretch a long way,' was the best advice I could offer.
Another day as I waited for noodle soup, a young mother joked, "It's unusual to see a tourist in here."
"I like Chinese food and it's not expensive," offering her a seat.
We chatted about the handover of the Colony.
"Why did the British build an airport and a new bridge before leaving?" I asked.

"A legacy perhaps."

"Actually most of the construction companies were British; the money would be going into British banks. Taking what they could before the end," shrugging her shoulders.

Lots of slurpy eaters around us, putting the bowl to their mouth for the last drops of noodle soup, not looked upon as bad manners.

I made a trip to Shenzhen, just over the border in the People's Republic of China. Less than one hour by train to Lo Wu, then walk across into Guangdong province. No visa was required for Shenzhen, originally a simple rural hamlet, now thriving and modern. The International Trade Centre was busy, traders buying perfumes and jewellery.

Baoon seemed to be a down-market community, stalls selling cheap clothing, gadgets and shoes. Ronmin Lu was the prosperous district, well dressed shoppers and businessmen, a few beggars sprinkled around. The main train station in a vast town square with lines running to many parts of this newly free market country.

Ferries continually flow back and forth to Hong Kong, Zhuhai and Macau which was once a Portuguese colony. A simple one day trip to see a piece of the mainland of the People's Republic of China.

I wanted to voice my concerns on the problems of the domestic workers. So two days before leaving I telephoned a local broadsheet and made an appointment with a reporter. The journalist was Philippine, living in Hong Kong for twenty years.

"Why do you have such an interest in the immigrant community," she inquired. A photographer must have taken about twenty-five shots.

"Are you putting my ugly head on page five, your distribution will drop," as I ducked under the table clowning around avoiding the camera lens. They were good humoured and served me tea and biscuits.

"I am intrigued that a foreigner has come to talk about this issue. We can blend this story in with the income tax issue," the journalist getting comfortable with pen and note pad.

I talked in detail about the many negative stories I was hearing. A high percentage of domestic workers were not happy with their employers, but nothing is said for fear of losing their jobs. The free-time written into the contract was not been honoured by employers.

Someone needed to speak-out, so why not me.
I was hoping the message would reach a wider audience through this newspaper.

HONG KONG PORK CHOPS

6 tablespoons soy sauce, 6 tablespoons hoi sin sauce.
4 teaspoons honey, 2 teaspoons Chinese chili sauce.
2 teaspoons minced garlic.

Marinade
3 tablespoons soy sauce, 3 teaspoons oriental sesame oil.
3 tablespoons dry sherry, 1 tablespoon minced garlic.
1 tablespoon minced peeled fresh ginger.
1 shallot finely chopped, half-teaspoon salt

6 thick, centre cut loin pork chops.
2 tablespoons honey, 2 tablespoons oriental sesame oil.

Instructions:
Prepare by dipping sauce by combining all the ingredients in a
medium bowl, divide among six small bowls and set aside.

Combine the marinade ingredients in a large bowl and add the pork
chops and toss to coat completely. Let rest, covered at the room
temperature for 2 hours, turning a few times.

Combine the honey and sesame oil in a small bowl. Place 2 non-
stick skillets, large enough to hold the pork chops, over medium
heat.
Brown the chops lightly, 5 minutes per side, basting with the honey
mixture.
Reduce the heat to medium low, cover and cook, turning the chops
after 8 minutes, then cooking through on the other side.
Serve each chop in a small bowl of dipping sauce.
6 servings.

Bombay → Mumbai

I would make a second visit to the world's most populated democracy. At Chhatrapati Shivaji international airport [a simple name that rolls off the tongue] in Mumbai, the arrivals terminal was downright dreary. Surely this nation's government could finance interior decorating to elevate a welcome for foreign visitors and their own citizens. [that has changed in recent years with new terminals].After getting through the normal formalities, I was bargaining at the hospitality desk with a bundle of baksheesh stuffed in my back pocket, two Chinese men in my company, who were seated next to me on the flight. Their English was sporadic, so I offered help, for it was their first time in the sub-continent. Slightly concerned that my new buddies were thinking five-star, en-suite, balcony sunset views and a la carte menus.

I settled for the Rockmount, $31 per night, pointing the location on a city map, my buddies seemed content.

"It is central and convenient for entertainment," the airport personnel assured me.

Promises, promises, that's India.

As we waited for the courtesy pick-up bus, I looked around contemplating refreshments, there was nothing available. It was not as if the cafes and shops had just closed, for by now it was 8:15 p.m. There would be more facilities on a deserted island.

We boarded a mini-bus, sent by the hotel and drove about two hundred yards. The driver stopped to answer natures call, behind a bush.

"Jack, this place shit." I laughed at my Chinese friend efficient linguistic, and such a truthful observation. From what I could see, everything looked derelict, rugged, a shantytown feel.

The Chinese lads were keen to socialize, so we checked-out the 'Irish bar' at the hotel. Two Bulgarian women served behind the counter, a third bartender from this metropolis resented our friendliness with his workmates. Guinness and Harp [Irish beers] were the only obvious connection with Ireland. We chatted with Sanjay, a local carpenter who exaggerated about India been a strong economic country and also about his many girlfriends. I listened and did not challenge, he recommended this Irish bar as a haunt for the Bombay female socialite. It was Saturday, almost midnight, I counted three women, all with male company. His alcohol was talking, we all need an escape, I guess.

I had a friend in Mahim, a central district, we corresponded for a couple of years. Shilpa, a school teacher, had sent me information on budget hotels in south Mumbai, a popular area for tourist. The following morning I checked my e-mails, then made phone calls on vacancies.
The Chinese had departed, a mid-day flight to New Delhi was on their agenda. In a renowned yellow and black ambassador taxi, with my backpack slung in the back seat we were manoeuvring through the chaotic streets. The Causeway in Coluba was my instruction.
The cabbie was quick to ask, "Any coins from your country."
A slick way to make a little extra money, I was not obliging. The beggars did not waste an opportunity at the traffic lights. Some I gifted, others I ignored. One individual stood head and shoulders above all other international vagrants. As we waited for a green light, I watched in amusement as he waived through the traffic. A six lane boulevard, we were a distance from been confronted. The vehicles ahead, their windows closing at high speed, 37 degrees Celsius, a roadside thermometer highlighted earlier. They would risk temporary heat exhaustion rather than a possible incurable ailment. As the pauper drew closer, suddenly we were in his frontline. A shawl dropped off his shoulder, wrapped around his waist. No shoes, hair unkempt. His body exposed, a loud and clear message of disease. From head to toe this man was covered in lumps.
"Is that leprosy?" I asked.
"It's a form of, it's veeree dangerish," the cabbie answered.
My gut was churning, I dropped baksheesh into his hand.
I pondered on futile efforts on appearance, deeply annoyed momentarily. Where is the justification of what passed right in my line of vision. Is it a sentence, a punishment. Have we got an example of bad karma. Who would display unconditional affection towards this sickly human?
'Ask and you receive' is a powerful directory from any spiritual literature. That's exactly what this man was doing. He did not get much change from me, twenty rupees may get him lunch at a street

vendor.

What about orchestrating an authentic difference, financing medical treatment in a hospital. Surely we westerners can offer more than the price of a mid-day meal.

My new sleeping quarters were like a secret enclave. Maybe used by Israelis on the run from the police in Goa, I'll elaborate later. The windows were all boarded-up to keep out sound and light. Air-conditioning was necessary in the stifling Mumbai heat.

I met with Shilpa, my correspondent, a carefree personality and very independent. She had great knowledge on European sport, a fan of Michael Schumacher, the Grand Prix race driver, also on the Premier league and the Arsenal football team.

An informed guided stroll through the locality was most helpful. We discussed local issues, "why are women held back, when the country had a woman prime minister at one time."

"It's one of the problems we have here," Shilpa shrugged.

"But Indira Gandhi was groomed from a young age by her father, Nehru," [who was this country's first leader].

I asked about the caste system.

Shilpa explained, "Hindus believe in reincarnation, so some people try to live a righteous life in the hope of been born into a higher caste next time. There are four castes: Brahmin, Kshatriya, Vaishya and Shudra. Brahmin been the highest and the others following suit. Beneath these four are the Dalits, who hold menial jobs like latrine cleaners and sweepers. The path you take in life can be influenced by what group you are born into. The higher your group, the greater the chance of a successful living."

This of course is a very unfair system.

The following day I went to buy a rail ticket. I love train stations in this country, watching the nation on the move, always seemingly carting too much luggage. Cardboard boxes tied with rope, linen, cotton and canvas bags. Trunk style suitcases, rarely a lone traveller, in couples, large groups or three generations. On the train, two people sharing a one-birth sleeping pad and why not. A simple trip to buy a train ticket can be a mission.

I enquired at one window where to buy a ticket for Goa.

"Go there," the clerk answered with a hand jester. Everything is, "go there," with a hand direction when inquiring about a location. You walk off, still confused. Suddenly a man began shouting. I glanced but ignored him.

"Sir, sir stop, one moment," the same man approached me.

"You need a ticket," he asked.

"I'm o.k." continuing to look for the appropriate office.

"Come, come sir,"

I remembered from my previous visit to this country that purchasing a ticket needs to be done at least one day in advance. The office had closed at 4 p.m., so I would have to come back the next day.

"Where are you going sir?"

"Goa, I want to travel tomorrow."

"Sir, this is the price, cheap for you," writing on a newspaper. A hefty commission added, it seemed. We argued, his price lowered considerably.

He wanted money and my passport up front, I adamantly refused. This is his territory, he knows the turf and could disappear at any moment with my loot. I give him twenty percent of our agreed price, he also wrote down my document details. Ten minutes later he returned, the deal was complete.

Next morning I was chatting with Greg, an Aussie, at Victoria station, cheese and tomato sandwiches with black tea for breakfast. Stacking up on fruits, biscuits and water for the ten-hour journey south. We departed on time, at 6:30 a.m. Seating was surprisingly spacious. In the next bay were two Scottish lads, on their last 'port of call' from a round-the-world trip before returning home. They were the most boring 'jocks' I've ever met. Most folk from the tartan country are never short of voicing an opinion with a touch of humour thrown-in. Perhaps these Ayrshire residents with the highlands in sight had the realization setting-in of how much dosh they squandered.

One of them said two words in the entire trip……..."uh, no" when I asked if he wanted a soda. Seated opposite me was Rolf, a mechanic from Berlin. One week in Goa, checking out the scene before flying onto Thailand, was his plan. Sanjay joined our company as we 'chewed the fat.' Sanjay was part of the national polar scientific expedition team. This seemed strange to us, Indian scientists at the Antarctic, South Pole. They had a departure base in South Africa,

where Sanjay always remained, logging the data information.
The toilets were the usual filth and stench. The kitchen was in full
swing, porters passing through every hour with food and drinks.
Vendors were stopped from entering the train at station stops. The
landscape was a shabby green, more rain needed.

Anjuna, in north Goa was the largest exodus. I opted for Calungute,
twenty minutes further south. A twenty-five minute taxi-ride shared
with Rolf. The driver nominated accommodation, he brought us to a
bungalow-style guest house. It was tidy and new, beautiful tiled
floor, double-bed with lamps, three-speed ceiling fan, en-suite
bathroom. $30 for six nights.

An early morning walk along the shoreline, it was deserted but
clean. The water was calm, two local women were bathing, fully
clothed. A jewellery seller approached, dressed in red sari and
cardigan. She was wearing more than she was selling; three rings on
her nose, several earrings, about a dozen bracelets on each arm.
Several chains dangling from her neck, a couple of ankle chokers.
The lady offered a number of items. I bought three beaded necklaces
for one hundred rupees. It was hard work, initial asking price was
two hundred rupees. The real stumbling block was the seller wanted
me to buy ten necklaces for three hundred rupees. Three was fine for
now, excess material can get lost or broken. For about two hundred
yards this woman pestered me to buy more. Eventually I turned the
tables and began trying to sell my sunglasses.

"One thousand rupees, very good price,....... o.k. nine hundred. You
must buy, my best price. The best sunglasses in the world, nine
hundred, you must buy. Nine hundred, come on only nine hundred."
She soon got tired of my blarney and strolled off.

In the afternoon I rented a motorbike, nothing extravagant, a
Yamaha 250. I cruised off to the Basilica of Bom Jesus. This is the
resting place for the patron saint of Goa, Saint Francis Xavier. His
incorruptible body has survived almost five hundred years without
ever been embalmed, placed inside the church in a glass cage in an
elevated position.

Frances Xavier, in 1541 went to spread Christianity in the
Portuguese colonies. It is quite remarkable because of the transport
situation in that era. He died in 1552 on the island of Sancian, off the
coast of China. A year later his remains were transferred back to
Goa. With the body perfectly intact, the locals were declaring a

'miracle.' The canonization came in 1622. Parts of his body were removed by 1636 to make holy relics which were distributed around Asia. This has probably contributed to the body partially decaying. Goa, is a state in southern India that was once controlled by Portugal. Lots of churches are visible because of the Christian influence. It was handed back to India in the 1960's.

Choices of nightclubs was minimal, but what was available was always busy. As I danced with Emma, an English girl who had a room down the hall from mine, local guys were copying my rhythm. I started doing silly moves totally out-of-sync with the 'house-music,' so like sheep they followed suit. The shanty bars had inexpensive beer, the sports channel was an attraction for European football viewers. I made a couple of trips to Anjuna, by taxi boat. It was much quicker for there is a shortage of good roads. It was the busiest beach for backpackers. A hippy feel at the local markets with ex-pats throwing their anchor out many years before, selling their hand-made crafts. Many Israelis floating around, ask any guesthouse owner, vendor, shopkeeper or taxi driver about who causes the most problems. The same answer comes-up every time, 'the young Israelis.' I guess it's all that testosterone.
Many of them go travelling after their compulsory military service. They may experience hostilities on home soil, but the aggressive attitude should not be necessary, they're on holiday. Some are on small budgets, money is tight, so they argue about prices all too frequently.
Outside my residence, dirt tracks shoot-off in different directions. Pigs, goats, cows and hens grazed near-by on rubbish.
Kids played, shouting "hello" as I walked pass. I bought them ice-cream, the vendor relaxing in the shade of trees. Other kids darted out of the cracks shouted "me, me, me."
Soon it accumulated to fifteen ice-pops, I couldn't leave anyone empty-handed.
Young Indian men play on the beach like kids, burying an individual in the sand, knocking each other in the water and always a cricket game in progress. Indian women will not be wearing swim suits, the few that did enter the water had tee-shirts and shorts.
Many of the locals stroll the beach in the evening as the sun begins to fade, most are dressed in street clothing. Banana boats are a busy

activity with no life jackets available. Speed-boat parachuting is the main attraction for extra adrenaline. Goa is a popular destination for Europeans, the local international airport makes it conveniently accessible.

My visa would expire soon, so I returned to Mumbai, travelling first class, a single-bed with a dirty draw-curtain for privacy. Every passenger in the carriage was in seclusion. An overnight journey I slept through most of it. Arrival time was 7:30a.m. Porters entered the carriage before the train reached the station platform, one grabbed my rucksack.

"Oi, Oi " I shouted, wrestling my only belongings.

Hordes of people were swarming onto every carriage for the next destination. I think they were daily commuters, off to work in the suburban areas. A ten-minute taxi ride and I was back in Coluba.

The hotel I picked had a variety of rooms, I opted for the cheapest, at 150 rupees. Paper thin walls, snores and voices annoyingly audible, I guess I got what I paid for. The next morning I transferred to a lower floor.

Situated one hundred yards from the waterfront, it was not the French Riviera. We had the sunshine alright, but not the five-star treatment with elegant surroundings.

The promenade had fortune tellers, Sadhus [holy men] offering blessings for money. Vendors selling musical instruments, watches and candy. Beggars, homeless families and tourist guides. There was a twenty foot drop to the sea, protected by a stone wall, the water was shallow and murky. A dead body could be seen one morning, the authorities were in no hurry to retrieve it from the water. There was also glamour, in the shape of the Taj Mahal hotel. Doormen dressed in traditional uniforms, glittering chandeliers and antique furniture in the lobby, wealthy folk passing through as I viewed the architecture.

One morning brushing my teeth, I heard banging. For some reason the lavatory and shower cubicles had locks on both sides of the door. I undid the latch, a Muslim woman exited dressed in her black rupush and headscarf, smiling with a lingering look. I muttered a reply through a mouthful of toothpaste. She was gorgeous, light olive skin, warm dark brown eyes. It was just a moment, thinking nothing more of the incident. Surprisingly for this country the restrooms were unisex.

Later in the evening we met again in the hotel lobby. I recognized her friend, Ahmed, we had exchanged greetings earlier. I accepted their invitation for a promenade stroll. Others in the company were two guys from Tanzania, on a business trip involving textiles, also Isabella and her cousin Ali from Yemen, they were always laughing. Miriam was the lady I rescued from the restrooms, from Iran on a ten-day holiday. She had a camcorder running, picking-up the action on the street. So I performed a five-minute stand-up show; joking about the Tanzanians and myself visiting Persia to help with the male shortage. I kicked-up an Irish jig and belted out a ballad.

It was my understanding there is an imbalance in the male population because of the eight-year Iran-Iraq war in the 1980's. "It's probably true, but is not highly noticeable on the streets back home," Ahmed confirmed.

"Besides, a man can have more than one wife."

Mumbai is an exhilarating city, high energy, India's economic powerhouse. It's an industrial hub, the centre for the Hindi film business. We booked a jeep for a guided tour. The following morning the driver started with the Indian Gate, an eighty-five foot stone archway [similar to the Arch de Triomphe in Paris]. It was erected quickly to welcome King George V1 and Queen Mary. Ironically less than forty years later the last of the British troops departed from here. Kamala Nehru Park was next, great views of the city from Chowpatty beach to Colaba.

Across the street are the hanging gardens, decorated with lawns, flower bed arrangements and designer cut hedges. Pensioners exercised, others relaxed. We sat amongst them, one was given full attention to Miriam, the immensely attractive Iranian. Who could blame him wanting to sing a duet.

We drove by the 'towers of silence' where the local Parsi community of the Zoroastrian faith dispose of their dead. Pall-bearers carry the remains to the top of a cylindrical bastion where it is left to be devoured by vultures and crows and decomposed by the elements. High walls and relatives prevent anyone from viewing. Mani Bhavan was an interesting house, in Malabar hill, on a tree lined street. The three-story yellow and brown home of Mahatma Gandhi, he lived here from 1917 to 1934. A library and a small museum on his life's work, his simple belongings are displayed in his room. The original copies of his bible, Koran and the Bhagavad Gata. Important letters to overseas leaders in his fight for independence against the British. Numerous photos adorn the walls. Gandhi, during his life had spent a total of 2,338 days in jail at various times. His wife, Kasturba died in jail in 1942.

The Dhobi Ghats at Mahalaxmi is quite amazing, an open air Municipal laundry. Rows upon rows of brick troughs, not a washing machine in sight, or a dryer. No fancy detergent or fabric softener here, just a large bar of soap. By hand, beat the dirt out of clothing brought from all over the city. 'Perhaps, including our hotel bed sheets,' Miriam suggested, which created nervous laughter. I could not see how they dried the washing, quickly.

Possibly the world's largest laundry. A drunk tried to hassle me about taking photos, he calmed down when I give him a cigarette. Last stop was the Crawford street market, a sea of fruit and vegetable stalls. The sheer numbers of people can be intimidating. The meat section at the rear was bloodied and no place for the queasy.

Next day the Tanzanians went north to New Delhi, I became good friends with the Iranians. In the evenings we would chat in a restaurant, they would have soft drinks as there is no alcohol sold in their country, larger for me. "What about the Shah and the American hostage situation in the late 1970's" I asked. Ahmed thinking for a moment, then answering.

"The shah was a friend of the west. He squashed all political opposition at home. Our country is rich in oil but the Shah left it in a shambles. He fled in 1979 which led to the hostage situation at the American embassy. He was not a good leader."

"What about the Ayatollah taking power?" I asked. [who succeeded the shah]. "It was one extreme to another, everything changed socially from a western style to Islamic way. We made enemies with other countries. There was an eight year war with our neighbour Iraq which accomplished nothing, too many got killed. Women should have the freedom, it's ridiculous, too many restrictions."

In 1995 the city of Bombay changed its name to Mumbai, a Hindu goddess. Originally it was a group of islands controlled by the

Portuguese. Later the British reclaimed land that is today a multifarious metropolis. It's got mind-boggling contrasts, exciting one moment, disturbing the next. Slum areas are evident, but just a flashing glimpse of the overall poverty for us tourists. We drove through Nariman Point. Executives, well dressed, returning to their office after lunch, while half-naked kids with malted hair scavenged in the gutter. This is a city of opportunity, it moves much faster than the rest of the country. People migrate from all parts of India; Engineers, Bankers, Taxi drivers, Labourers.

"I'm a farmer from Gujerat," one cabbie told me. He returns home during harvest.

With a population of one billion and not slowing, Mumbai, the largest city has 16 million, that's just 1.6%. So this country has a number of other highly populated cities, the countryside also has a crowding problem.

I was continuously approached by beggars. If I give a little every time, will it make a difference?

"Of course it will. What if I ignore them all?

One night I was walking back to the hotel after a few drinks, while watching European football. Someone began shouting 'sir, sir, mister.'

I looked to my right.

A young man came towards me, holding a child that was half-asleep. He asked for money in a mild tone. At first I couldn't look at him, he scared me a bit. His eye-lids were deformed and he had a cleft-lip.

A moment of silence, I stood there, contemplating. Then a girl arrived, his sister, and mother of the child.

"Separated from her husband, their parents had passed-away," she was quick to tell me.

"What is the matter, what is wrong?"

"We have nothing, we are beggars."

"Are you from Mumbai."

"No, we are from Pooma [which is a couple of hours south]. Our home is a plastic hut. It's no good, there are no jobs. We make more by sleeping and begging on the streets here," she explained without hesitation.

"You sleep there in that corner," I pointed.

"We sleep at that church, sometimes at the other one down there."

I give her what was in my pocket, a handful of rupees, but it wasn't much.

Next day I was thinking, perhaps I can make a difference. Whether their story was truthful or not was irrelevant, the young man certainly needed help. I went to the church, I wanted a trust-worthy person to monitor the situation.

"Bring them here, we can evaluate their circumstances," was the response.

I walked around the area, they were nowhere to be seen, the chance was gone. My visa had expired, I was heading for a departure lounge.

Perhaps a weeks' salary for me, could correct the problem. Would this be the best way to offer 'real help.' Take a single individual, give them a new lease on life. Unfortunately this could result in a whole new set of obstacles. Possibly ironic that his deformities are his survival, a continuous trickle of financial handouts. Looking normal with little education, how would he earn a living? But surely the corrections are the best option.

At 2a.m. I bid farewell to Ahmed and Miriam, the 'Persian goddess' as I teasingly called her. By 10p.m. Bombay is calming down, so we had a clear run to the airport. The taxi driver waited outside, as I had personally booked him earlier. I joined a lengthy queue in the terminal and I never really came out of it until I was seated in economy class a long time later.

Since September 11, 2001 governments and aviation authorities are extremely worried about airport security. Would a change in foreign policy not be a more agreeable road to take? But perhaps someone is making too much money. With communism gone, is a new enemy needed? In western countries the media is weak, most don't really challenge. The current answers are not correct.

In a constant slow moving line, chit-chatting with Bruce on his way to Dubai, where he worked as an engineer. In front was Elizabeth, who elaborated about her flight home, "Hong Kong, Tokyo, Los Angeles and finally Che-kargo."

One security machine check was followed by another. At passport control, seven bays were open. When I reached the top of the line, I stepped to the left, optioning for bay six. The officer in cubicle five was asking nervous-looking passengers too many questions.

"Stay clear of number five, he is looking for promotion," joking with Bruce.

Quickly passing through I was walking a medium length corridor, down an escalator, that was switched off. Then surprise, surprise another queue which was access to the boarding gate. One café was opened, there was little choice in food and drinks. Now I realize why there are no shops, when you are literally in queues the entire time.

"You did not go through customs" the official informed me.

I shrugged, "where is customs?"

"Follow that man."

In which I joined a group of eight sleep-walkers who strolled passed the two desks with no signs or indications. Receiving the appropriate customs document, returning to the gate, the last check or so I thought. Inside the barrier, luggage was been openly searched, I went to the only employee who was not causing a fuss, avoiding my backpack been emptied.

I entered the terminal at 3a.m. for a 6:05a.m. flight. Three hours and twenty-five minutes later I relaxed for a moment as others boarded.

I actually feel sorry for the airlines and their staff, on edge looking for dubious intent.

Bombay Aloo

Ingredients:
3 potatoes, peeled and chopped into bite sized pieces.
Half an onion, finely chopped.
Half an onion, chopped in large chunks.
Half a green pepper, finely chopped.
2 tablespoons tomato puree.
Grated root ginger.
4 cloves garlic, sliced.
2 teaspoons curry powder.
1 teaspoon cumin powder.
1 teaspoon chilli powder.
1 teaspoon turmeric.
1 tablespoon Worcester sauce.
1 tomato quartered.
5 tablespoons chopped coriander leaves.
Vegetable oil.

Method:
Boil the potatoes in water with a little salt and tumeric added until cooked.

Fry the finely chopped onion until translucent in oil. Add the curry powder, chili powder, cumin powder, sliced garlic and grated ginger and stir fry for two minutes.
Add the pepper, tomato, tomato puree, chunks of onion and Worcester sauce and stir. Add the potatoes, mix in with the sauce and serve immediately, topped with the coriander.

Thailand

ONE NIGHT IN BANGKOK MAKES A HARD MAN HUMBLE, CAN'T BE TOO CAREFUL OF YOUR COM—PAN—Y

As flight cx750 began to make it's decent into Bangkok international, I was in trouble, a pain like no other in my forehead. I closed my eyes, tried to relax. It intensified, trickling down the bridge of my nose. I massaged the throbbing area...........and prayed.
Relieved when we finally landed, the pain eased considerably.
Where did that come from I was internally questioning. Sometimes it takes a threatening moment, to look at ourselves. To realize we are not invincible.

Thailand is the most popular Asian destination for European holiday makers. The airport was surprisingly quiet, I opted for a pre-paid taxi to Koh San road, a western base camp. I followed the information of a British tourist who was on the same flight. "Go to the church at the bottom of Koh San road, stay in that area, it's better for a good night's sleep."
I asked two guys carrying backpacks about a cheap hotel.
"Take the next left and go three blocks, you'll find something there for under ten dollars."
"Thanks guys," as I wearily strolled with a heavy load.
Having second thoughts, I needed sleep, was in no mood to be a neighbour of late night revellers in a five dollar room with just a board of sheetrock between us. Stopping to read a window sign, 'rooms at $14/night,' this will do me.
Slumber is a great leveller. The following morning, feeling totally refreshed I joined a trip to the Klong Damnoen Saduak floating market, a ninety minute drive into the countryside. The group was chatting excitedly. The Kiwis asking a Canadian, questions on Vietnam, their next flight was to Hanoi, others talked about trekking in Chang Mai, in the north of this country. The countryside looked swampy in parts, we passed a number of fish farms. A couple of kilometres from the market our driver dropped us off.
"We take scenic way," as he pointed for us to enter a long-tailed

boat, a canopy overhead for sun protection. The engine revved, soon we were darting through dirty waterways. Little villages with restricted road access, wooden framed houses with balconies. At the entrance to the market we were advised to take local market boats. But this was nonsense, the waterways were too congested.

Some customers shopped by taking a boat. For me, it was more convenient to walk the river bank. Long narrow boats, packed with fruits and vegetables, it all works well despite the initial chaotic impression. The boat vendors; most were women, wearing loose cotton shirts and Chinese style hats, looking aged but cheerful. They had a utility instrument, a fishing rod with a net for passing items and money. I would point to my desired request; two of them, three from that basket. Exotic fruit, I'd not seen before, unknown names; Jackfruit; a yellow wary texture, semi-sweet when ripe. Rambutan; red with hairy green strands, translucent sweet flesh on the inside. Custard Apple, Mangosteen, Japanese pair.

"Try this one Damien," who was part of the group, as he clicked away, photography his passion. It was the controversial Durian fruit, I cut it open with a utility knife, mushy flesh on the inside. It stunk, like the bad smelly socks of a former flatmate who was good at making rasher-stew.

Damien threw it in the garbage can.

"Buy plenty of them," I said sarcastically.

Later we visited a wood carving centre; animals, birds, boats and statues all slowly but surely taking shape by patient craft workers. The Japanese tourists were doing most of the buying.

Returning to Bangkok in the early afternoon, the group had changed as others with this tour company were off visiting a museum. On the mini-bus, Damien and I chatted with four Korean women.

"We want to visit Patpong"

"Pat who," I asked.

"Patpong" Lu repeated, giggling.

"That sounds like a Thai sports game," I responded.

"We need men to come with us," she whispered.

"Are you applying for a job," I teased.

"Yes, I will be a policewoman, I will arrest bad men like Irish people."

We met later in the evening, sampling the local cuisine. Vendors on

Koh San road set out their stalls as the day becomes cooler. Thai food can be extremely spicy, a test to your system. Damien was giving advice on the less spicy stuff, but my mouth was burning anyway.

After dark we hailed two Tuk-tuks [three-wheeled motor taxi]. Destination: Patpong. The Koreans produced breathing masks that looked nerdy but sensible. Traffic jams were horrendous, the noise and fumes filling the night air and my lungs.

The neon clouded district was not overly sleazy. An open air market atmosphere, stalls line the streets; food, clothing, jewellery, toys and souvenirs. Many bars looked respectable. We entered 'Magic Moments,' crowded with patrons: married couples, dating partners, single men of course. We were immediately offered seating. An attractive young woman came to us; the Koreans got nervous and wanted to leave, but we politely refused. We just observed, no wise-cracks, showing no romantic interest. Thai boxing been shown on a large screen.

We strolled through the district; two men came rushing out of a flashy lit lounge. "Don't go in there; they tried to charge us one thousand baht for a beer, we didn't drink anything."

We had seen a confrontation between beefy looking doormen and young tourists. They were arguing over money and the price of drinks. Suddenly re-enforcements and the backpackers were outnumbered.

Damien got propositioned by two women, then two more as we turned into another busy street, I think they were lady-boys. Two of our Korean friends were sticking very close to me and whispering, "let's leave."

We had seen activities involving beer bottles, darts and balloons, it's not an Olympic sport, but uniqueness was displayed.

As the song goes, ONE NIGHT IN BANGKOK MAKES A HARD MAN HUMBLE, CAN'T BE TOO CAREFUL OF YOUR COM-PAN-Y.

Our short-term Korean friends returned home the next day. I hopped on a bus for the fifteen-minute ride to the Grand Palace. A local man interrupted as I tried to figure-out the main entrance.

"The palace is closed today, we take you to good markets for shopping."

"I telephoned the king, he is waiting for me to have lunch," I joked.

"The palace not open today," another repeated, cab drivers looking to con a naive dopey tourist. This was not their lucky day.

The entrance gates were wide open. Massive gardens with many temple styled buildings. The Wat structures are extremely colourful. Gleaming gilded stupas, orange and green roofed tiles. Mosaic styled pillars and marble pediments. Murals illustrate the Chakri dynasty, the current ruling family name. The Grand Palace is used only for certain ceremonies by the king. It would take three weeks to absorb the entire splendour, I was breezing through. Borobiman hall, a French inspired structure, it's sometimes used for foreign dignitaries. The grand hall palace is the largest of the buildings, a blend of Thai and Renaissance architecture. Each wing is topped by a mondop, the tallest contain the ashes of Chakri kings.

The Wat phra kalw or the emerald Buddha, this image sits in a glass cage about thirty inches in height. It seems small to the ignorant visitor like me, but of great importance to the Buddhists of Thailand. It has changed hands over the years, on display in Chang Rai in the north, Laotian invaders captured the image. Two hundred years later the Thai's recaptured it when war was waged against Laos.

Wat's are sacred places, some female tourists were refused entry because of their revealing clothing.

I moved on, catching a ferry across the river Chao Phraya to visit Wat Arun. The temple of dawn, named after the Indian god of dawn. It had housed the emerald Buddha before king Rama transferred it to the Grand palace, unique and spectacular in design. An eighty-two meter Khmer-style tower, a mosaic of broken multihued Chinese porcelain embedded in brick plaster, a common temple decoration in the past when Chinese ships called at Bangkok for usage of old porcelain as ballast. Steep stairs reach half-way up the tower to a look-out point, excellent views of the river activity.

Inside the temple, murals date to the reign of Rama V. Images of prince Siddhurtha encountering examples of birth and old age, sickness and death outside the palace walls. This experience led him to abandon his glamorous life.

Bangkok has many waterways, in the past this was a way of transportation, it still is but on a much lesser scale. Many were filled-in to make roads, as a result major traffic snarls and floods in the monsoon season.

I approached a bus stop, two young monks were there; short tight haircuts, long orange robes and sandals. I tried to converse with them, they half-smiled and avoided eye-contact, not willing to break their silence and why should they.

I had a 6p.m. flight booked to head south, perhaps I was moving too quickly out of the capital, it almost took off without me. The shuttle bus had a number of pick-ups. The airports, International and domestic are next to each other. The driver ignored my request to make the domestic terminal first stop. As Sue, a young backpacker from London and me rushed through the security check, with the help of a uniformed guard. We skipped scanners and queues to receive boarding passes. A mad-dash to the mobile steps, which had to be repositioned for our convenience. The doors of the plane were closed and needed to be reopened for us to board. Some passengers applauded as we panted down the aisle.
A one-hour flight south to Ko Samui, I was seated between a Canadian businessman and a German backpacker. With no guide book I was quizzing these guys about this southern island. Tom from Toronto was a regular visitor to Thailand. "Give it four or five days, if you like it, stay, otherwise move on."
Olie from Hamburg said "I am not interested in Ko Samui. I was there nine years ago, it's too commercial now. I'm going to Ko Phan Ngan to meet real backpackers."

****

Ko Samui airport was the most exotic I've ever encountered. Palm trees lined the runway on both sides, mixed with nature's natural heavy growth. Bright texture trolleys waiting to transport us as we stepped off the Technicolor air-shuttle. The arrival and departure terminals were open wooden structures with thatched roofing, trimmed greenery leading to the car park, a romantic tingle in my gut.
I prodded the mini-bus driver for cheap lodgings as we drove through Chaweng, the biggest town on the Island. They normally have a hidden agenda, like commission, for bringing customers to their recommendations. In fairness he pulled-up at three different hotels, the cheaper rooms were occupied. It was dark and raining lightly, with a heavy backpack I settled for a chalet at twenty-two

hundred baht, certainly above my budget.

Next morning I was dressed by dawn. It was chilly, a high tide had me wondering, 'where is the beach?'

Stefan, a Swede, the only other guest for breakfast, he'd just completed a thirty-minute jog. He was paying eighty percent less than me for a beach bungalow. Everything was booked solid for the week ahead. Stefan took me to Charlie's Huts, a cluster of buildings in close proximity to the beach. They had vacancies, paying for two nights, not wanting to make a commitment too quickly. A single room, old wooden style thatched building, a wooden framed bed with closet, table and two chairs. Community toilets, surrounded by palm trees and green hedges. The soothing sounds of the ebbing tide, a primitive coziness with a romantic edge.

Dubliners from Ireland, were next door. Jason, a Canadian the other side. Willie, across the way with a thick Belfast accent. By the second night the comfort feeling dropped dramatically. The mosquitoes liked me too much, nasty bites, embarrassingly visible on my arms and legs, not to mention the itching. The ceiling fan was no deterrent; they lived in the straw roof.

'Yea, we'll have a piece of this guy, fresh Irish meat.'

With such exoticness, I couldn't allow these insects to spoil the holiday. An early morning search for new lodgings led me to a bar that leased motor-bikes. At a cost of two hundred baht per day, why walk. The bar owner was most helpful; with one phone call I had a new base in the centre of town.

A beautiful furnished room with on-suite bathroom, ceramic tiled floors, soothing on my feet. Air-condition, cable television, a balcony and clean linen every day. 6000 baht per week [U.S. $60]. These conditions would be taken for granted in the western world. Thailand, despite it's popularity is a developing country.

Some evenings Jason and the Dubliners would drop-by for a few beers and watch European football. A cool room was ideal after a hot day on the beach.

For nightlife, the Reggae club was recommended. Palm trees mixed in the seating, an open-air floor to boogie. There was a competition in musical chairs. 'Big Jim,' from the 'west of Ireland hit the top prize. A bottle of Rum and drinks on the house his award, sharing his winnings with Jason and me. A group of Germans joined our company, they were rooming in the same block as Jim. Later a mini beach party developed, a song contest continuing until sunrise, no sun-tanning that day.

The Reggae club was a desirable joint, situated three kilometres from the town centre. You better not forget your parking spot, rental motorbikes in abundance, all looking the same. It was the dangerous side to this holiday island, drinking and driving was rampant. A motorcycle license was not necessary, amateurs speeding on narrow roads with no head protection. I had seen many with limps and bruises.

I was talking to Sammy from south London at breakfast one morning, he was all scratched on his left arm and leg.

"I had to swerve to avoid a collision, mate. The other geezer took the corner too wide. I ended up in the ditch, mate," showing me his wounds. Sammy had arrived two weeks earlier to comfort his brother who had a teaching job. But his dream working-holiday was put on hold, a broken leg from a road accident.

Stefan, the Swede had been to Ko Phan Ngan, a less developed island, thirty minutes away. He took a taxi from the ferry to his lodgings and witnessed a terrible accident. The roads were rugged, unpaved in parts. Up ahead a tourist lost control of his motorbike and was killed instantly, going off the road. Stefan and the taxi driver were first on the scene, the victim a German national.

One local nurse I met in a night-club confirmed, "everyday there are accidents, it's too much. If you go to Chaweng hospital, there are many casualties."

I met two Islanders on the street selling real estate. Dear and May were agents, looking for foreigners to buy local land or holiday homes. They needed clients to at least look at properties to justify their salaries. I obliged, as did Matt, a new friend from Chicago who was thrilled about recently receiving Irish citizenship. At the property office our interests quickly dwindled when the flash American behind the desk began talking in millions.

"It is baht, your quotes are in," I interrupted.

He gives me the rolling eyes expression, "the currency of the world is U.S. dollars."

"It's not the French Riviera, sir," I told him straight-up. But our pretension remained as we viewed property photos.

We looked at other plans with another developing company. More lavish ideas on paper, wanting us to buy before anything is built.

These guys were all out to make fast bucks, I believe.

The real estate sales girls invited us to a gig.

"My brother plays guitar with the band," Dear informed. The venue was just off the main street. I had not noticed this place in my first ten days. Rock n' roll music with four alternating lead singers. Matt and I got acquainted with a number of natives through Dear and May, a brilliant atmosphere with few tourists. We treated the locals, two bottles of whiskey, a couple of mixers, a bucket of ice and glasses for $23. At these prices it's no wonder people keep extending their holiday visas.

We moved next door to do some Karaoke with our new friends. I belted out a few notes but others with proper singing voices were much better than me. Matt, meanwhile got cornered, all I could see was long hair, mini-skirts and stilettos. The microphone was thrust into my face and I was struggling with 'Maggie May', the hoarse voice [Rod Stewart] just wasn't coming through. I bought a couple of beers and give one to Matt.

"Them two are lady-boys," I whispered.

"Yea, yea, I know."

But I think he didn't because he wasn't smiling anymore and a few minutes later he was using the 'F' word and then he was back in the Karaoke group.

The 'lady-boys' were not in short supply, very much accepted in this country, wanting to attract the attention of foreign men. At night they perform in cabaret shows or perhaps some are prostitutes. Someone is interested in them, otherwise they would not exist in such large numbers.

Not always easy to detect, if one is even remotely suspicious that they are talking to a lady-boy, you are probably right. Giveaways; are the voice, adams-apple and their walk. Yes, the lady-boy will try very hard to duplicate the female strut, never quite mastering it.

Saturday night arrived; Matt and I were watching live European football in Scruffy Murphy's. With a new Irish passport he was making plans to live and work in Europe. Jamie, an Aussie joined us. A group of Thai women walked into the bar.

"I'd go for one of them, mate. I met a cool chic last night in Bangkok. She took me to a party; we had some good smoke man," Jamie yapping about his activities.

"I'm looking to get married guys, take a nice Thai lady back to Sydney. A good housewife that can cook and clean and look-after me, would be cool."

"Sounds like you're looking for a maid."

"Nah Jack, she'll have a nice place to live, I've got a pad near the beach."

"You Jamie Dundee and the Thai princess, she can put a bit of croc' on the Barbie' for you dinner."

"Yea, sounds good, man. I live alone, so I need a chic to complete the process."

"Seal the deal, over a meal."

"That's the plan dude; I have sixteen days to put it into action."

"Wait a minute, there are plenty of single Sheila's back in Aussie, you're a young fella, what's the hurry, mate."

"Ah Jack, I've been up the garden path twice before, I need to try new pastures. I'll soon be thirty."

"Up the garden path, it didn't bring much happiness ever after, buddy. Misery it seems, are you looking for more misery, Mister Dundee."

"I didn't tie-the-knot the second time, we lived together but there was always a blue about moolah."

"About what?"

"The shekels, we never had enough and the bloody credit cardies got abused first time round. It's gonna be third time lucky, I can feel it. I've no kids, no baggage, man."

"Matt, whadayah think, is he on the right track?"

"Guys, my aunt is a lawyer, she actually deals in divorce cases and I have learned many things from her."

"O.K. here we go, we have the expert legal advice from the yanks."

"If she were here now, Jamie, she'd kick your butt. Guys, why is divorce so high. In both the U.S. and Europe it's quite high."

"It's low in Ireland."

"Is it? o.k., Jack you take Jamie to Ireland and find him a partner."

"I'm bloody not going all the way to Ireland, Thailand is far enough."

"He's only joking Jamie."

"Seriously guys, one in three get divorced and another twenty percent are stuck in a bad marriage. I think it's the same in most western countries. That's more than fifty percent are failing. Most of

the time there is financial problems and that leads to stress and unhappiness. Jamie, you need to chill-out, hang loose for five years."
"I'm chill, but should I re-write the plan, Jack you're just grinning there."
"I'm listening, but let me put another prospective on this.
I used to live in an apartment building with many tenants. One of my neighbour's was a professor."
"Professor of what?"
"Em, English and Psychology and would also counsel students privately.
Anyway, he covered many issues with me because he liked to chat. He told me if you can reach thirty and are still single, you have done well. You may have a few emotional scars but that should make you stronger. In your twenties, many people 'fall-in-love' but at times with the wrong person. You go with the flow, you let it happen, duplicate your friends. Or you go for the safe option, Mr. Bland but that will lead to a monotonous life and inevitable divorce.
Into your thirties most people become more stable and have a better chance of finding someone that fits you better. You are more practical, a job and an income. Yes, there has to be an attraction, but also a sense-of-humour, good conversation and strong work ethic. It's no good looking all-nice, if you have no personality."
So Jack, the professor was your mentor."
"No, no, he wasn't schooling me. This was in New York, Americans are friendly people, so there can be lots of gab."
"What about women, my sister back in Boston is thirty-eight, single and a teacher, what would the Professor have for her?"
"Eh, well, it looks like your sister is on the right track. He didn't really differentiate between the genders. Basically get your own life in order before pursuing a serious relationship, having a balance in life; work, social activities and homestead. Too many people 'patch things up' and it all 'comes out in the wash.' Yea, that was one of his favourite sayings, 'coming out in the wash.' That's one of the problems; people are slow to end relationships, especially women. Lots of men are not good at been single, they nest themselves into a relationship, like squatting. He told me many stories about people coming to him for advice. He was precise."
"He took no prisoners, that professor. You put his philosophy into action?"

I laughed, "gee, it's not something I wrote down in stone. I didn't stick ideas on the kitchen fridge."

Chaweng, the largest town on the island has a beautiful white sandy beach, eight kilometres long, one guide book quoted. The water, turquoise in colour, beach bungalows, in brick or wooden. Bars, restaurants and clothing stores in abundance. Cafes, internet shops and financial businesses. Massage outlets, a detailed neon sign of human feet at their entrance. Stretch out on a bed alongside others and let the masseur take control.

Matt told me, "that it's not exactly a pampering, a Thai massage can be painful. The lady twisted and pulled to distribute energy through my nervous system. She was using her hands, thumbs, elbows and knees to apply pressure. I didn't like it at first and was embarrassed to complain, but then it became bearable. Afterwards every muscle and bone was loose and flexible. It is healthy, you should try it."

Tee-shirts I bought had to be xxtra large because the average Thai is smaller than the average European. One shopkeeper had many football jerseys of European teams. I bought one for just $5, but then changed my mind when I realized it had a sports logo. The shopkeeper offered to make a jersey for me with no advertisement. I agreed, his wife got busy on the sewing machine.

Slavery was abolished many years ago but it seems it does not apply to some sports companies. They pay top sports people large sums of money to wear their products but their employees get a pittance in salary. If just one, high profile footballer, golfer, basketball player or tennis professional took a stand on this issue, it would make a massive difference to thousands of sweat-shop employees. Surely one of them has a conscience and will step-up and do the correct thing as a human being. Meanwhile, you the public should not buy these products, no excuses.

Modern-day slavery is alive and well across Asia. Millions of jobs have been lost in America and Europe and are now in Asia, mainly China and Bangladesh. Financial experts and the media call it globalization.

That's totally wrong, it's Extreme-Capitalism packed with employees who are pushed into doing long hours, no overtime pay, tough conditions and almost no rights. In reality, it's slavery. Employees in any country should be paid a fair and honest wage.

The people of America and Europe, if they have a conscience should simply stop shopping and live on the basic necessities. This sends a genuine message to the bad leadership in the political, business and banking world to put things right. At the moment, the future of America and Europe looks very bleak, for you and the next generation. Wake-up people of the western-world, if shopping is all you want to do, then you are doomed. If it's not made in your country, then think twice, before you buy. People first, then money, then things.

In 2006 while living in New York I was discussing economic issues with a couple of friends. Forecasting a serious recession was about two years away and stating some facts to justify my opinion. My buddies in total disagreement, that the U.S. would always be financially strong.

Sadly, but predictably a massive economic collapse in September 2008, but it was not a world recession, as many sections of the media and so called experts told us. Australia, Canada and some central and northern European countries dodged the crisis with sensible national planning which in reality is not difficult. The Irish Times and New York Times newspapers are good at getting to the truth. If you didn't see the financial breakdown of 2008 on the horizon, you were dozing.

The notorious full-moon party could not be missed. From the big Buddha statue, which attracted a lot of viewers, sea transport was departing to another island, Ko Phan Ngan, a forty-five minute ride in a small speed boat. It was the worst water crossing I have ever experienced. Seating for eight, seventeen were squeezed on board. We bumped along at a nifty speed. The further we went out into the open waters, the waves became higher. We had some nasty bounces, everyone was getting soaked. Seated on the floor with a plastic cover I brought was ample protection from the splashing water. The wind got stronger; I could sense the scared feelings, I certainly was worried with no life-jacket. If this boat hits a wave the wrong way, it will capsize. I don't want to test my swimming abilities in the choppy waters in the gulf of Thailand. One girl began crying and roared for the boat to stop. The pilot slowed, keeping the engine running. To continue at a slow pace was not logically possible, the waves were impeding our progress.

"We must go fast, the weight will help the boat," one guy advised. "This man has crossed these waters many times, we must trust him," another shouted. I swapped places with the girl, there was no smooth safe passage. The throttle was slowly released, we increased our acceleration. Lights were visible in the distance, as we got closer, the waters became calmer. A major sigh of relief, as we got our feet on dry land. Returning on a ferry boat was the unanimous banter.

The music was pumping, lights flashing, a massive canopy tent, the D.J. in good voice. Vendors with bins packed of beer and ice. Smoked filled the air from food stands. On the beach the aroma of hash was evident. Watch for the undercover cops was a regular low tone warning. Every adventurous traveller in southern Thailand may have been there. A loose friendly atmosphere, no aggression. Smiley happy folk, grab a few beers, mingle and enjoy. Techno, house and a dash of reggae.

Fortunately the water was shallow, drunks entering for a dip, sadly it became a toilet for some idiots. Many here for a one-night shindig, others had arrived too late for vacant accommodation. Had hidden their luggage, so would be sleeping rough or not at all. Fire crackers were shooting off, a dreadlock raver on the receiving end of one that went too low.

As day begins to break it rejuvenates the mood. A second-wind and suddenly the masses are animated again. Who would want this party to end. This was phenomenal, an unpretentious location, an international gathering without hesitation. The food vendors were still there, so I stuffed myself with rice and chicken.

The cool morning began to fade, a cloudless sky brought high temperatures. Thong Sala was the choice of destination for the return journey, a much calmer ride back to the island of Ko Samui on a middle-size passenger boat.

As I strolled from the warm waters to my beach towel, the following day I noticed 'Big Jim' play-acting with snorkel gear and flippers, clowning with the sun bathers around him. Roy, one of the Dubliners clicking his camera, Willie relaxed on a deck chair reading a day-old European newspaper, moaning about Liverpool losing in football. "I thought you guys had gone home," I said. "We went to Malaysia, for one day, so we could get a new thirty-day-visa. We're all staying a bit longer," Roy enthusiastically basking.

An ice-cream seller comes-by carrying a full cooler, heavily clothed with hat and scarf protecting her against any further skin damage. As we sit around eating our purchases, this bloke strolls by who had a strong resemblance to one of my school teachers from the past. I mentioned this.

"Maybe it's him, Jack," Roy joked.

I laughed, visioning the possibility. This guy had Bermuda shorts, Hawaiian shirt and Ray-bans. Head held high with a young chic on his arm probably about forty years younger.

Ray shrugged, "he's got a woman and is twice our age."

"I know a couple of ol' fellows who come here every year, they drink in my local back home," 'big Jim' interrupting.

"Ahh, you've been listening to the exotic pub stories, so you jumped on board for a piece of the action," Willie could not resist.

"I've been behaving myself," responded 'big Jim.'

"Yea right, what about that one on the back of your scooter today," Willie raising his voice as he stood-up.

"Are you the new security guard around here," Jim replied.

"Everyone seen you, it's not that you are easily missed," Willie shouting back.

"She's a respectable person, a Dutch school teacher actually, just giving her some driving lessons," Jim defending his corner.

Later as we all dined at Scruffy Murphy's, an elderly guy went by with two young women, one on each arm.

"He's a bit greedy," nudged 'big Jim'.

"You see plenty of that in Patatya," responded Willie. "I was there last year, I'm thirty-one and at times it looked like I was the youngest tourist around.

With just two days left on my visa, I would say bon-voyage.

An early morning taxi on a Song Taos pick-up truck with seating on each side and a canopy for sun protection. Off to the town of Na Thon for a ferry to the mainland. Four passengers had no choice but to stand on the rear bumper of the truck, everyone needs to reach their destination.

A quick cup of thick black kopi with a pastry as the boat was inching towards the dock. About fifty backpackers to board an already full vessel which had sailed from Ko Phan Ngan; the venue for the full-

moon-party four days earlier. It was reminiscent of a refugee escape boat. Haggard, weary looking folk sprawled on the top deck. Dreadlocked, tattooed, eye-brow pierced, stinky arm pits crew, the odd fresh smile. Stumbling across stretched-out legs and piles of luggage, I managed to reach the steps to the lower deck. Further progress impeded, a full-house down below. But enough shade from an increasingly hot rising sun, I relaxed and stared into the open waters for the next two hours. On reaching Surat Thani I helped a middle aged Multiple-Sclerosis sufferer, losing control of his right arm and shoulder. "The warm climates help my condition."
I wished him well.
Confusion as to which bus to board to take us to the main station, six kilometres away. I purchased a ticket for Penang, an island on the west coast of Malaysia. Others were going to Kuala Lumpur, a few to the southern point of peninsula Malay, which is Singapore. Our transport would be going straight through, no changing vehicles at the border. At Surat Thani bus station I boarded a mini-fbus which took us to a café, ten minutes away. We sat around for about an hour waiting to continue our journey. This is Asia, so we expect delays. I chatted with English lads about football, Spurs and Watford supporters.
"Maybe Watford and Spurs should join together and make one good team," I sarcastically tested.
"Oooh, this geezer is pushing his luck."
"I know what he means but that would be a step down for Watford," the other one stuttered out through his laughter.
It would be nine hours driving before we reached the border. Southern Thailand has rugged mountains and forests. Fishing and shrimp farming is a large part of the local economy. Coconut trees, giving an exotic look.
A pit stop in Hat Yai, the town centre seemed to be dominated by Chinese jewellers and restaurants.
When we got tired reading we played cards, Shit-head is a popular game, 'Nomination trumps' is good also.
No problems with the border exit stamps. A couple of miles down the road, the Malaysian immigration, their outlet was cleaner and modern. More food take-outs to ease the hunger. Ten minutes later a surprise spot-check from customs, opening the side door of the mini-bus. They were armed and looking straight at me.

"Chicken is very good in Malaysia," I said as we chewed on our first meal in new territory. They seemed to soften their stance and wished us a 'happy holiday.'

"A bit of charm did the trick there," said Watford.

"Well, with two kilos in my bag, I didn't want to look nervous."

Two German women expressed a shocked expression, the others giggled understanding the wise-crack.

South of the border, houses and roads looked more superior. Night fall came quickly so our views were minimal. At Suberang Prai [formerly Butterworth] a transport change, a luxury coach for the five Brits and two Germans continuing south. The mini-bus driving straight onto a ferry for the twenty minute ride to Penang island. After docking, I shared a taxi with Sam from Kansas [U.S] and two Swedish blondes who unfortunately were meeting their boyfriends. Yes, the Vikings with their perfectly flawless features, some of us a distant second in that category. But what about their extrovertness or sometimes lack of it.

PHAT THAI FRIED NOODLES

Fry chopped garlic and onion until yellow. Add chicken and fry until cooked. Pour in shrimp, pickled white radish, soy bean curd.
Break the eggs into a pan and scramble. Add sugar, fish sauce, vinegar, ground dried red chilli and stir well.
Pour in the noodles, stir fry until mixed well.
Add onion, half-cup of bean sprouts and stir fry until cooked.
Spoon onto a platter, garnish with ground peanut, bean sprouts, carrot, cabbage and sliced lime.

Ingredients: 3 cups of narrow rice noodle.
Half-cup sliced chicken meat[small strip].
1tsp. ground dried red chilli paprika.
Some Sugar. 4 tblsp. Fish sauce.
4 tbslp vinegar. Half-cup bean sprouts.
1 lime for garnishing.
4 shrimps, 2 eggs
Half-cup soy bean curd.
1 tbslp. Pickled white radish. [chopped].
Half-cup cooking oil.
1 tsp. garlic [chopped]. 1 tsp. shallot and onion [chopped].
Quarter cup carrot for garnishing, sliced thinly.
Quarter cup cabbage for garnishing, sliced thinly.
2 tblsp. Ground roasted peanut

Malaysia

Malaysia can be the overlooked nation, it is rarely mentioned by Backpackers. Used as a transit country, travellers making the connection between Thailand and Singapore for their next flight. Others will tip across the Malaysian border when their thirty-day Thai visa has expired, then return a day later with a new visa. In this corner of south-east Asia, Thailand is the main attraction. Vietnam and Cambodia are also popular choices.

In Penang I had a late night snack and a few beers with Sam. We stayed at the same hotel, the Island City. He was checking-out early. Along Lebuh Chulia street there are lots of cafes and restaurants to choose from. After a Malaysian breakfast of sweet rice noodles with coconut and jaggery, I rented a bicycle and headed for the beach. It was deserted, I was the lone swimmer on a west coast shore, clear blue skies and thirty degrees Celsius temperatures. O.K. so let's see what else is here.

Georgetown is the capital of Penang. As I cycled around, some areas were dominated by Chinese traders, others more populated by Indian folk. I approached a mosque, the garden flowers blooming, palm trees dotted the path which was spotless clean. A young boy of perhaps no more than ten years old greeted me, "Welcome to Malaysia," shaking my hand with such elegant manners. Most mosques are brightly coloured as this one is, with high ceilings and no seating. Long mats carefully placed for the worshippers, when the call for prayer arrives non-Muslims must not enter. I meditated momentarily in the large open spaces.

Back on the bike I cycled through a Chinese trading area. Narrow streets, open shop fronts, vendors well stocked. A temple nearby, Buddha statues at the entrance. Inside joss sticks smouldering, the aroma filing through to the thoroughfare.

I returned to my hotel, an open-air bar at the entrance. I took a seat and had a few beers with Bill, he was from the midlands of England, travelling in Asia with his wife and eighteen year-old son.

"I struggle to walk, my legs are weak, but coming to the tropics has helped. The heat has strengthened my muscles," he explained.

"Where are you going Jack?"

"To Kuala Lumpur and then Singapore."

"Listen Jack, go to Medan, in Indonesia. It's just across the water. Take a boat from here, you'll be there in a couple of hours. They just had a war, but it's finished. Lovely people, they are. What do you think Jack?," Bill encouraging.

"Oh maybe, it's tempting."

"Look at this Jack" in a low voice, referring to the lady-boys who had just planted themselves at the next table.

"Hi, you come to Malaysia for fun time," one said.

"What's happening around this town, where can we go," I said, with Bill chuckling.

"What are you looking for?" the other answered in a female tone.

"A place to party, an exciting night-club" I shrugged.

"We can give you a good time, a really good time."

"Relax, all we want is to hang-out and have a few drinks," I shoot back.

"What is it, you folks are looking for," Bill challenging them.

"Some white guys from overseas," the short one answered.

"You won't get them here," I gestured.

"Oh, we can give you a new experience that you will never forget," the other one offered, in a bright red sweeter.

"Go to Thailand, you will find lots of white guys there," I told them.

"Oh, I have been to Thailand and had great fun."

"I bet you had," Bill muttered.

Bill and I laughed though the conversation, keeping it humorous. I saw both of them on the street corner that night looking for business. The red sweeter lady-boy had an almost perfect feminine face. Certainly an unsuspecting drunk customer could be caught in an embarrassing situation with a lady-boy, taking the bait as he staggers back to his hotel after midnight. Malaysia surprisingly had it's fair share of gender alteration.

I caught the mid-day express south to the capital Kuala Lumpur, the following day. As the bus leaves Penang island it crosses the four-mile bridge to the mainland, mouth watering views of the harbour and the skyline of residential and commercial buildings. A new motorway was built the length of peninsula Malaysia which is just one part of this country. The scenic rolling hills, covered with trees, a jungle feel to the countryside. This came to be as an experiment in the British-rule era. Seeds were bought from Brazil, tested in

London, then transported to Malaysia. So today rubber trees dominate the countryside.

In the past rubber, tin mining and later oil-palming dominated the local economy. Then the Mahathir ruling years brought new prosperity. Engineering, technology, gas and oil have enabled the government to attract foreign investment. The standard of living has risen greatly. Whatever the western press opinion of Doctor Mahathir, he certainly made a massive difference during his twenty plus years as prime minister, surely most of it is positive.

The guy seated next to me on the bus worked in Penang, returning home for the weekend. With a spicy breadth, which can be foul, we didn't chat much, I was reading, he was sleeping,

A cab to the Badok lodge in K.L.[Kuala Lumpur], one room was available for one night, then booked solid for days. I decided to look elsewhere, the cabbie took me to hotel Nova. The heavens opened, a heavy thunderstorm progressed. The receptionist allowed me to view a room, but at $45 per night, I'd keep my options open. I relaxed in the hotel lobby waiting for the torrential downpour to ease. A drenched western guy dashing-in, we exchanged pleasantries. Rene, was his name, from Sweden. We agreed to meet later, for a Friday night prowl. One block away, a hotel with no name over the entrance had rooms for $16. In the lounge area three native women were watching a 'Westlife' concert, gushing with admiration at the young Irish male singing group.

"They are from Ireland," I informed.

Looking puzzled one of them said, "they are American, right."

"No, no Ireland" I repeated.

"Is that in America," she asked.

"Europe," finding a world map and pointing out the geographical location. Some folks automatically think, if you are foreign, you must be American.

The porter escorted me to the top floor. I refused room seven, pointing to the large bug on the pillow. Thoroughly checking room eleven on the fourth floor before accepting.

JL Sultan Ismail, JL Petaling and JL Bukit Bangtang; the streets in the 'Golden Triangle' district. Bars, restaurants and nightclubs; Pop, rock, house, hip-hop, reggae, DJ's and live bands, this was the happening strip. Determined for a varied sample of the clubs, to avoid paying at every venue, we introduced ourselves as travelling journalists from Europe eager to taste the K.L. entertainment. Rene producing identification, associated with a local weekly newspaper back home where he worked part-time. The doormen were always accommodating, at two clubs, the Emporium and the Warp, drink charges were waived, fat chance of receiving this type of hospitality back in my hometown. The locals were out to enjoy themselves but I sensed a touch of conservatism and shyness. In the club, Manara Pan Global as I danced with a Japanese chic, Rene was off getting the drinks-in. Three others came into my vicinity, we were just rolling to the house-music. When Rene returned, he whispered in my ear, "I think one of them is a lady-boy."

"Is it this one in the black on my left?"

"Yes definitely that one."

Moving onto the Hard-Rock café, Lee from Manchester England, who worked for an oil company, explained.

"I visit this city once a month for a long weekend. Locals are reserved initially, but once you break through that barrier, you begin to notice the friendliness. Let me get those drinks lads, it's on the company."

Rene and I managed to sample the action in Bangsar, another popular area of the city. Narrow streets, less flashy establishments than the 'triangle.'

Irish and German theme bars were not missing in this a predominately pub scene, we mixed more freely with the patrons. Dignity and respect was evident, in six nights out socializing, not once did I see a couple showing affection in public, everyone been very respectful.

Rene told me an amusing story. His friend was refused entry into Malaysia because the immigration authorities noticed there was a page missing from his passport. So his buddy Freddy returned to Bangkok to organize a new passport at the Swedish embassy. He shrugged when questioned by the border officials. Saying "he could not understand there was a fault with his documents." But the real truth is that after a heavy night partying, back in his hotel room he decided to have a smoke, using a passport page for his roll-up. Their plan now was to meet in Singapore for their next flight, to Australia. On Sunday, I hit the suburb of Subang Jaya to visit Chak, a correspondent for three years. He was of Aborigine background, sharing a pleasant two-story house with four guys. Chak was a fashion designer. A few blocks away, his three sisters and a brother resided, whom I also visited in their detached house with driveway. One sister, Sarah worked for a daily broadsheet. We discussed the major event in town, the 'Non-Aligned Movement.'

The N.A.M. conference had representatives from over one hundred countries. Security was heavy, streets were sealed off. It is mainly countries from the southern hemisphere. Mahathir, Malaysia's leader at that time, in his opening speech talked about, 'prospering thy neighbour.' It makes sense to expand the prosperity. Also 'take the moral high ground,' reminding leaders to do the right thing. 'Take a look at yourself, don't point the finger at other countries. Put your own house in order, first.' as I quoted the newspaper.

Sarah agreed, responding "Our country has improved a lot in the last twenty years and most of the credit should go to Mahathir and people around him."

I would hope some of the leaders in attendance would take a good look at themselves and their actions. Robert Mugabe of Zimbabwe who has done a good job of ruining that country. Also some of the oil countries who do not reinvest enough into the infrastructure of their own nation, just filling their own pockets.

I wanted to talk more but we had to rush off to another big event. We attended a concert in the commonwealth stadium in protest of the threat of war in Iraq. The U.S.A. government had threatened to invade Iraq and remove Saddham Hussein from power. Chak, Rene and I reached a packed arena. Local musicians and celebrities provided the entertainment. A slogan 'Malaysians for peace' was everywhere. As we clicked our cameras, people in our vicinity pushed their way into the photo-shoot. Muslim women dressed in jeans, sweater and a head scarf of their chosen colour. Fashion is conservative, but trendy.

Kuala Lumpur is organized, not the major traffic jams of other Asian cities. A mixture of old and new, Islamic style buildings, colonial architecture in Merdeka square, Chinatown is near-by, teaming with activity. Shops, vendors, customers, a jungle of signs and noise. Temples on the side streets, rarely a quiet moment. Little India; an abundance of sari shops, a number of Muslim restaurants. As Rene and I strolled around these areas, making our way into the Golden Triangle which has a lot more than just nightclubs. It's very much the supreme business district. Home to one of the world's tallest buildings, eighty-eight stories, the Petronas twin towers, something this country can be proud of. The first six floors consist of shops, cinemas, an elegant concert hall, art gallery and museums. The visitors viewing point is on the forty-second floor, a pedestrian bridge linking the towers. Stainless steel and glass structures dotting the skyline. Fashionable lighting, a balanced blend of nature. The landscape garden at the rear in immaculate condition.

Monday is sluggish and irritating for the working-class. For travellers, the start of the working week is totally oblivious. Rene departed for the five-hour bus trip south to Singapore. I went to the Australian embassy, they stamped an electronic visa.

Later I popped in for a drink to a place called the Paradise club. I got talking to a fascinating character from Scotland, in town on business. Euan, his meetings were complete. Now he had two days and an expense account to play with, generously including me in his perk. During his teenage years his family lived in Canada. At sixteen, Euan had a solo holiday in Liberia, in west Africa, who at this age would have heard of this country. Rugby is his sport which we discussed at length over many tiger beers.

"Tanzania was my favourite country, where I lived for six years. We taught the locals to play rugby and started leagues, me and a bunch of other ex-pats."

He knew a lot about chicken farming.

"I set-up local people in business, to own chicken farms. I was the market, I would buy their chickens for export. They would pay me back monthly from their profits."

Euan continued, "I met western charities in Africa, they don't always get it right, they try to change people too much. It's like this Jack; I had a very good worker, one time. I made him foreman and doubled his salary. The guy was always punctual, never missed a day. When he became a boss, he started missing a lot of time, working only half-a-month. So I asked him one day about his absenteeism. He took me for a walk to his village. Now, believe it or not he was earning too much money. When I give him a rise in wages, his relatives heard about his pay increase. So they decided to come and live with him and get a piece of the money. Ironically, he told me he had enough money, he didn't need an increase. He had enough to buy food, beer and tobacco. There were no banks, there is no where to put the extra cash."

"So did you make some changes?"

"Instead of giving higher wages, I looked around and talked about what the area needed. We built a small school for his children to get a better education."

The vitality of one man can be phenomenal.

An e-mail from Rene influenced my decision to change plans, not for the first time. I'd take my next flight from K.L. instead of Singapore.

"There is nothing here, just a big clean city with shopping malls. It's not exciting, by-pass it if you can." This common duplicated message from many travellers.

On the way to the airport I threw-in a few questions about the country. Who better to ask than a native taxi-driver. Malaysia gained it's independence from the British in 1957. It was rich in tin which attracted Chinese immigrants. The British East Indian tea company brought many Indians for labour in the rubber plantations. This country is in two parts, peninsula Malaysia, the other is Sarawak and Sabah which became part of the country in 1963. After world-war-two the British regained control from the Japanese. In the 1960's the Chinese dominated the economics, but the Malays had the upper hand in political strength. Tensions erupted in the 1969 general elections, hundreds were killed in the capital. In the aftermath greater economic and political reforms were introduced. In the 1970's Malaysia began to develop into a more mixed economy. Oil and natural gas were discovered in the South-China-Sea. In 1981 Mahathir became the country's fourth prime minister. His radical reforms, no nonsense approach enabled the country to be a major player in the 'Asian tiger' of the 1990's.

In the traditional sense Malaysians were brought up to believe 'British is best.' Mahathir turned this on it's head. 'Malaysia can do it.' He entrusted a belief for the natives to believe in themselves. Engineering projects sprung-up, bridges and roads were built. Sky-scrappers are common in downtown Kuala Lumpur. The K.L. tower is in the top ten largest building's in the world and of course the Petronas towers completed in 1998. The technology industry blossomed as did automobile and heavy manufacturing. Foreign capital poured in and the stock market soared. Mahathir has survived two recessions and has led the country into modern age. He may have moved the goal posts in the political arena many times for his own benefit. Outsiders may look at this as too authoritarian. His political party keeps winning elections comfortably. The common feeling on the street is he has done more good than harm. His deputy Prime Minister Ibrahim was jailed in the 1990's for corruption and homosexuality, this sparked large protests. The taxi driver told me that Ibrahim should have been more patient and not be making leadership challenges. By 'biting his tongue' he would have been prime minister today.

At least the general population seems to have benefited from the economic growth, unlike other developing countries that are rich in oil. These vastly corrupt leaders with western petroleum companies jointly pocket much of the profits, leaving the general population in continuous poverty.

My family, relatives, friends, neighbours and fellow comfortable citizens of the world could make a stand by buying petrol from conscientious companies. No excuses, do your research and take a stand.

Nasi Lemak [Coconut flavoured rice dish]

Ingredients:
2 cups rice, 2 pandan leaves [tied in knot].
1 shallot-chopped, 10tsp. thick coconut milk.
1 small piece sliced ginger. Salt and pepper to taste.
Half-cup dried ikan bikis[anchovies].
4 shallots, 1 small piece belacan [shrimp paste].
1 clove garlic, 1 large onion-sliced.

Half-cup tamarind juice, 8 dried chillies—soaked

To prepare rice:
Wash and clean rice.
Add two cups of water and coconut milk.
Add shallots, ginger and pandan leaves.
Bring to boil, lower heat—simmer for 10-15 minutes, until the water
has been absorbed.

To prepare Sambal:
Heat oil and fry ikan bilis until crisp, then keep aside.
Add oil in wok and fry pounded ingredients till fragrant.
Add sliced onions, tamarind juice, salt and sugar.
Cook till gravy thickens.
Add ikan bilis and mix well.
Remove from heat.
Serve with Sambal ikan bilis, garnished with cucumber slices.
Sliced hardboiled egg and roasted peanuts.

Brazil (Brasil)

London to Sao Paulo was the best long distance flight I ever encountered. No blanket or pillow tucked in around me. No lights out at the midnight hour. No stewardess stepping carefully down the aisle. No tossing and twisting in search of the impossible snoozing position. No heavy breathing or stifling bad breadth from people in my vicinity. No delaying a toilet visit to avoid disturbing your temporary neighbour. We were accelerating down the runway at 10:30a.m.

A vacant seat next to me, the only one on this flight, then a couple on their second honeymoon. The lady was well prepared; eye mask, neck support, airline socks, glassy sweets for take-off, personnel music with headphones and guide books. Me, there, with just my sense-of-humour.

What is an enjoyable flight? Punctuality, good food with snacks in-between, plus conversations with a variety of passengers. A steady flow of free liquor and maybe an invitation for lunch with an air-hostess.

Touching down in Sao Paulo I had no idea what to expect. This country is the best at football, they get hot weather, have lots of beaches and a famous carnival. That was it really, my knowledge was limited. My imagination profusely stagnant, one step at a time, try to enjoy as I go, absolutely abstaining pre illusions.

At Guaralhos airport I was quietly excited, through customs and out into the arrivals hall. I'm hoping to be noticed, my eyes searching through the crowd, it's more difficult from my perspective. Suddenly a radiant lady jumps in my path, Alana greeting me.

I reach for the handshake, her nervous manner was noticeable, quickly introducing me to her sister Cristina and her partner Bruno. We strolled to the revolving exit doors.

"I need to change travellers checks."

So my host escorted me upstairs to the appropriate office. An American is trying to negotiate a transaction. It's unsuccessful, he's pacing back and forth.

"What's the matter?" I asked.

Raising his hands in disgust, "I'm in the wrong country, we're on our way to Argentina. With the stopover here, we got off the plane to

196

browse around the duty-free, somehow we have passed through immigration. Now they say we need to pay a departure tax." Technically they had entered the country and now they were leaving, this guy from Chicago, needed local currency. He was arguing the point that his travellers checks were in his hand luggage, which was on the plane. He changed the cash he had in his pocket but would it be enough for two.

Jacarei, was Alanas' hometown, I was given my own room, there was no awkward rules, a very comfortable start.
A Caipirinha shot was slapped in front of me as we relaxed in the shade at a recreation park the following day. Farm animals of cows, two bulls, horses, pigs, goats and hens were the residents. Locals were picnicking and fishing by a lake, others played games at an indoor arena. Caipirinha is the 'poor man's drink,' about $3 a bottle. 'It would take the paint off the door.' A couple more came my way, with larger as a chaser. My insides were gasping for a halt. We later played a pool competition with Alanas' sisters and their partners. There was no clear winner as intoxication was setting-in.

Many Brazilian homes were brick with tiled floors to keep cool, concrete driveways with a porch for sun shelter. The early days I was awakened by the local security at 4a.m. A man would cycle through the streets whistling in a distinctive way, this was to let the community know that he actually does his rounds. But surely burglars would figure his movements and there was no surprise arrival. Also dogs would begin to bark and then it would escalate. So at 4.18a.m., I'm wide-awake, thanks to the community hired lookout-man. Alana was an excellent host, giving me the freedom of her home. Breakfast was refreshing, papaya and water melon, brown rolls and tea.
Brazilians love the sweet taste, not shy with sugar. Cooking in oil is common, salt is never missing. This Portuguese speaking nation is exotic, good-looking and have an zest for life, plus sensuality is quite evident.
The extended family was most hospitable, inviting me for evening meals. Everyone was willing to be a friend despite the language barriers.
The Rio carnival was imminent, so a venture on my own in the

largest South American country. 'Be careful in Rio,' everyone kept saying. A six-hour bus ride, seated next to a middle-aged woman. Our contact was limited to a few smiles of acknowledgement. The countryside was mostly flat, but hilly in parts. The landscape off-green in colour, it seemed much of it was not put to good use. Open fields with little activity along the Via Dutra linking Sao Paulo and Rio de Janeiro.

Arriving at the clamouring Novo bus station in Rio, I opted for a prepaid taxi. I had made a reservation at the Copacabana Praia hostel.

Gus, introduced himself as I entered the dorm room.

"Be careful, there was stuff stolen here last week."

We chatted briefly, "a group from the hostel are meeting at nine, at the front door. They are going to a Carnival ball, be there if you are interested."

I was eager to walk the sands of the Copacabana beach. Ten minutes later, there it was, in all it's glory. A number of beach volleyball, soccer-style games in progress. Vendors carrying coolers, full of beer, soda or ice-cream. Bathers stayed close as the high waves broke near the beach line, scantily-clad bikini females in abundance. To the left was the magnificent Pao de Acucar, Sugarloaf Mountain. Further back was Cristo Redentor, Christ the Redeemer statue, the highest point all around. I slowly walked the promenade, beach front cafes catered for a steady stream of customers. On the opposite side of the street, bars and restaurants stand next to apartment buildings which had high security gates with inter-communication systems and cameras visible. I stopped at the Copacabana Palace and gazed at its elegance. I was in awe of been in this town, energy was building inside me. I wanted to jump around, do cartwheels, hand stands, an Irish jig.

I noticed rough characters eying me, 'here's a dumb tourist, perhaps an easy hit later.' With all the warnings I had received, I built-up a resistance in my mind.

I spotted a vendor, selling tinsel wigs. I settled for red, just the ticket for tonight's event. Back at the hostel, the shower was busy after a sweaty day on the beach. I was introduced to the room crew and suggested a wig gang of different colours, but they are too inhibited. Gus arrived with a case of Bohemia beers, after knocking back a few the lads loosened-up. I give them spray cans of yellow, green and blue, the national team colours, so room 205 turned into a hair and facial salon. Taxis transported the international nomads to the 'anything goes gala.' A mixed crowd of young and not so young. Just express yourself, it was easier to dance on the higher platforms, the main floor like sardines. The orchestra played continuously without interruption. The Aussies in our group had their cameras rolling, a documentary for a travel show back home. Helena, a local from the Flamingo district became my boogieing partner, my rhythm certainly was not in tandem with hers. As night-clubbers, Brazilian women are brilliant shakers, the hip movement is phenomenal.

A late night means a 3p.m. breakfast, the next day with fellow hostellers, Sonia and Marla from Norway. Omelets on toast all round, a touch of guilt as you realize the day is half-over. Eased considerably when you notice the beds next to you are still occupied. Determined not to allow the late nights devour my enthusiasm for daytime activity.

A clear blue sky, ideal for a Cristo Redentor visit. Two, 583 buses passed without stopping, a hand signal we belatedly discovered is necessary for the bus to stop. Sonia took off walking seemingly disgruntled.

"What's the matter," I asked Marla.

"We've been travelling five months together, there is nothing more to say to each other."

"Split-up after carnival," I suggested.

"The trip is finished, we fly home next week."

Arriving too late for the last tram up the mountain to the statue, we strolled the busy streets, making a pit stop at what would become a favourite haunt, a Suco [juice] shop. Avocado, Pineapple, Cheery, Plum, Beetroot, Peach, Lemon, Cashew, Star fruit, Chayote apple, Guava, Jackfruit, Orange, Papaya, Mango, Watermelon, Strawberry, Passion, Grapes. Also Caldo de Cana from sugarcane, Guarana and many others from the Amazon. Straight-up with ice or a mixed request. Sugar is normally added by the Cariocas [residents of Rio]. Fabulous tasting fruit drinks.

The following day I bumped into Sonia and Jonathon, a roommate from Manchester at the hostel reception, so we took off to Copacabana beach. I had just stretched out on a sarong when Sonia started running, she didn't stop until she reached the street about one hundred yards away.

"What's she chasing now?" Jonathon looking amused.

"That chic is giving you the eye, Jonathon, in the white tee-shirt, she is constantly watching you."

"What can I do, my schedule is full," he beamed.

"Hot date tonight then," I asked

"I hope it's hot," grinning to himself.

Make the effort to chat with strangers on the ocean front and you may have new friends. It wasn't just the bold and the beautiful. From expectant mothers to senior citizens, all shapes and sizes, no one was covering-up, everyone accepted. Could I find a notch and live here, the temptation is growing. About twenty minutes later Sonia returned wearing a flashy aluminous green swimsuit.

"I suddenly realized I was the only woman without a bikini," she said, "That's unique then," I complimented.

"No, no, I feel better now."

Sonia could play the guitar and would enter our room with a morning tune, making sure to wake everyone. Jonathon had a soft spot for her, so I steered Sonia in his direction. But a few days later he was retreating.

"She's clinging too much to me," Jonathon moaned.

"Well, she's all yours now, she can sing you to sleep at night," I teased.

He soon became happily occupied, meeting a beautiful young journalist from the Amazon country. He had the perfect job to continue the relationship, working for an off-shore oil company, off the coast of Angola. Six weeks on, six weeks off.

The promenade on Copacabana was crowded each evening, the foreigners were a tiny minority. I bought ice-cream for Carla, a local girl I'd met a few days earlier. As we strolled on the beach after dark, making our way towards the water, I noticed a guy approaching on my right, almost from behind.

I turned my head to look in that direction.

"Hay gringo" he called out, with two friends joining him.

I could smell danger; Carla suddenly scampered off in a scared reaction towards the street. I raised my fists letting out an almighty roar of bad language, I clearly stunned these wise-guys. A second group of young men were in close proximity, not sure if they were all together. I slowly moved to the safety of the masses on the promenade. The 'hay gringo' guy and his mates stood motionless, so no bruises from that possible encounter.

Carla explained, "Copacabana no good at night, many crazy people."

Next day, I told my roommates about the incident. Dave responded, "they tried to jump me last night, the street was crowded, but that didn't stop them. I noticed one guy looking at me, planning to attack from behind. He actually jumped on my back, but I was ready for the fucker. Knocking him off, he landed on his ass. Another challenged me head-on, but I swung at him, not connecting, he ran-off. He was about to get the beaten of his life."

"If they attack guys like you Dave, [who is six feet tall and muscular], they have no fear," I observed.

A Danish guy got mugged twice, his friend laughed as he told us. "He is small, an easy target, they took his camera the first time. The second time he give them his sunglasses, he had nothing else."

A Canadian got lured into a side-street by a local woman, only to be jumped by three men, taking his wallet.

On the beach a designated look-out had to stay and watch the gear, as the others were swimming and body-boarding. When it was my turn, I literally had to stand and be diligent. One guy approached looking for a cigarette light, clearly trying to distract me, I waved him away. But he was lingering, then pointing down the beach for me to come and see something. There is hundreds of Cariocas relaxing around me, he decides to approach a possible dopey foreigner. Then the bloody ice-cream seller is giving me the hand signal, five real for a frozen pop, I refused the purchase. He tries to create a scene by yelling, I smiled and remained calm. A senior citizen sitting on a deck chair with his wife and grandson backs me up, the vendor takes off.

"I see he try to, you high-price. For me, a-a-a two real. Next time I buy for you. Before many tourist from Europa, Amerikaa come here. Now today crazy people, they cheat, cheat. No good, no good. Tourists come, no."

I nodded understandingly, thanking him for his concern.

Larry, an Aussie with distinctive bleached hair from Queensland came back from Ipenema beach with an annoying story.

"They mugged me, took my money belt. It's almost certainly a young woman. She was lying close to me, wearing sunglasses, probably pretending to be sleeping. I turned away to retrieve a ball, minutes later I noticed the money belt was gone, she was gone as well. They're always fucking watching me on the beach. They got about fifty bucks, no more."

I haggled with Raul at the hostel reception about tickets for the carnival parade, $40 was his one and only price. 'Go at midnight and we can buy from scalpers,' was the word from other travellers.

From the metro station to the Sambodromo, [carnival parade] a continuous pedestrian jam. 'Coo-caa-Coo-laa, cer-vej-a, aq-qua' was the common chant.

A sea of vendors; burgers, sausages, onions and chips frying, a dark-haired shirtless local flipping the meat. A grandmother sitting next to a Marlboro dominated table. Honey smelling roasted nuts, Dave stopping because of the temptation aroma or more likely, a female cook with a gorgeous wide smile. Corn-on-the-cob; on wire mesh over a burning flame. Ice-cream in a cooler, cevaja [beer] in a bin full of ice, regular Cariocas making income.

About fifteen in our group, no one was straying, aware that foreigners are possible targets, safety in numbers.

This is the Rio carnival, the show begins at 8p.m. and ends around 4a.m. It's a competition of fourteen samba schools, over two nights. Each one taking more than one hour to complete the half-mile cat-walk extravaganza. Women and men of all ages lounged on the grass embankments, perspiring contently, carrying part of their costumes. Their school had passed through the finish line. The game was complete, looking a little exhausted, but jovial. We'd politely approach, requesting photos, refusals were non-existent. Most wore beach clothing with additional decorating. Spears with feathers, exotic laced boots, string waist garments, apache head gear.

Geno trying to organize a ticket price for our group. Three hundred dollars for fifteen tickets, Gus joined the deliberations, the dollar figures quickly dropped. Other scalpers were on the fringes, ready to pounce. Settlement at two hundred was the deal, a surprisingly low price. A short eruption of fireworks was the signal for the next samba school to start. The opening group will display a message, usually a political commentary or economic criticism. This is normally followed by a group of elderly men who are been honoured for their years of contribution. Floats of all shapes and sizes populated with samba dancing folk. About four thousand revellers in each school, the action is non-stop as they pass through. It's phenomenal, a constant flowing rainbow.

Section thirteen, we were seated near the finish line. I passed a couple of beers to the people behind us. A plastic cup full of caipirinha and lemon with ice came back. "No ingleis," shrugging their shoulders.

Dave and I moved higher on the terracing where there was more room to dance. A black girl approached, requesting a cigarette light. Dave obliged, she motioned for us to join her friends. Clicking the camera with three women hovering around Dave. He mustered broken Portuguese, unsure of the answers from the attractive dark skin locals. I complimented one in Spanish, a heavy peck on the check was her response. An elderly lady introduced herself, "I'm Larisa's grandmother," who was all eyes for Dave.

"I was a language teacher for thirty years; English, Spanish and French. I have taught students from Canada in an international exchange program.

I expressed our delight on such a magnificent event.

We were seated a medium distance from the parade. The music pumping-out, the drums and saxophones were the dominant sounds. As the crowd slowly dispersed, Dave and myself mingled in a local park with our new friends. Our hostel buddies having already returned to their sleeping quarters. Dave was becoming a handful, he was pissed, so when he fell in a heap breaking a park bench, it was time to call it a night.

It was a struggle getting him into a taxi.

Back at the hostel, two English guys had just arrived.

"We're off to the beach for sunrise."

"I'm too knackered to join you."

My sleep was interrupted by Sonia, the Norwegian guitar player. Strumming to a melody, there was no welcome gestures. Moans and groans from Geno and Gus in the bunks nearest the door, I placed my head under my pillow, Sonia got the message and left.

Larry, the Aussie was organizing a trip to the Maracana football stadium, supposedly the biggest in the world. Certainly, this country's most famous, where Brazil shockingly lost the 1950 World cup final to Uruguay.

5:30p.m. the meeting time at the front of the hostel. I skipped off to a

Churruscuria for an afternoon meal, where one could stuff
themselves without the risk of indigestion when the check arrives.
They had lots of dishes on display, mashed and roast potatoes, pasta,
vegetables, Brazilian beans, salads, rice. The waiters and waitresses
would repeatedly come to your table with meat on a skewer, offering
more and slicing with shape knives. One could not complain about a
miserable dinner. The best feed I ever got in a restaurant, anywhere.
Back at the hostel the crowd was swelling for the evening match.
Meredith from California was waiting anxiously for her friend,
Marilyn to return from the beach. I stalled, willing to hang back, ten
minutes passed.
"Don't miss the game because of us, thanks for waiting, but I can't
go without her," Meredith conceding.
"O.K. see you later."
I took off running to catch the hostel crowd. Seconds later, unknown
to me Marilyn turned the corner, so the girls linked-up with the gang.
I was moving at a fast pace, wondering how I had not caught the
group. A left turn, not sure it was the correct street. Finally out of
breadth reaching the metro station, I must have run a full mile.
"Well that's just great," thinking aloud, the bloody thing is closed. I
slumped onto a wall, accepting that sinking feeling of missing out.
But it was more than that, a football game in the Maracana, in Rio de
Janeiro, now that would be a top-ten best moments, [venue for the
2014 world cup final].
I walked like a wounded animal, slumping. Stopping at a suco shop
and ordering an Amazon fruit drink. This will cheer me up, albeit
temporary. I didn't want sympathy from the crew returning from the
match, so I headed to the night market in avenue Atlantica, near
Copacabana beach front. Browsing through the colourful clothing
stalls. Scenic paintings of the favelas, souvenirs of the more famous
landmarks. I purchased a Brazilian harp, a simple wooden frame
with ten strings and the music notes of songs for guidance. I sat by
the beach practicing, passers-by stopping momentarily. Perhaps if I
had a hat, I could be officially busking.
I moved to a miniature promenade bar, ordering Brahma beer.
"Haaayy, what are you doing here, where did you go."
"Hi mate, there was a lot of people chasing you."
It was Larry, Dave, Jonathon and Geno, hostel companions,
suddenly appearing throwing comments.

'Pull-up a chair lads, Caipirinha, four" signalling with my fingers to the barman.

"Easy Irish" laughed Larry, "we just came out for a beer mate."

"I know you Aussies are fit for anything," I responded.

"We seen you running, where did you go, four guys chased after you, Sean," Larry asking, lighting a cigar.

"I ran into a supermarket, I thought you went in there," Jonathon jumping in. "Gus and the Danish guys tried to catch you also."

"I zoomed all the way to the train station, the feckin thing is closed on Sundays. I was Forrest Gump for fifteen minutes. Running, running, running like an idiot."

"We were all at the bus stop, you went the wrong way."

"I'll stay a bit longer and go to next week's game. Who was playing anyway?"

"Botofoga beat Flamingo 2-1, the stadium was half full, about sixty thousand."

I beckon for another round.

"Wait a minute, I'm calling this one," Larry stood-up. Let's cool it down, cinco Brahmas, por favour."

An unplanned social evening, the best way, jokes, intellect and blarney flowed.

Two days later I was having lunch in a pizzeria, I shouted at Dave who was across the street.

He joined me, "Geno went out last night and never came back. But he phoned the front desk to say he's fine and he'll see me later."

"Ah well, I'm sure he's having fun."

Twenty-four hours later Geno was still missing, in the dorm room we joked with Dave.

"That's it, you'll be returning to California alone, he's hooked-up with a hot babe," Jonathon said, fetching a couple of beers from the fridge.

"Maybe he's in the favelas tied to a pole in a backyard with six dogs around him. The next phone call will be a ransom," I offered.

"Yea, have you any money Dave, we can always make a collection around here, Dollars, Real, travellers checks, Peso," Jonathon fetching a sombrero from under his bed.

Gus was stretched-out listening quietly, decided to offer his summation. "Have you guys ever been to 'Help'?"

"I have………with Larry," responded Jonathon.

"Ooooohh wait a minute, so that's where you guys go when you disappear in the evening," Dave looking envious.

"We didn't pay, the doorman waved us through. We had a laugh with some of the clients doing their rounds," Jonathon defending his corner.

"It's part of the scenery, the same as going to Ipanema beach or Sugarloaf mountain. Going to 'Help' is allowed once. If you go a second time, then you're a sleaze," Jonathon continued.

"As I was saying" Gus intervening, "he probably skipped off to that night-club and hasn't stopped partying," Gus standing to express his opinion.

We laughed and applauded.

We put notices on Geno's bed, 'Missing in action.' 'Copacabana mystery.'

It was a clear afternoon, we grabbed the cameras and went for a photo session. A very steep climb of 710 meters on the tram. Inside the tram, the seating is sectional, in a step form. So passengers are not seated at an angle position. The Corcavado [hunchback] as it's known to the locals, Cristo Redentor [Christ the redeemer], it shouts out Rio. This 38 meter statue is a huge grey concrete structure. I had seen it numerous times in magazines, travel sections of newspapers and movies.

We duplicated the image with outstretched arms, we jockeyed for mug shots, this been the most visited attraction. The left arm points to the north of the city, where the Maracana stadium and the international airport are located. The right arm extended towards the suburbs of Jardim Botanico, Gavea and the horse racetrack. Ipanema and Leblon beyond. On front of the statue is the beautiful Pao de Acucar [sugarloaf] peak, about three hundred meters below. A light haze was developing which made it difficult for clear photography. We sat on all sides viewing this compact metropolis of seven million inhabitants. Mountains, sand and sea combined, are a recipe for charm and splendour.

As we disembarked from the descending tram, Jonathon suggested we visit Sugarloaf. A couple of taxies had us there in five minutes, making sure they went the shortest route. The first cable car rolled up over two hundred meters to an area called Morroda Urca. Here,

there was a restaurant, souvenir shop, a theatre and a helicopter landing pad. Rising to almost four hundred meters above the streets, the second cable car was special. As the daylight faded the city lights began to flicker. The Copacabana beach and promenade curving in the foreground with the Corcavado Mountain looming overhead.
If there is a top-shelf romantic view of a city, this is it.

****

Back at the ranch the 'lost soul' had returned, Geno was reading papers on immigration to his country. Dave got on his case about some presentations they needed to prepare and wanted an explanation about his absence. [Dave and Geno were in this country doing talks at universities promoting student exchange-programmes for California].
Dave planted himself on a stool, "so you decided to come back, I was thinking of calling the Police and report you missing."
"Take it easy, Jonathon butting-in, "let him be."
Dave continued to quiz him, so he relented.
"A couple of days ago, I was just walking along the beachfront as the sun was going down. There was a girl walking about twenty yards in front. You had all these joggers 'checking-her-out.' Young guys hanging-out were shouting at her. So I increased my pace to get a closer look. As I passed her, I said hello and made a comment that she was receiving lots of attention.
"Ahhh, Brazilian men, they're like this," she said.
I admired her beauty and the colour of her skin.
"I like your colour," she replied touching my arm.
"Yours is much nicer, it matches your eyes," I shoot back.
"Actually I am white, pulling down her bikini top."
"She bloody flashed," Jonathon said.
"No, not really, just a little."
"So the hormones are jingling now, what did you say," Gus jumping-in.
"I'm not sure what I said. That's beautiful, I think. We talked for about ten minutes and agreed to meet that night. She lives in Flamingo with her parents, they're really nice people."
"Good man Geno, you're the man," everyone cheering.
"Hang-on, wait a minute," Dave raising his arm.

207

"What's all these papers for?" looking like an annoyed father.
"She wants to come to America," Geno answering with a chuckle.
"Are you mad, you just met her," Dave challenged.
"She's gorgeous, you'd do the same," Geno looking for approval.
We started singing love songs, Dave left the room shaking his head.

Giselli, a girl Gus met on the beach, telephoned to invite him to a
party. "Guys, I need back-up, who wants to come?"
No one was coming forward. A few of the lads were next door
making themselves known to new neighbours. They were getting
louder, so probably getting drunk.
So I volunteered.
As we waited in a downtown designated location, I was moaning to
Gus about his friend been late. Giselli arrived running and smiling.
Her English was weak, but Gus and myself had a translation
dictionary which was our bond. The party was a low-key affair, one-
hour drive in a public mini-bus.
The problem for us was each invited guest seemed to take along their
dog; Alsatians, Labradors and Boxers. The animals received most of
the attention especially when one became excited, which was quite
often. It seemed to me it was a get-together for the animals. I had a
miserable night's sleep, the dogs were restless. Also probably
developed an unhealthy bladder thanks to one Alsatian who during
the night took up residence in the hallway blocking the route to the
bathroom, my first and last visit to the suburbs.
Gus was more optimistic, taking one of the Labradors for a morning
walk. What is it with this nation and the canine animal? What's the
first thing Brazilians do when they get married? I think they seek-out
a dog. A year later a second dog enters the home because the first
one needs company. Then they decide on kids. A dog is great
company but here there is an infatuation. I'm joking of course, with
a dose of reality.

"Don't go to Santa Teresa alone," advised Lourdes, a waitress in a
café that I frequented for breakfast.
"I will escort you, I'm free in the afternoon."
We took the bondinno, a mini train across an old stone bridge that
looked like it was about to collapse. We disembarked at a junction as
the train veered right. We briefly strolled through the hilly cobbled

streets, killing time for the next train to come.

"See these people are watching you," Lourdes whispered. She entered a miniature police station asking, 'should we go higher up the mountain.'

'Be careful, do not get off the train, come right back down.' was the advice from the cop. The second train was destined for Santa Teresa, A bohemian district, artistic surroundings, bars and restaurants. My escort repeatedly reminded about the young men who were riding on the outside of the train to avoid paying the fare. They will try to steal. This is the favelas, they have no jobs, crime is high. Just a minimum taste of life in the poverty areas higher up the mountains.

On Sunday and Monday nights are the carnival parades with the samba schools. Then it's Ash Wednesday, the beginning of Lent on the Christian calendar. It's a party before the forty days of fasting begins.

The following Saturday, the top five placed schools perform in the Champions Parade.

On the metro train to the grand finale we mixed with samba school members. The women had laced boots with shorts and adverts on their tops. Men wore flowered silky pants and speckled waist coats. Yellow and blue were the dominant colours. They performed mini-demonstrations of Samba movements, we pushed a few drinks their way. Exiting the station, vendors were out in force. Brahmas seem to be going cheap, everyone were buying them. We stumbled upon one group, they were edging towards the starting line. Glamorous women of all ages in dazzling costumes, red the main shade. My heart rate steadily increased as we were embraced from all sides during our photo session. The scalpers were shouting high prices for tickets to get inside the Sambodromo. We delayed another round of beers. One lady accepted ninety U.S dollars for ten tickets. Zone four our location, miniature and clustered, but a prime section. This was the final night of carnival and locals were making the best of it. Four elderly men stood in front of us sharing a homemade cocktail, pouring from a flask, swirling to the deafening beat. Each school had many sections that display unique outfits and varied choreography. Massive floats passing through, surrounded by guides maintaining coherency. Even the sweepers at the rear looked decorative in flashy orange boiler suits. As the fourth placed team passed, some spectators shouted 'champion, champion,' disagreeing with the Judges decision.

As the night wore on, spectator numbers began to dwindle, allowing our group to mingle in the front row. One could almost reach out and touch the dancers, the energy and sound-beat keeping everyone jovial. Back on the street several mini stages were packed with performers. Each individual determined to better the next, strutting their stuff. Audiences grew as dawn began to appear on the horizon. We were grooving, locals from Leblon putting us in the correct motion, or at least they tried. The carnival was about to end but many were not going quietly.

The exodus began with Jonathon flying north to Belem. Gus had a long bus ride to the coastal town of Salvador. Dave and Geno were heading inland to Belo Horizonte on their presentation talks. Larry was staying for another month.

As quickly as people were departing, the rooms was been refilled. Americans working with the Peace Corp arrived from Bolivia. "I need this holiday, we're living in primitive conditions." "Is that a third-world country?" I asked. "It's another world, helping the locals in education and agriculture. We are there fifteen months, every week I get ill," Ron slumping onto his bed. "From what, the food, the water?' I quizzed. "Sometimes it's that, but the altitude is my main problem. We are living high in the mountains."

Kick-off time was approaching, I could sit among the thousands in the Maracana stadium. The fact that I missed the game a week earlier was actually a blessing. Because this time, it literally would be one-hundred-thousand. The final of the Rio-Sao Paulo tournament, Vasco de Gama, the home team against Santos, a coastal town in Sao Paulo state. The best teams in the country are from this area, a two-leg affair. Unsure what type of ticket to buy, Marilla, another traveller, fluent in Portuguese took the lead, asking locals what ticket to buy, "Brazilians can't answer a question," she moaned. Suddenly I found myself at the front of one line, stuttering to the sales clerk.

"Ask for an eight real ticket," one helpful fan interrupted.

"I think you are Irish, trust me," he sensed my confusion.

"I know Dublin, O'Connell street, Trinity college," Ordering six tickets for me.

"I'm sorry my friend, we get different information," apologizing.

"I hope the Dubs give you a cracking time."

"What, what was that?"

"Did you have fun in Dublin?"

"It was great, I want to go back and live there."

A senior charity match was in progress, as we surveyed our seating choices. Marilla was originally from Mozambique, in southern Africa, controlled by Portugal at one time, she was now a Danish citizen.

I wore a Brazilian shirt, that can't offend anyone, as did Garrincha, who graced this turf numerously. Not the most recognized name but he overcame physical adversity. Zico, Socretes, Romario, Ronaldo, Ronaldino, Revellino.

Pele, probably the most famous but off the field lacked conviction in tackling the issues of the populace. This country gives it's footballers one name and the world remembers.

The teams for the main event entered the arena, a sea of swinging black and white shirts, the host's colours. Not a silent voice, not an empty seat. Fire crackers shot into the night sky, smoke bombs filled the air, toilet rolls sailed onto the field.

Santos threatened early, the crowd became anxious, three times the visiting team stretched the Vasco defence. A drunk behind us spilled beer on Marilla, who retaliated with a tongue lashing. Santos continued to press, half-time came as a relief to the home supporters. A ravine divides the football pitch from the spectators, how's that for an idea, no mass crowd invasions here.

The home team kicked-up a gear in the second period, constantly pressurizing the heart of the Santos defence, who continually fouled. Free-kicks in dangerous areas led to the inevitable, a twenty-five yarder into the top corner, the goalkeeper stranded. The celebrations had barely subsided when a second goal was scored. The party could begin, beer and pop corn rained down on us, Vasco were victorious 3-1.

Now the dreaded journey home, traffic jams all around the stadium, taxis going nowhere, buses packed. We help to push one, it's engine stalling. Finally squeezing onto a 683, the atmosphere and noise continued. Chanting and banging the roof, it was relentless, but this is what we came for.

The following morning I left Rio. It certainly has it faults, one could be mugged on a quiet side-street or your camera stolen sunbathing among the multitudes. But it has an edge that would definitely draw one to return. Soccer, samba, sunshine and sand, sensuality, suco drinks not to mention it's stunning scenery.
Sharing a cab with Harry from Berlin to the main bus station, a delightful lad, he had just completed a year of studying Spanish and business in Buenos Aires. I absorbed his information on Argentina where my next check-in would be. The bus station was modern in parts, drab in others. Harry went to the Brasilia window, San Jose dos Campos was my bay.

****

Returning to my host Alana, meeting me at the bus terminal. A pleasant change, having a bedroom to myself, a proper kitchen and living room to relax. Each morning I'd take an exercise walk by a river that was more stagnant than flowing. Stopping briefly to watch football on a marked cement playground, there was always a game in progress with a woman referee.

An attraction was developing with Alana, should I test the waters on romance. I quickly pushed that thought into the distance. But over a few drinks by a riverside café, sparks did fly, continuing to erupt much longer than a volcanic mountain. It was a warm summers evening, then a sub-tropical storm developed. Thunder and lighting, combining with a heavy downpour, the salivate didn't drop. Three hours later there was no hiding place, the rain relentless. We walked through the water logged streets, accidentally by-passing the appropriate right-hand turn. I wanted to stop the clock, halt the earth's axis. This was a deep magical moment, through my veins and into my bones I could feel truly alive. It was not just crossing a line, clashing head-on, propelling into a different atmosphere.

Alana and her family had a few days off, so a trip was planned to a relatives beach house. Ninety minutes drive to Caraguatatuba, the latter part was a beautiful slow descent to the coast. A modest three bedroom brick house, a sheltered patio at the front. This is the Ubatuba shoreline, the Paulistanos from San Paulo flock to these beaches during the summer months. We had many to choose from, visiting Praia Vermelha, Flemengo and Domingos dias. Clean white sandy beaches with turquoise waters. Food stalls, souvenir sellers, snorkeling equipment, banana boat rides. The house population increased dramatically on the weekend, Alanas' relatives arrived. On Saturday the beach was cancelled because of cloudy skies and cooler temperatures. But visits to Cachoeira das tocas, a variety of waterfalls and deep pools raised our spirits, the adults been more enthusiastic than the kids. Playing cards and board games in the evening, keeping us occupied. I was unbeaten at checkers, so they conspired against the foreigner, creating new rules.

Back at my base in Jacarei, I strolled through the old town on hot afternoons. I could notice the effort to create employment. In the shops there were too many employees, one to answer your queries, another to wrap your purchase, then the cashier. In the evening Alana would drive to the modern town of San Jose dos Campos. We'd visit the cool air-conditioned shopping centres, taking-in a movie, or played bowling.
A couple of solo trips, breaking my enjoyable routine took me to Sao Paulo and also to the Panthanal area in western Brazil.
Sao Paulo, the most populated city in the southern hemisphere. Teresa, an ex-flat mate of my good friend, Aussie Al, from their days living in London. A few phone calls and I would be meeting Teresa and her sister, Juliana at Clinicas metro station. I'd be wearing the national football shirt, there were no dramas, as a very cute girl shouted my name.
Juliana would be the pilot during my ten-day stay. She was always clicking the button to lock the car doors when we stopped at traffic lights, crime is a problem. Meeting her many friends, challenging the Paulistas at pool with Enzo as my partner. Our opponents, most were big strong muscular guys with lots of tattoos but were crap at shooting pool, so we remained unbeaten.
Friday evening socializing, hooking-up with Teresa and her buddies after work. Ron, an English guy married to the beautiful and pleasant

Marilene was part of the group. The bartender rang up a tab of fifty-one real, about $29 U.S. At these prices I should relocate permanently.

Downtown areas off Paulista Avenue were busy with street markets and fairs. Sampling the Bauru, a famous Brazilian sandwich with beef, tomato, pickle and a delicious mix of melted cheese. As I was munching into this tasty food, I noticed the horrible site of a sickly human being. So wretched looking, I cringed and looked away. Not sure if he was blind, certainly was diseased with infections on his face and all along his legs. What did I do? Nada, zilch, nothing, looking and reflecting just doesn't cut it.

Sao Paulo is the resting place for this country's 'dead king.' Juliana reluctantly drove me to a cemetery in Morumbi.

"I no like," shaking her head and stayed in the car, while I went to search for the resting place of Ayrton Senna.

Killed in 1994 at the Italian Grand Prix, a simple lawn graveyard, no lavish headstones, scripted flat cement plates on the ground. A caretaker pointing to the middle, in the centre Senna rests in peace. A few withering flowers in a bottle of discoloured water, a dark moment for this nation that many Brazilians will not forget.

In this city, Cathedral Metropolitana was my favourite street hangout. An area of many buskers, where I performed a comical ceili jig for a banjo player. He'd been to the folk festival in country Clare on the west coast of Ireland. "Watch your pockets around here," he muttered.

The weekend is action time in Ibirapuera park, two stages set-up for local musicians. Sport activities were in full swing. Across the street a monument which would surely challenge for the world's biggest, dedicated to the pioneers of the city. Unknown to me I'd visited this city at the right moment. Enjoying a drink downtown at Finnegan's, the owner asked if I was Irish.

"That's correct."

Introducing himself as 'Danny the Dutchman.'

"You must come tomorrow night for our Saint Patrick's day party."

A can of green spray was a necessary purchase. Teresa, Juliana and a bunch of their friends came along. A sprinkle of Irish amongst the crowd.

Ex-patriots from Canada, America, Germany and the U.K., many employees of foreign embassies. The vast majority were Brazilian of course. A stage was erected on the street; the Irish band played mainly traditional tunes to fit the occasion. I tried teaching Irish dancing to Juliana and others. Encouraging them to lift their legs higher, Juliana ripping the ass of her jeans in the process. A borrowed sweater to tie around her waist got her in the mood again. Danny does not trust his bar staff. They stamp your customer card every time you are served a drink. Payment is made to a cashier when your evening is through. It was past midnight, Teresa was doing a roll-call for the transport home. It was an effort to push through the crowd to re-enter and pay my bill. With a card full of beer purchase stamps it would have been easier to go straight to the car, but that would not be honest, bad karma.

Teresa lived on the eleventh floor of a sixteenth-story apartment, I had the benefit of the spare room. From the kitchen window I could view the contrasting living standards. Comfortable bungalows, two-tier homes with driveways, shrubs and painted tall gates. Two hundred yards away a group of huts, under the cover of trees, a small shanty community, families cooking outside with gas cylinders, kids mingling in need of a proper bath. They migrate from the countryside to the city as many do in developing countries, but the road to a stable life is tough. Easily visible during the day, after dark I could barely see a flicker of light.

Back at my base, happily rising each morning to have breakfast with my host, Alana, who was part of an administrative team at a manufacturing company. Conversations in the evening on current issues such as education, the economy, government incompetence and family life. There was much to learn with two people from different continents. The high-school system was interesting, with alternating schedules. One could begin class at 7:30a.m., terminating at lunchtime. Afternoon students can begin at 1:30p.m. and finish five hours later. This gives the opportunity to have a job which may be necessary to finance your schooling. But also in some areas there are too many students and not enough schools.

Brazil is a country that has suffered economically because of corrupt officials and military leadership. In the 1960's the military came into power, twenty years later they still had a grip on this country.

Throughout the world the evidence is clear that most ruling military generals have little conscience, filling their pockets and that of their crony friends.

One month before I arrived, the national currency, the real, collapsed in value. One Brazilian real was equal to one U.S. dollar, now it was 1.7 to one dollar. It was a massive gain for me with my foreign currency, tragic for the natives.

"Watch now, prices will increase," Alana frowned.

"The weekly grocery shopping is steadily rising, imports will be very expensive."

I stumbled upon a newsagent that sells foreign newspapers. While browsing through, delighted to have a chance to read a familiar broadsheet. My contentment was short lived, $18 U.S. for the Sunday New York Times. It stayed on the shelf, I'm sure they were over-changing.

But today, more than a decade into a new millennium the Brazilian economy is vibrant, because of a demand for commodities and discovery of more oil. Also the cost of petroleum is not a problem for this country. Many of the local cars are run on alcohol, which is made from sugarcane. This idea started in the 1970's when there was a world oil crisis. In recent years Brazil paid off its debt to the World Bank. Government corruption still remains a major problem.

Alana picked-up a statistics book and explained the land problems. One percent of landowners own nearly half of the cultivated land. About forty percent of this land is left idle. There are sad stories through the years, Alana remembering incidents, as I filled the coffee maker to brew some.

"Peasant leaders, trade union people, church workers have been killed by estate owners. The government introduced land reform, but it's never enough."

So much land is not been used in this country. Brazil is the fifth largest country in the world, it occupies almost half of the South American continent.

A seventeen-hour bus journey through the night to a town called Campo Grande, the state capital of Mato Grosso de Sul. The miss-use of land was evident in the flat countryside. I would just sleep and read, been the only foreigner on this bus. Upon my arrival at 8a.m., I was approached three times by travel agents promoting Pantanel trips, with booklets, pictures of birds, animals and sunsets. I refused, Bonito was on my itinerary. Relaxed and rested by mid-afternoon at the Tunis hotel, two blocks from the station. A stroll around town, reading the entertainment section of the local newspaper. The weekends could be fun, but this been a Monday, I opted for a 5p.m. departure to Bonito, about five hours away.

A three-quarter full bus was soon vastly over crowded with a stop at Aquidauana, about an hour into the journey. Landscapes were almost invisible through stretches of woodlands, on unpaved narrow roads. Pleasantries exchanged with Israelis.

Stopped at a traffic light, suddenly got nudged through the open window. A guy speaking Spanish, quickly changed to English upon noticing my puzzled expression, offering accommodation.

"I'm going to Bonito," I told him.

"This is Bonito, we have a good deal at our hostel."

"O.K. I'm coming," informing the Israelis who followed me off the bus. Brendan was a hawker for a local hostel.

'Munito Bonito is a good place to stay' talking like a holiday rep. without the glamour. Been the off-peak season Brendan arranged that each guest had their own room with no added cost. Mario, the owner, gregarious and helpful, had five languages. But what about Gaelige [Irish language], teaching him a few words. A trip was organized the following morning. We hiked through the countryside, over hills and peaks, into valleys and woods, stopping at waterfalls to swim, our guide demonstrating a safe area to dive.

If there is a top-grade place to live in the Brazilian countryside, this is it. Mario visited ten years earlier from his native Argentina, the next year he arrived back to stay. Breakfast was included in the price; Porridge, cereals, bread rolls and coffee. Many of the local eateries did not open until mid-day. Excursions had to be organized, booked in advance. The land is private and visitors are limited for preservation. We took-in the subterranean caves with an abundance of stalactite. A Steep treacherous descent to a small lake inside the cave. Divers had tried to find the end of the lake, but it possibly extends for miles, perhaps all the way to Bolivia.

Later we rented equipment for a swim in a natural spring. A wet suit and snorkels had to be worn. Extra terrestrials on the move, we viewed varieties of fish that didn't react to our presence. Their phenomenal colours of blues, pinks, greens, gold, orange, black. A sinister looking creature known as the 'shark' seemed to have a threatening presence. The other species scampered away. I tried to reach out and intimidate, the bugger was too quick, this was his territory.

In the evening the 'taboo bar' was a popular haunt, not that there was many other choices. One evening we met Bianca, an Italian charity worker, involved in local education.
Bianca explained, "many of these people do not have higher education, the facilities are not here. In recent years the situation has improved, but Campo Grande is where most must go to further their education, which is five hours drive."
At Munito Bonito the majority of the guests were Israeli. Unsettling the status quo were two Danes, a German, Ari the Greek and myself. We rented scooters and took off to a public recreation area, a lake for swimming and boating. We challenged a local group in volleyball and won. Noam, an Israeli friend chatted with three women using a translation book, they give him their address, inviting him for a visit. That evening he asked me to go with him.
"Go over there and ask Mario for directions to that place," I urged. Suddenly Mario burst out laughing, then said quietly "this is a drug-den." Embarrassed was putting it lightly, he threw the note in the bin.
I was giggling to myself, "Good man Noam, you can pick-em."
I laughed all evening with little teasing comments.

Ari the Greek was a journalist, on a trip to this country for a new millennium issue, to find the top ten holiday destinations.
When Ari spoke everyone listened. He could talk about many places: New Delhi, Mauritius, Costa Rica, the Caribbean, Bahia, in north-east Brazil, Patagonia, in southern Argentina and north Africa to name a few.
"It's verrie ny-ice, it's verrie beauut—ifull,' was his common response.
He had brilliant photos, catching the moment.
"As the sun is going down is the best time to take shots, that's when the light is best."

I went off on a cycle, one afternoon with Abbi, an Israeli. Arriving at a crossroads, Abbi opt to go left to the lake district. I continued straight, deep into the countryside. Narrow roads with little traffic and even less houses. The fields were empty, the grass a parched green. Then a minor disaster, a flat tire.

"Shit, shit what the bloody hell can I do now," expressing loudly. With no pump I had to start walking, but which way. I must have cycled about fifteen miles, I had no watch to check the time. To walk towards Bonito, my only hope was to hitch-hike, but I had not seen a car in the last hour. I could see cows in the distance, perhaps there is a farm up-ahead. I continued on in search of life, passing the cow field. Buildings were visible, making my way up a lane-way. The house about two hundred yards from the road, broken windows, the roof sunk, doors missing. No truck tracks or house pets roaming, simply derelict. The sun was setting, another hour would bring darkness. I'll sleep in an open field if necessary. Then I heard a noise in the distance, gradually growing louder, a red truck was coming. As it drew closer, I began waving, this is my only hope.

A rough-looking middle-aged man stopped alongside.

"Hello, bom dia, habla Ingleis" I said.

"No ingleis" he answered in a hoarse voice. I showed him my bike problem, "Vive en Bonito, vive en Bonito, comprende."

"Si, si senor" he answered, signalling for me to load the bike, then motioned to take the passenger seat.

"Habla espanol," I asked.

'Si, waving his hand in a so-so gesture.

"Come se llama."

"Oooh, Carlos."

"O.K. me Jack."

He began speaking in Portuguese. I was lost, but nodded in agreement. After about fifteen minutes we turned left and soon arrived at his house. With white gates, a small open barn with a shabby looking truck parked inside. Two women appeared at the door as Carlos shouted something. I was beckoned inside, the kitchen was busy, the evening meal in preparation. I sat at the dining table and Carlos' wife bought a translation dictionary and a globe. So we managed to communicate, explaining my situation. His wife responding that I could stay tonight and Carlos would drive me in the morning into Bonito. Feeling relieved but slightly awkward that I was intruding.

Dinner was served; Rice, Brazilian beans and chicken by an elderly woman, dressed conservatively with a long skirt and apron.

Afterwards Carlos put a bottle of Caiprinha on the table and poured a small glass for himself and me. He knocked his back like an old pro.' Well, I had to follow, no wimpy sipping, 'down the hatch,' his wife watching, laughing loudly and clapped. The grandmother disappeared, then returned with sugar and cut limes, the appropriate mix for this native drink. Soon we were all sharing the bottle. Surprisingly a continuous conversation with the dictionary and world map.

I was giving a room downstairs with a single bed.

I awoke to rattles and chuckles in the kitchen. The grandmother acknowledged my presence, signalling to the bathroom. I give the thumbs-up. 11:20a.m. on the wall clock, the morning half-over. Carlos was gone but not before fixing my puncture. I offered money but they adamantly refused. I slowly drifted out of sight, waving as I went, how about that for hospitality towards a total stranger.

Most of my temporary buddies were heading west to Bolivia. I returned to my hosts, near the south-Atlantic coast. The countdown was on for my departure. An intended two-month-stay, was now more than three. I volunteered to lead an open discussion at an English language school attended by Alana. A teacher absent, so I stepped-in to be a temporary replacement for the evening class. Questions were thrown, but football would be the dominant topic. The class became a little agitated when I admired France for winning the world cup, in 1998 [France beat Brazil 3-0 in the final].

"It was a fix, the competition was in France, they wanted France to win. The sponsors wanted Ronaldo to play, so he did. But he should not have played, he was injured," one girl commented from the back. [Ronaldo, Brazil's top goal scorer played badly that night, questions were asked about his fitness and mentality]

"How could we do so bad, we let France win," another comment which was the general feeling among the class.

So I opened it up, I picked out a football statistics manual from a book shelf. It explained the history of the world cup. Brazil winning the tournament in 1970 and then there was a twenty-four year gap before the next title. Was it a fix during the 1970's and 1980's when other countries were winning, of course not. Brazil normally has special players who are a joy to watch but periodically they get undone by a European country.

Brazilian recipe: Picanha na Tabua

Ingredients:
3 lbs picanha, 1 tablespoon garlic paste.
3 tablespoon margarine, melt. 1 bay leaf, chopped.
1 teaspoon salt
Ask your butcher to cut the Picanha out of the top of the sirloin.

How to prepare:
In a large bowl, combine salt, margarine, garlic paste, bay leaf and mix well. Rub this seasoning over the entire piece of meat. Do not rub over the fat, as you will discard it after grilling. Let it marinate for 2 hours in the fridge before grilling.

Grilling:
Cover grill with aluminium foil. Brush with margarine and place entire meat with fat facing up. Also cover meat with aluminium foil and bake it in a covered gas grill for about 45 minutes or until done.

Caiprinha: 1 lime [quartered], 1 tablespoon sugar, 1 shot of Cachaca, half-cup of ice-cubes.
Prepare: Lime and sugar in glass, crush and mash with wood spoon. Pour the liqueur with ice.

Argentina (Don't Cry)

The last person to board the bus, we didn't converse much, gifts were exchanged. I slumped into the back seat, avoiding direct air-conditioning. Staring into space, reflecting on the high level of compatibility, this was truly a satisfying friendship. Time together was quality and interesting, it was good-bye to Alana, her family and friends. Sadly a concluding hug for princess Barbara and princess Milena.

I was hitting the road, the high-road.

It would be a long journey through the night slipping in and out of consciousness. The roads were good, the countryside generally flat with brick or stone white-wash houses.

Reaching Foz de Iguacu, sixteen hours later, at the bus station agents were on hand to offer accommodation deals. Viv, a fellow traveler and myself decided to stay at the Alberque Paudimar Campestre, on the Brazilian side of their border with Argentina. At seven dollars [U.S.] per night, always looking for the inexpensive bed. The Campestre was refreshing, like a club-med resort. A bar, good food, swimming pool and an immaculate football pitch, perfect for seven-a-side. Each evening, kick-off was 7p.m.

The Latinos cruising to victory against the tourists. A different story twenty-four hours later, a European selection kicking their butts on their own turf. Nick, the Dane rattling the net with spectacular vigor. Our sweeper Klaus, a Hamburg fan, clearing everything, nothing got passed him.

A fifteen minute bus ride earlier that day had us at the Iguacu waterfalls. Split between two countries, a national park dominated by rain-forest swarming with birds, mammals, insects and reptiles. The river Iguacu receives water from about thirty tributaries as it flows across the country from the Curatiba hills in the east. It widens and sweeps around a magnificent section of forests, passing over a basaltic plateau that abruptly ends. It divides into many channels with hidden reefs, islands and rocks before reaching the falls. Numerous distinctive cascades are visible that form the waterfalls. At three and a half kilometres wide and ninety meters high, 275 falls occupy this area, a natural wonder. Wider than Victoria falls in

Zimbabwe and higher than Niagara falls on the U.S.-Canadian border. Think about that for a moment, almost unknown in the western world. This is truly a spectacular sight.

To stand, watch and listen, the water gushing and crashing, photos will never justify the scene. Typically South American, wild and exotic. The Brazilian side offers a whole panoramic view. Steep drops, inches from your feet. One walkway branches off, stretching out into the choppy river, offering an up-front scan of the Garganta do Diablo [devil's throat]. A tolerant soaking in the process, the rising sprays creating majestic rainbows.

The next day we crossed the Ponte Presidente Tancredo Neves bridge into Argentina to view the waterfalls from another side. The first thing I noticed was a blue and white sign, 'Las Malvanas con Argentinas' [The Falklands belong to Argentina]. Referring to the war between Argentina and Britain in 1982 on ownership of the Falkland Islands.

"Stop, stop, por favor" I shouted, this has to be photographed.

The driver Pablo following, "I take photo, give me camera," he shouted.

"Show that to Margit Thatch-chor," [the British leader in 1982] Pablo joked with a roar of laughter. So that's the message loud and clear.

The Argentine side offers closer views of the individual falls in their forest setting. We would approach the Devils throat from above the waterfalls. Evidence of a concrete walkway is scattered, swept away by the sheer force of water. Boats transferred us to a platform, an overhead position view. Fast photo shots to keep the lens dry, a constant heavy spray blowing. One hundred and thirty thousand cubic-feet of water per second, plunging ninety meters. Fourteen falls in this tight pocket. Swifts would drop like rocks, lightning quick into this chasm to catch insects, moments later darting out to perch on a cliff. In the distance hawks and parrots cruising over the greenery. We took an engine dingy underneath the falls, a deafening audio in addition to a drenching, staying a safe distance from the heart of the action which we would be no match for.

Downstream, about 20k.m. is the confluence of the Iguacu and Parana rivers. This forms the tripartite border of Paraguay, Argentina and Brazil.

Driving across the Ponte da Amizade bridge into Paraguay, the town of Cuidad del Este is chaotic and grubby. It attracts con-artists, smugglers and money launderers. A hive of frantic shoppers from the neighbouring countries seeking cheap goods. One of this continents' largest shopping hubs. Much of the merchandise illegally transported into a neighbouring country, avoiding import duties. Klaus and Nick stocking-up on cigarettes.

"If it's cheap, you buy it, they're getting no duty from us, right lads." Returning to our base camp, on the Brazilian side requesting our mini-bus driver to take a detour for a quick glance at the world's largest hydro electric plant. Supplying Paraguay's energy needs and 25% of Brazil's. This is a dam, 8 kilometres long, a mass of concrete. This costly joint venture has been a burden on the finances of Brazil.

Another short journey………….. fourteen hours by bus……………. to Buenos Aires…………. 'We'll be there in a flash.'
It did start anxiously, then entertaining. Waiting for a local bus, taking me to the international station, half-hour later I'm still standing at a downtown bus stop, fretting, grumbling to myself. So I flag a taxi, "pronto, pronto." Surprisingly a 6k.m. ride, the last few passengers were boarding the express bus to the capital.
A short ten-minute run then a mass exodus, a border checkpoint. The Argentinean customs were taking no chances, not in a charity mood. We had to exit the bus, walk through the checkpoint with our luggage, then board the bus in the new country.
My gear neatly organized, now annoyingly a thorough search. My backpack totally emptied, poking their noses into a plastic bag of toiletries, underwear and smelly socks in another, which he quickly pushed aside. Ahead of me in the queue was a tall beefy guy, shoulder length hair and a thick curved moustache. With his deep voice, he protested constantly as his bags were opened by the customs officer. I watched amusingly as he had more junk than a scrap yard. Pots and pans, small household goods, a traditional record player, ring dial telephone. Tins of food, desk lamps, used tools.
I later discovered that the big guy was been deported. He could talk, and through the night on this journey his was the one voice that would be heard.

At the rest spots, I joined a Buenos Aires couple who spoke broken-English. "The big guy, habla, habla mucho," I said.

"Talk shit, shit" Ricky and Adriana responded, followed by collective laughter.

In the capital, the Retiro bus terminal was massive and modern. The metro underground train station, ten minutes walk as the hospitable couple escorted me. The Friday morning rush-hour was in full swing. Not wanting to be a hindrance to speedy morning commuters, I relaxed over coffee and a facturas pastry near the token booth. A well dressed middle-aged man sat at the next table, a brief case and the Buenos Aires herald, an English daily. He nodded, acknowledging my presence.

"Howya doing," offering to converse.

"Have you just arrived?" he asked.

"Yes, from the Iguacu waterfalls."

"Oh, a magnificent sight" he beamed.

"Yes, Phenomenal, are you here on business?"

"I come down here about three times a year."

"You're British, right," interrupting him.

"Actually, my father is Irish, like yourself, I spend time in both countries. I've scheduled a meeting for nine," checking his watch.

"But I'll be a little late. They're not punctual in this country, it's a strategy to keep you waiting."

"Does it work in their favour?"

"I let them think that way," with a wry grin.

"Best not to damage their ego, the president can't be trusted. This continent is not financially stable, do business with caution. I must go now, hope it's not too expensive for you."

Taking the metro train to Constitution station, using my guide book to find an international hostel on Brazil Street at the rear of the station. It was an old building with high ceilings, wide creaky stairs, wooden floors and second-hand furniture. Winter was just around the corner, but the heating thermostat in the hostel was not rising. I stocked-up on some food and a few hours rest. The evening meal made by the hostel cook brought the global society out of the woodwork. I latched onto a small group of Aussies and Germans planning a night at a bar called 'the Kilkenny.'

A thriving crowd at this Irish bar with live music, a pint of Kilkenny beer cost six peso. I could get two for that price and a packet of nuts back in Ireland. The creamy Irish beer had lots of takers as I surveyed the bar. Who arranges this pricelist, a weeks' budget could disappear, in the mix with a guzzling cultural team.

"This is the place to meet English speaking locals," Mick shouting in my ear, he had an arrangement to meet a local girl. The Germans were getting smashed having been drinking throughout the afternoon.

"Come and talk with these people, I'm on good terms with Gabriella, I'm a bit nervous, you'll be doing me a favour."

"O.K., where is Pete?" I asked.

"Ah, mate," shaking his head. "Every time he has a few beers he calls this girl in Santiago [Chile], he's talking about going back to see her."

Mixing with this night crew, they were saying things like;

"We are the same as Europeans, other countries in South America have more poverty. We are a good country."

I listened and nodded, but this was not necessary, I wasn't making judgments.

The Portenos [Buenos Aires folk] are social owls, normal to dine at 10p.m. Enter a pub at 8p.m. and you may only have the bartender to banter with.

A weekend of sight-seeing was the order but not without warning.

"Don't visit La Boca alone," was the message from the hostel staff. It certainly is a unique neighbourhood, with its colourful houses; reds, yellows, greens, blues, orange. Home to the famous Boca Juniors football team, whom the local community adore. Not forgetting Maradona where he once plied his trade. This football genius adorned many bars and restaurants. Rough tough looking characters on the street had us on edge. Unemployment was high, we didn't dwell to become another statistic.

Recoleta cemetery is probably a place visitors get nervous about. Upon entering this above ground graveyard, I could sense wealth and elitist. Presidents are laid to rest here.

"Where is aeee, donde' Mick trying to ask.

"Evita" the ground worker responded.

"Si," Mick answered.

Pointing us in the right direction, he must do that fifty times a day.

Mausoleums in all shapes and sizes; row after row, some designed in spectacular splendour. Tainted windows, others had plain glass in which we could see through the curtains, the caskets visible. It sounds eerie, but I don't know these people so my emotions are not stirring. Duarte was her maiden name, Evita Peron, her resting place had a jungle of flowers and messages.

"I think it was her birthday recently," one lady commented.

It took more than twenty years to arrive at this resting place, the remains returning from Europe in 1974 against the will of political enemies. Evita was the second wife of Juan Peron, who was leader of this country for nine years. She reached out to the poor and underprivileged, much to the annoyance of the established nobility. Her early death from cancer at age thirty-three was a devastating blow to the lower classes.

San Telmo which was walking distance from our hostel, is top of the list in outdoor entertainment. A charming antique outdoor market, a collectors paradise. The birth place of tango, the famous Argentine dance, performers, professional and otherwise are not shy to demonstrate. Jugglers, clowns, elderly singing groups, human statues are all providing street activity.

If you dropped into this town from another planet not knowing anything about this country, the first impression would be a wealthy society; elegance and panache. Women in the park walk their dogs dressed in their Sunday best. Saturday afternoons on avenue 9 de Julio pensioners are decked out in suits with aristocracy flavour. Incidentally, it took us three hours to cross this street, only joking, maybe three minutes. With fourteen traffic lanes it was an eternity, the widest street in the world.

Enormous old buildings dotted around the city, European comes to mind, particularly Parisian. Stylish inhabitants frequent Florida and Lavelle streets, pedestrian shopping areas, our scruffy presence embarrassingly more noticeable. Actually most men in the western world do not have interesting dress-sense, they lack imagination and courage in this area.

My short stay unintentionally been extended, rolling my clothing carefully, creating more space in my backpack. Looking at my ticket, this does not seem right.

"Here check this, I think I missed my flight."

Lenny, an American looking at the document, "what's the date, today guys?"

Checking his watch, "Yea dude you've missed it alright."

That feckin plane had departed fifteen hours earlier, confusing the dates. Laughter from the others present as I stood there, scratching my head, momentarily pissed-off. Initial annoyance changed to the satisfaction of a couple of more nights on the streets of this Latin capital. No extra charge from the airline.

We stumbled upon a massive demonstration as Mick, Pete and I viewed the parliament buildings, a huge grey structure with a weather-worn green coloured dome. Students were protesting against tuition hikes. I wondered about the military and how strong they are today, perhaps lurking in the background.

"The military are gone, no army thank god."

"We would not be allowed to march if the military were here."

Students informed upon my inquiries.

Amongst the crowd were the 'Madres of Plaza de Mayo,' [The mothers of plaza of May] voicing their disapproval of the military governments of the past, tumultuous applause for this group of women.

Every Thursday afternoon these mothers protest at plaza de Mayo square, in front of casa Rosada, the presidential palace, a unique pink in colour. Used by previous leaders to rally the crowds for approval. The 'Madres,' their sons and daughters went missing during the military junta regime between 1976-1983. One lady explained through an interpreter.

"My daughter went to college one day and never came back. The police, the government did nothing to help."

Another said, "My son went to meet friends on a Saturday night, he never came home. He played football with people who protested against the government. Videla is responsible, [the Argentine leader at the time], he is a very bad man."

Many of the women wear a headscarf, white with blue dots. We embraced these pension folk, wishing them luck.

Videla, Messina, Galtieri, and Viola, all top governmental officials were sent to jail. In reality, it was luxury accommodation in a military prison. But later president Menim who ruled for ten years, until 99' pardoned these murderers.

One morning I rushed off to Teatro Colon, this is a world-class venue for ballet, opera and classical music. The building occupies one whole block, in immaculate condition despite periods of national economic hardships. Seating for twenty-five hundred, unique architecture, a massive stage for performers to express themselves. Our guide led the way to the basement workshops where sculptors, costume designers and wigmakers are located. Another room stocked a mass of shoes.

On Saturday night we were back at the Kilkenny bar, the hostel gang went before me. When I arrive it was jam-packed. As I walked-in, a girl came towards me. She grabbed my arm and said hello, throwing compliments. Her English was minimal, I smiled and tried to advance to the bar. Something is not right here, she is on to me too quickly, I'm thinking. I coyly eyed her movements as she talked with a couple of local guys, all wearing black tee-shirts. Were they plotting a trap, I was not about to be snared. The music was pumping from the live band, then bag-pipers came on stage, the crowd were chanting and clapping. One guy next to us was giving-off loud whistles and heckles.
Mick, the Aussie, whispered to me, "he just tried to pick-pocket me, I felt his hand in my back pocket."
"Let's say something, there are plenty of us," I urged.
"No, no" he got nothing."
He was wearing a black tee-shirt.

Jake had just arrived from Chicago. He was telling me about Central America, "I'm not impressed with El Salvador. Tomorrow we fly to Lima in Peru."
"How long did you stay in El Salvador?" I asked.
"Two days, but it was enough, I can tell. I love to travel, last year we did sixteen countries in thirty-eight days."
"That's just enough time for lunch and a walk down the main street in each capital. I think you like to fly," I joked with him.
Many Portenos were of the opinion that the Falklands should be ruled by Argentina. One couple I chatted with in a San Telmo café were adamant. "You are Irish, you know England. Why do they want our islands, the Falklands are so near us. England is thousands of miles away. We should have control of these islands."

I listened to Caesar as more coffee was ordered, this was the general opinion in this city.

"What do you think Jack," looking for my approval.

I shrugged my shoulders. I knew what I wanted to say, not sure, he might be offended. He was pushing for me to say something substantial.

"O.K. this is how I see it. Who was the Argentine leader? Galtieri, right." Caesar nodding. "This guy was not elected by the people, he was a military man. Sometimes they become a leader by force. Some military generals can be ruthless and not good for the country. If you invade and take a place by force, that's not always a good idea."

"So what is the answer?" Maria jumping in.

"Negotiate, start with talks. It can be a slow process, does not happen overnight. Then maybe ten, twenty years later the deal is signed. Keep talking, keep chipping away. At this moment Argentina will not get these islands. I'm sorry, that's the way I see it."

They looked at me with disappointed expressions.

In the hostel, the evening meal of mince, potatoes and vegetables was been served, Mick sat next to me. "The last supper, I fly to New Zealand tomorrow," I said.

"We leave tomorrow as well," he shot back. "This place is putting a hole in my bank account. We go to London, hope I get a job, we're planning a year there."

"I think most travellers pass through quickly, the expense probably scares them. How can the locals survive?"

Surveying the situation in this country, I questioned. "We come from countries that are in decent shape and it's expensive for us. Everything is overpriced."

Mick agreeing, "Bloody sure it is, the peso is equal to the dollar. This is not a strong economic country. Unemployment is eighteen percent," showing me a clip from a newspaper.

"I wonder how much money a working person has in their bank account. This is New York prices but they don't get New York wages. The system will crack, it can't sustain," I predicted.

Unfortunately, two years later the Argentine economy collapsed. The peso devalued and the country was in turmoil. Latin America has had too many dictators. Thankfully these days democracy has blossomed on this continent and economies have stabilized.

Argentine Beef Stew

Ingredients:
2 pound of beef, cut in bite size cubes.
1 small onion, finely chopped.
2 garlic cloves, minced
1 tablespoon, olive oil.
2 large potatoes, coarsely chopped.
1 green bell pepper, chopped.
1 red bell pepper chopped.
1 teaspoon black pepper
1 tablespoon oregano
2 teaspoon of basil
1 teaspoon crushed red pepper [optional]
1 teaspoon sugar
1 cup of dried apricots, chopped coarsely.
3 medium potatoes, peeled and diced.
3 sweet potatoes, peeled and diced.
2 cups of beef broth.
1 medium large pumpkin.
Butter or margarine, melted
¼ cup dry sherry.
1 lb. of whole kermal corn, drained or defrosted.

In the olive oil, brown the beef with the onion and garlic.
Add all the remaining ingredients, except the corn, sherry and pumpkin.
Simmer for one hour, covered.
Cut the top of the pumpkin and discard. Scoop out the seeds and stringy membrane and discard them as well.

IT WILL TEST YOUR COURAGE.....ELEVATE YOUR SPIRIT

A flight leaves Buenos Aires, Argentina at 12:30a.m., just after midnight on Monday May 17th.The flight path was across South America and the Pacific ocean. Fourteen hours later we touched down in New Zealand. So what's the local time upon arrival? Don't read on. Stop and think, ask a friend. Please stop, you may surprise yourself with the right answer, which is about three minutes ahead. Don't cheat, work it out.

Across the south-Pacific, I slept through most of the journey. What would I stay awake for, endless obfuscate darkness.

At Auckland International, no chances were taken, the sniffing dogs were on the prowl, they mingled around my backpack for more than just a few moments. After passing through 'passport control' I was directed by customs, 'to the right.'

"They just put the dogs on me," I stated.

"To the right please," the uniformed official repeated more forceful. I noticed an airline pilot leaving the search area as I entered, perhaps no one is exempt. It's a nuisance when the Customs officer begins to pull everything out of your backpack. In this case they all looked like front-row props [rugby forwards], so I didn't give them any lip. I boarded the 'Air-bus' that leaves every fifteen minutes to transport visitors to the city, destined for Auckland central backpackers [A.C.B.] on the advice of Marty, a fellow traveller.

As we stopped at the different hotels, Pat from county Clare, a fellow compatriot was pointing out the entertainment spots, seated next to me at the back. He had previously lived here and was returning for a wedding.

"This is 'K' road, there's lots of night-clubs here, that pub, the Dogs Bollix, good craic at the weekends."

"Is that the real name," I naively asked.

"Yea look, ah you can't see it now. Murphy's on this next street, check it out on Saturday nights."

"Auckland central backpacker is the next stop," the driver announced.

A huge hostel of seven floors, a bar and restaurant on the top level, two large kitchens, a study and television room, lots of toilets and showers. I checked into an eight-bed dorm room. Other occupiers were Stan, a South African, Joe from Boston and Salma from India. "This is rare to meet a young Indian female backpacking." She agreed, on her way to attend university in California.

First thing I noticed, was the friendliness of the locals, always having significant time to say hello and willing to help, the shop assistants been most pleasant.
New Zealand, Aateoroa to the Maoris. 'Where men are beer drinkers and the sheep are not nervous.'
A land of hills and mountains, rugby and horse racing, Kiwi fruit and wool sweaters, outdoor life and bungee jumping. Not forgetting women Prime Ministers.
Back to the question, as we touched down on New Zealand soil the pilot announced "It's 5:15a.m. Wednesday May 19th."
He repeated this several times. This is more than 48 hours later. How can this be, it's two days later, we missed Tuesday. We crossed the 'day-time-line' in the Pacific ocean, but I had no idea the time would change this much. One girl told me later that she missed her birthday because she had taken the same route.

I had buddies in this town. A few phone calls and we're off cruising, Milton calling the shots, Rachel been the driver and me, the vagabond. Auckland is full of hills, so we started with the biggest one, Mount Eden at 96 meters high. We drove to the summit; this was the best view I ever had of a city. Turning slowly, three-hundred and sixty degrees, nothing is blocked from the naked eye. The entire Auckland area and it's bays are visible, no clouds or haze to cheat us.
Many volcanic formations dot the landscape. Pointing at one, which looked sparse and isolated with a lone tree on top, which would be our next stop. Known as Maungakiekie [mountain of the kiekie tree] or the more common name of 'One Tree Hill.' Named after a totara tree which stood here until 1876. It is replaced by the current tree, a pine, which is braced with steel cables and a six-feet high metal fence surrounded the bark. A Maori protester unhappy with this particular plant attempted to chop it down. Actually, after I left New Zealand, there was another attack with a chainsaw that resulted in

this symbolic tree, changing. Also on the hill there is a monument dedicated to the Maori community. It's a sacred area to the Maoris and the terracing dugouts are still visible.

We drive across the north shore bridge to Devonport. Victorian style buildings are highly evident. We chilled-out at the waterfront promenade with shops, cafes, art and craft galleries, with Mount Victoria and other peaks in the background. Many islands on the horizon, Devonport is truly beautiful.

Later that evening we were clinking glasses in the 'Dogs Bollix.' Milton, Mark, Penny and Rachel, not forgetting the gregarious Diane, all Kiwi friends I had met in London. It was Saturday night, Irish and rock music, packed to the rafters. The only 'Pacific island girl' on the premises was receiving lots of attention, numerous white guys approached. Why not chill-out in an 'islanders club' where the opportunities were greater, I thought. Manchester football shirts were on display, so we later squeezed into the 'Immigrant bar' where the English cup final was been shown live at 2a.m.

I was chatting with Gary and his sister Shelly from Nottingham, England, they had emigrated three years previous.

"Come here tomorrow" they encouraged. "Every Sunday afternoon there is a music session and Irish dancing."

It did not disappoint, the band hitting all the right notes, bantering with the crowd in the process. Six women and two guys dressed in costumes, stepped out for three Ceili sessions. It was a shivery afternoon, the wind too brisk for a site-seeing wander, the perfect place to knock back a few.

Milton offered me a room in his house as one resident was out of town. There were no radiators, the house was freezing, as we were in the winter months. I packed a stove type fire with wood and soon had a warm blaze. Coal is illegal in Auckland, so if it's used in this hearth the grate will buckle. But I didn't intend to sit around. I planned a trip to the Bay of islands in the northern part of the North Island.

The bus pick-up at Auckland central backpackers [A.C.B.], helping Susannah with her luggage, a Brazilian domestic worker studying English. The bus, three-quarters full, this been the off-peak season. Nationalities of nine countries; Germans, Scottish, Irish, Japanese, Dutch, English, Canadians, Aussies and Brazilian. The Bay of islands has charm and is unspoiled with balanced development. We stayed in the Paihia-Waitangi area. The highlights: swimming with dolphins who come alongside momentarily, then shoot off rather quickly. I could get a better observation from the boat deck. Also a speed boat ride to a rock formation and Cape Reinga with it's ninety mile beach. The bus drove on a stretch of sand for many miles. It's hilarious, driving on a beach, locals casting their fishing rods. They call it Ninety Mile Beach, I think it's actually ninety kilometres. We reached Cape Reinga, which is at the top of the north island. Here the Tasman Sea and the Pacific Ocean meet. We could see these two bodies of water clash, creating a choppy current. As I looked out from a lighthouse, a sense of isolation is evident. We were almost at the bottom of our planet, you could feel it. There was a signpost reminder of just how far away other cities in Europe, Asia and North America are in mileage. Nearby the sand dunes was an exciting stop, "Let's go sand-boarding" the bus driver shouted as he unloaded a bunch of mini surfboards from the trunk. Jump on a board and go head first sliding down a steep hill, over one hundred meters in distance. Wearing sunglasses and keeping your mouth shut was necessary from the splashing sand. A few got stuck halfway down, dragging their feet, fear of the speed. Others lost control and tumbled. For me it was smooth and exhilarating.

****

Back in Auckland, I had a directory on Organic farms, where one can volunteer to work. As it was winter, the quiet season, making a number of phone calls before been accepted onto one. The deal is four hours work per day in exchange for food and board. Jane on the other end of the line gave me directions and expected me on Sunday. I took the bus north to Whangarei. At the bus station they pointed the road to Green Creek, about a thirty-minute drive. Just five minutes hitching in the rain and a car stopped. The driver was going my way but not to Green Creek.
"Jump-in, it'll be easier later. I'm going to the marina, you'll get a lift from there." Nancy was here name, from California, came to New Zealand for romantic reasons. That relationship had fizzled-out, but was in-love with the country. She set-up a business, making boat covers.

"Sailing is popular here, I'm going out today, the weather isn't stopping me," dropping me off at the marina.

"It's about seven miles from here, someone will take pity on you." She had a lovely free-spirit personality, my kind of people.

A continuous drizzle, a damp and overcast feeling, but sure enough the first car stopped. An English couple, living in Auckland, on a Sunday afternoon drive.

"We're not familiar with this area but we'll get you there mate." They enjoyed the outdoor life this country had to offer, camping, fishing, hiking, swimming and hunting. A post office, grocery and hardware store all in one was my destination.

"This is Green Creek," the shopkeeper assured me.

Slightly concerned initially, this was a stress-free journey.

"I'm here and I'm knackered," the code message as I called Jane to come and meet me.

Driving on a narrow laneway for about four miles, stopping momentarily to talk to the horses she owned.

"Horse-riding is my passion, these days it's too wet."

She lived in a large two-storey house, introducing me to her three beautiful children, aged fourteen, eight and four, also to three lady friends drinking tea in her kitchen. One was analysing her recent trip to America.

"Too many guns, crime is so high. Everything is big over there, I could never finish a meal."

My lodgings would be a caravan, up the embankment behind the house, surrounded by thick growth of grass and weeds. It was cold and I needed four heavy blankets to keep the blood circulating as I tried to sleep. The following morning instead of taking the path around the long way to the house, this idiot shot down the steep hill as a short-cut, slipping on the wet ground, landing on my arse. Muttering obscenities to myself, my jeans were covered in muck. With only one other pair of pants, for good wear, there was no choice but to use them. After breakfast of cereal, tea and bread rolls, time to clock-in.

The first part was grab a sledge-hammer and knock down part of a concrete wall, making an entrance wider for her car to park, in an open garage. I quickly worked-up a sweat, continuing into the afternoon to complete this chore. With no man around to do heavy work, I wasn't bothered about the four-hour work rule. When the kids came home from school, I helped them with their homework. We exchanged card games and I tested them with riddles. Jane was a jolly individual, looking younger than her forty-five years and the kids had impeccable manners.

The next day, the weather was more pleasant. Four women dropped-by in a station-wagon with a trailer attached. I went with them to collect second-hand furniture. Two of them had just moved into a new wooden structured house, ten minutes walk from my current residence. Heavy loads to carry through a narrow pathway and then up a staircase. The main living room looked too big, how could you heat this place, I thought. A pot of stew was simmering, a hearty meal for all the helpers, about twelve people by now. A sunny day and half the community arrive for lunch. There was a hippy feel to their personalities and dress code.

Eric from Denmark, another woofer [which organic volunteers are called] was painting the interior of a neighbouring house. We managed to borrow bikes and went cycling, discovering the coast was just beyond the periphery. Eric's plan was one year as a Woofer, dividing his time between this country and Australia. His family had a farm back home, he wanted to learn about organic methods.

Over the ensuing days I cleared an area of weeds, this was a bloody nuisance, bringing back memories of my youth, working in Taaffes, a strawberry farm in Ireland. But also a sense of satisfaction, cleaning-up a space for banana trees to be planted. After ten days I returned to Auckland, for Jane's dad was ill and would reside with her through the remainder of winter.

Booking into the A.C.B. yet again, but this time I asked for a room at the rear of the building, they were smaller, warmer and quieter at night. My original plan was to pass through New Zealand in six weeks, but Auckland was growing on me. There was lots of construction in progress, preparations were in full swing for the 'America's cup boat race,' it would begin in nine months. The previous prestigious race was won by New Zealand, who now had the honour to be hosts.

A new Imax cinema was been constructed on Queens street, the main thoroughfare in the downtown area. I seek out the electrical company, asking for a job. The foreman assured me I would be hired, 'just call the office,' he insisted.

238

Two days later I was pulling cable and installing pipes. Neil was my working partner, near-by was a beefy looking Plumber, he talked all day.

"I've been to Ireland three times, my grandfather was Irish, I love it there. They know how to live, just like us. What's that word they say? They use it all the time. Ah, ya know."

"What's the craic," I answered.

"The craic, yea that's it, the craic. We had great craic," he continued.

A few minutes later, the plumber shouting "hay Irish look at this, look at these toilets, Neil here."

We walked into the finished lavatories.

"The juvenile urinals are way at the back, around that corner. That's ridiculous, you can't see them from the entrance door. It must have been designed by a bloody paedophile. Have you ever seen the like of that, bloody unbelievable, isn't it."

Opening day for the cinema was approaching. Most of the work was complete, but still lots of lighting fixtures to mount. It was ten minutes walk from the hostel, perfect travelling time.

I checked my bank balance, three weeks in the country and I had spent too much money, brunch and evening meals in expensive joints. I was now working, so I settled into a routine, using the hostel kitchens for cooking my meals and leaving socializing to the weekend.

During the winter months the hostel is only half-full, so guests are allowed to stay long-term. A number of travellers had free accommodation in return for a couple of hours daily work, mainly cleaning rooms, toilets and the kitchens.

Friendships were developing with the hostel residents. Rica had brilliant humour, many of the guys fancied her, but she had a soft spot for the 'Poms.'

The kitchens were communal in the evening, travellers passing through, staying a few days, then moving on. I would introduce a new friend to Rica.

"Hay Gunther, this is Rica, sorry mate she's off-limits, you are the wrong nationality."

Rica would mock the guys in the television room in the morning.

"Sometimes I have to go in there and give it a quick cleaning, but the boys are lying-up like old men. Oh, I've got a hangover, oh I feel shit."

"Which guys are in there?"

"Mike and Ricky…….. and big John as well."

"I went into that room a few times, Mike is always on the armchair, right."

"Yea, yea he sits on that chair," Rica agreeing giggling.

"Actually before, that was Eddie's chair, the Scottish guy. I think he give it to Mike," I sarcastically pointed out.

"Yea Eddie would be the same, oh I drank too much last night," Rica continuing the imitating.

My room was 304, the first two weeks, roommates changed rapidly. Then Dillin moved-in, a Canadian, who got a job with a carpet company. His hours were 9p.m. to 6:30a.m., laying carpets in shops and businesses after closing time. A couple of days later Arun arrived, he was from southern India; a doctor, planning to immigrate to this country. Arun had a series of exams to complete, so he studied a lot. As long term lodgers we became good buddies. Canadians will always have their national flag sewn onto their backpack, they do not want people to think they are Americans. I would test Dillin on this.

"What is it with the Canadians and the flag. Do the airport authorities stick small replicas on your pack before leaving your country? You want your own identity from America, but you all live as close as possible to the U.S. border. Go to northern Canada, it's deserted. What would be the difference if you just scrap that borderline?" I continued with sarcastic banter.

"Dillin has no flag on his luggage," Arun observed.

"Hay man, you want to see a flag. I'll show you a real one."

Pulling his backpack from underneath his bed, producing a huge national pennant. That was it, hung on the wall, with all it's glory. After he went off to work I made a U.S.A. poster to cover the new emblem. Other times I'd tear out adverts and pictures of the U.S. from magazines and newspapers and stick them on the flag. Each evening when I returned from work they'd be strewn across my bed, it was all in good fun.

One Sunday afternoon he came into the room celebrating, he'd met a girl from his hometown the evening before. His older brother and friends pursued this girl but she always acted as a snob.

"I can't believe she is interested in me, I'm seeing her tomorrow night." He was doing laps of honour around the room.

At work, I would do ten, sometimes twelve-hour shifts. Christy, was one guy at the job, originally from Bradford, England. He immigrated to New Zealand twelve years earlier. He was an electrician in the coal mines in northern England, but didn't like what happened
"The government closed the mines and killed employment in the north of England. After that I had to travel miles to get a job," he explained.
"There were so many police opposing the coal miners' picket lines, I think that was impossible. I'm sure many of them were army, dressed in cop uniforms," he continued to explain. He had that distinctive Yorkshire accent, 'It's almost lunchtime I'll go put kettle on.'
In the mid 1980's the Thatcher government in England began closing coal mines, so there were mass protests by the coal miners. In Yorkshire, Christy had his house, living as a bachelor. He went to Thailand on holiday with friends. The following year he returned to the same destination. Each time he met ex-patriots who had a local business and married to a Thai woman. He was offered the opportunity to marry a local, so he took the plunge. Now twelve years later he was divorced.
When the mines closed, jobs were scarce, so immigration was his answer. They settled in Auckland, his wife got an evening job in a Thai restaurant. She began visiting the Sky tower casino when her shift finished. This was her weakness, gambling. Initially, money trickled from the family bank account, later at a faster rate, so divorce was inevitable. In the settlement, a woman judge ruled his wife to be awarded his house in Bradford, surely an unfair verdict. He was now involved with another Thai woman.
"Is history going to repeat itself mate."
"Next time there will be a pre-nuptial," he shot back.

Another workmate was Bashir, originally from Baghdad, Iraq. Of course I asked the inevitable question about Saddam Hussein, the former Iraqi leader. He was reluctant to answer the question directly.
"In the Arab world people stay in power for years, it seems to me that healthy men are picked. Perhaps there are outside forces behind

this," he commented. He also explained that in 1980 when Saddam came to power, he built war-sirens all around the country. He was in the Iraqi army during the eight-year war with Iran [1980-1988]. He seen a lot of death and destruction and was not willing to talk about this.

The Kiwis [local folk] were great to mix with, always friendly, in good spirits. If it's not done today, it'll be finished tomorrow was their attitude. They seemed to enjoy life at their own pace.

Auckland folk are discipline pedestrians, patiently obeying the traffic signals. Exiting a bus, passengers always acknowledged the driver with a 'thank you.' In the bars they were open to meeting new people, been Irish I always got a warm welcome.

But there is a problem and it showed in their favourite sport. Australia came to town for the tri-nations rugby and left with their 'heads hanging.'

South Africa and more recently Argentina are also involved in this competition of southern hemisphere countries. The hostel had organized two buses for transport to the game in Eden Park, been Saturday evening, a real buzz around town. The staff at the A.C.B. sprung into action. Face painting in the bar, the fern leaf [local crest] was sufficient for me, got to support the home team.

This was a bit special to see the world famous 'All-Blacks' [New Zealand national team, they wear an all black strip] on their own territory. Andrew Mehterns, the New Zealand number ten kicked successfully all evening. With the All-Blacks in control and stretching their lead, the Mexican wave got the fans more animated. Around the stadium until it reached the main grandstand, a sudden jolt, no participation. That's a 'let down' in my book, too stuffy to show emotion. Periodic hollowing from a few brave souls, but no real singing. Where is the All-Black fan base who could lead the masses with a chorus. A late try for the Wallerbies [Australia] made the score respectful. In truth the northern hemisphere supporters show more passion, actually the atmosphere was more electric on the bus ride to and from the stadium, Celtic ballads were bellowed out, the free-spirit flowed.

Arun, my Indian roommate had more knowledge than an encyclopaedia. Mention a country; Lebanon, Chile, Angola, he was there with the information. Entering my room after a days' work, a conversation would start, two hours later I still would not have made it to the kitchen to cook a meal. Covering issues from politics to world history to medicine. Explaining the problems in Sri Lanka to life in his home state of Kerala, in southern India. He became more energetic late in the evening, making his way to a designated study room or the reception area which was quiet after ten.

The fourth bed in our room would become occupied once in a while. One occupant was a guy who didn't speak. Every time I entered the room, if he was there, he was sleeping.

"Who is this man?" Arun asked, pointing to the bed.

"No idea, I guess he doesn't want to mix. Maybe he's a fugitive, keeping a low profile," I answered.

"Oh this guy, I was talking to him," Dillin commenting, breaking from his book. "He's from California."

"What's his name, is he here on holiday," Arun throwing questions.

"Don't know, it was a quick introduction."

"Maybe he is America's most wanted," I interrupted.

"I'll find out," Arun been determined.

"I bet you will."

A few days later, California was gone.

"Hay there has our cheerful friend skipped it," I said entering the room.

"I do not understand," Arun sitting up straight on his bed. "I was here yesterday, I said hello sir, where are you from?"

"America," without looking at me.

"Do you have family in the U.S.?"

"Everyone in the U.S. has family, he answered."

"Then turned around and went back to sleep."

Dilliin and I laughed, "ah well, we were due a strange one."

I went to the laundry room to do washing. Returning three hours later to put my clothes in the dryer. But, what do you know, they were missing. I searched all around, finding nothing of mine. Shit, this is crazy, my washing has been nicked. It's not as if I had overrated duds of Giorgi Armani or Gucci. Mainly stained dusty tee-shirts, socks with holes and underwear............well, I won't go there. Momentarily upset, then I just laugh it off. There'll be more room in my backpack. A Scottish girl told me that her lingerie was stolen from her room.

"Someone is wearing my knickers, can you believe it?"

****

We give Arun tips on cooking; pasta and stir fry, Lasagne, Chili con carne, Irish stew, fried breakfast, omelettes with varies ingredients thrown-in.

"We always had a maid when I was growing-up," Arun explained. The kitchen in the hostel was a place of congregating, banter and jokes. Ali was a friend, English with Hungarian background. Two South American geezers were getting frisky with her, making room calls which annoyed her. Confiding in me, I had a 'quiet word' with the lads. They were seething and ignored me for a week, the Latino machismo coming into play.

Greg had a job in communications, his girlfriend Janice from Cornwall, such pleasant folk. Stan from South Africa, Gary and Ray from Bristol.

John, who is Welsh and Tony, a Geordie, taking yachting lessons. Jimi, the Indonesian cleaner, Kim from Tokyo. Canadians; Karen and Marie from Montreal, Tom and Kay of Toronto, Johnny, an avid Thin Lizzy fan from Amsterdam. Heidi, when asked, 'where is he from?'

"Nobody likes my country. Bad news every time my country is on the television," a very humble Iraqi.

All happy campers and enjoyable company at the hostel.

Rica entered the kitchen one evening, "Oh someone stole my vegetables." Ding, a Korean student was at the fridge.

"Hay the Koreans are always taking the Japanese food," I said laughing.

But Ding didn't not see the funny side, responding with an outburst. "You do not know my people. You do not know what Japan did to my country."

Rica came to me, "be careful about the jokes."

The Koreans had suffered in the past as a result of Japanese imperialism. Ding accepted my apology the following day.

There were many Japanese in Auckland, Studying English and working part-time. I noticed they don't acknowledge space. If ever there is a pedestrian jam, almost certainly Japanese folk are the cause. If you sense people behind you, trying to pass, one will give way. But not Japanese folk, they will doddle across your path, no urgency. This is not criticism, just a fact, Kiwis agreeing with this summary.

Lenny from California, made me laugh every time I talked with him. He was a Chiropractor. Had visited friends in Ireland, the local Chiropractor became ill, so Lenny filled the job vacancy for eight months in county Clare.

"I want to retire and live in your country, great community spirit. Ennis was my base. I would drive out to the 'cliffs of Mohar,' then up through the 'Burren' to Galway. Strangers would greet me, a sense of belonging. That's what is missing in California, everyone living behind high walls."

"Well thanks for the nationalistic compliment."

"I'm off to the Philippines on Monday for two weeks. I'm looking for a wife, I need a partner," Lenny openly speaking.

"Hang-on, are we really talking about marriage here," I said grinning at him.

"Oh I'm serious, I was married at twenty, divorced at thirty. I'm ten years on the loose, it's time to get someone. I'll keep you posted, I've been there before."

Rica had a constant giggle when 'sea horse' was around. He was from Sri Lanka and wore a cowboy hat with 'sea horse' written on the front. He would seek out Rica and myself, 'come, come, let me make you tea,' he'd say. A big wide smile, dressed in black.

'The lone ranger' we'd joke.

'Sri Lanka, no long-term peace,' he'd say. He was planning to immigrate to New Zealand.

The opening date was fluctuating on my job at the new Imax cinema complex. They finally came to an agreement, but it wouldn't be finished. The prime minister was to cut the tape. As the first invited guests began to arrive for this Black tie and long gown function, grinders and drills were still operating.

Our foreman scurrying around, "clean up lads and go home, leave by the back door."

Open to the general public the following day, work assignments took much longer than normal. Safety a top priority, it's not easy to install lights when mothers and kids are walking underneath, carrying equipment and ladders up stairways with teenagers coming down. Thankfully I was transferred to another project at Auckland hospital, a smaller and more organized crew. Strolling across the Grafton street bridge each mild morning in mid-winter, views of the harbour and downtown areas. Walking groups and joggers passing in the opposite direction. Fresh flowers placed at a miniature memorial, someone too distressed to continue in this life, jumping from the bridge.

A leisurely stroll back to the hostel in the evening, sometimes I'd take the Auckland Domain, part of which is a war memorial museum with natural sweeping lawns. Popping into the museum for cultural education, displays of Pacific islands and Maori life. Also on wars New Zealand were involved in. It's believed that Moriori, Malanesian people were displaced by the Polynesian Maori. The Europeans began to arrive, with Abel Tasman, the Dutch explorer in 1642. He didn't stay long, but he christened the country, Niuew Zeeland, after the province of Zeeland in his own country.

James Cook was the next navigator to cast an anchor almost one hundred and thirty years later. Claiming the country for the British crown, he then continued onto Australia. Disagreements broke out but it was not until the treaty of Waitangi in 1848 that the Maori chiefs and the British came to a settlement. The deal, promised to benefit both sides, with settlers arriving from Europe and acquiring land. The Maoris didn't receive payment from the British government. This resulted in many family wars, finally ending in 1872. New Zealand became a self governing British colony in 1856. It was almost one hundred years later that it became independent in 1947.

Meanwhile back at the living quarters our room was changing. Dillin departed, driving south with six other nomads in a van. Arun moved to a house near a hospital where he was doing trial work.

Their places were taken by Luigi, a middle-aged Italian and Gary, an American, well over six-feet tall, a tough looking guy with plenty to say. Luigi worked locally on a construction site. Gary was on a mission to buy a boat and sail around the world, trading in merchandise was the plan. He was married six times, each one ending because he was in the bar too much.

"If you want to walk down the aisle, don't go looking in the bars. I was lying to them and they were lying to me. I'd discover the real truth after I put the ring on her finger," Gary informing.

In the past his family had a transport company which he was planning to float on the stock market. But bigger forces prevented this by manoeuvring illegally against them.

"I protested in the U.S. in the 1960's, the country was moving in the wrong direction. I went to the south and helped the civil rights movement."

"What about today," I asked.

"No one should be above the law. If the president messes-up, he should go."

Gary lived in Fiji for a year. "Go to Fiji Sean, you'll find a beautiful partner in the villages. At the moment all they get is older guys like me, the backpackers pass through quickly. Stay a while, mix with the locals and experience how they live."

"Look at this, that's Mimi, I took her from Fiji to Australia. She wanted everything, jewellery, clothes and chocolates. It was too much, the transformation from her village lifestyle to a modern city. I sent her to a Fijian community in Queensland. She can work there and get accustomed to a new country. If I buy the boat, I will take her with me. I will have a crew for the first six months to teach me how to navigate."

In the television room one evening, the news was on, reporting on the U.S. dominating the world. Two Kiwis began criticizing America.

"They always have to stick their noses in," one said.

"They act like the boss of the world, yea, we know what's best," the other responding. This was the tone of their comments.

Gary was there, I was expecting him to react any moment. He listened for a while, finally he let rip.

"Hay, hay that's my country you are talking about, you guys are talking shit. Americans are always the first to the rescue. In natural disasters, earthquakes, flooding, droughts. We offer financial and practical assistance, many countries around the world receive our help, and America is expected to intervene. Whatever we do, we get criticized. I'm sick of people knocking my country, where are you from?" Looking at the blond guy stretched out on the couch.

"New Zealand" he meekly answered.

"Shall we talk about your country, New Zealand and Australian companies are cutting down lots of the forestry in Fiji. Destroying the environment, but you wouldn't know anything about that."
A heavy mouthful from Gary and the room fell silent.

Auckland has a large Pacific islands population, they are big framed people, so going head to head would not be wise. I did see a number of fights, too often it seemed to be Maoris and Samoans involved. I had seen scuffles in bars, night-clubs and sometimes on the street with the police. There seemed to be this on-going confrontation between the two groups.
Johnny, from Amsterdam wanted to date a Maori or Pacific islander. On Saturday night after a few pints in Murphy's, he was at me, wanting to check-out a club frequented by this group. White folks were the minority, we were not feeling comfortable. Talk to the wrong person and trouble may come your way, were we too conscientious? So he quit chasing this fantasy and then it materialized. Johnny enjoyed having a drink in the Sky tower casino, not for the gambling but the live music. One night I was with him as we joined three Maori women at one bar. They were welcoming, the conversation flowed. Johnny was hitting on Marie, the tallest one. Word came through about a house party so our new friends invited us. We were in amongst about thirty Maoris in Parnell park, a suburb of Auckland, everyone having the craic with us. I lost contact with Johnny but I know a year later he was still living there and involved with that girl. Penetrate the local culture instead of running away.

Everyone in Auckland has a car, a boat and a pair of sunglasses…………. or so it seems. For strangers, public transport is questionable. One is never far from the water. The ozone lair has a gaping hole, skin cancer is a problem.

****

So after four months in the largest city it was time to move on. Make my way to the south island, the 'Magic tour bus' would be the choice. The Waitomo caves, south of Hamilton town, our first port of call. I listened intently to our guide, inside the caves numerous formations of stalactites, as we floated down river, glow worms were highly visible. They're similar to a large mosquito but have no mouths. Their luminous organs give off a greenish light, they weave sticky threads to catch insects as food which are attracted to the glow worm light. Because they have no mouths, the adult life-span is short. The caves have suspended overhangs, insects to eat and moisture, the perfect combination for the worm to breed. The ones that shine most brightly are the hungriest, they all looked hungry to me.

Further south is Rotorua, a popular town with visitors. It has energetic activity with bubbling mud pools, marshes and belching geysers, which were helped along by our bus driver who poured Sulphur into a spring to spark a reaction. A heavy stench, like rotten eggs as Sulphuric gases shoot into the air.

The highlight for me was a taste of Maori culture. It certainly is a touristy event with two shows every day. After sunset in a medieval garden with huts, with burning torches overhead. Dressed in traditional costumes, music and dance is displayed by Maori folk. Afterwards, a hangi [meals cooked in an earth oven], a great feast with many choices, traditional beef stew for me.

Returning on the bus to our accommodation, the driver decided to have a sing-song. A representative from each country using the microphone at the front, our compare was adamant, no nation would be overlooked.

Canada reluctantly stepped forward and embarrassingly stumbled through a Brian Adams number or most of it. An English girl belted-out 'Parklife' by Blur, but there was too much chorus as she was forgetting the words. An American was singing half his national anthem and got a few boos. The French, I think we're doing a nursery rhyme but because it was in his native language, received a higher mark. In reality, some of them should have been thrown off the bus and made walk home. With enough 'red lions' consumed I was brave enough to blast out 'Twice Daily' [an Irish ballad]. The crowd responded to the chorus, participation increased as the song progressed.

With a coach filled to capacity, the driver was a bit special, testing his own memory by naming each person and their lodgings. Thirty-eight people and he got everyone right. Getting off the bus, a Maori hongi exchange [nose to nose contact].

Friendships were developing with fellow travellers. Simon, his father a well known sports columnist in London. Louise, an Aussie, two Irish sisters from county Wexford, Carol from the English midlands and a couple of Germans.

Turangi was the next designated pit stop, a sprawling metropolis, of four thousand inhabitants. A mountain walk or skiing were the opinions.

An early rise at seven to catch the mini-bus. Simon, Louise and myself opted for the white slopes, above Whakapapa village. On the way we dropped off trampers for the Tangariro crossing, which had spectacular rugged views. 'Were we making the wrong choice?'

On the slopes I was cruising on the lower levels. At higher elevation, a couple of tumbles dented my ego. Blizzards began rolling in at noon, by 2p.m. announcements were echoing to evacuate, visibility was minimal. The rest area, I wasn't sure, little black dots in the distance, some were rocks. A local skier led a group of five, me included in the right direction.

I have suffered sun-burns in the past, now I had to endure the pain and fuglyliness of wind-burn. I look bad enough on normal circumstances, I laid low for a couple of days.

Simon was in jubilant mood after a night of guzzling free beer and shots, courtesy of the local bartender, as we made our way to Wellington.

"This is where Wellington boots are made, right." Only joking with the locals, Gum boots is the name down under. The least populated of the three major cities in this country.

The capital and government headquarters, with it's geographical position, the southern tip of the North Island, this is about right. I visited parliament, the Beehive is one building, because of the appearance. As we strolled through listening to our guide, a Maori politician stepped quietly to retrieve folders, he was introduced to us. He made a few comments about himself and who he represented, so the floor was open for a few minutes to this civil servant. I took the opportunity to ask, "what is the benefit to New Zealand by remaining in the British commonwealth?"

"None in my view" he unsurprisingly answered. "Trading today is mainly with Asian countries," he continued.

I interrupted, "so if Australia becomes a Republic, New Zealand will follow."

"That's possible, but I'd like for us to do it soon, regardless of what happens elsewhere."

'Downtown Wellington backpackers' was our base camp. I made new friends in Tanya from London and Paul from Lancashire. 'Courtney place' was the partying street. The All-Blacks were playing England in the rugby world cup been held in Europe. With the time difference, kick-off was 4a.m. local time on a Sunday morning, so the Saturday night crowds were out in force. Into the second half, the scores were level, then Jonah Lomu got the ball. He seems to thrive against the English, two tries by the big man and New Zealand had control. The roof was lifting with enthusiastic chants. Prior to the match Simon and I were digging the house-music clubs, no shortage of venues, roaming one to another.

Wellington has a picturesque harbour with Victorian wooden buildings on the steep hills, cafes are plenty. The massive Te Papa [museum of New Zealand] was the most interesting building for me, it dominates the waterfront. Inside Maori, Pacific island, European, natural history and environment collections, definitely a museum that added a modern touch which enlightens your energy to absorb more.

Sometimes I feel it's too soon to move-on. Certainly, Wellington was a place where I could 'hang my coat,' find a job and stay six months.

With the weekend becoming a misty memory, we boarded the ferry for the crossing to the south island. At one stage no land was visible on Cook strait, the body of water between the north and south island. It was by no means smooth, my stomach was rumbling, a nauseous feeling was common within the group, the toilets were busy.

A three hour journey brings us to Picton, on the South Island. Paul noticed a car for sale in the ferry car park. '$NZ 275' the sign read, for a 1965 triumph. Purchase was made after a test run, Simon and I offered to pitch-in, he refused.

"It's probably a piece of junk, but we'll give it a go for a laugh."

So a change of pace from the early morning bus schedule pick-up.

In the south island, Nelson would be the first destination, a town of over fifty thousand inhabitants. The Nelson region is fortunate to have the most popular national parks and great beaches. The fruit growing industry is an added attraction for cash strapped travellers.

A 6:30a.m local bus pick-up for Abel Tasman National park was squashed, a room to room search for Simon was fruitless. The trampoline was his choice of slumber, after a night of cider and failing to charm his way with a girl who was much taller than him. The following morning there were no dramas, we were on a three-day walking tour of the National park. But thirty minutes into our ramble, I realized my jacket was missing. Jogging back to the starting point, relieved to find it hanging on a store front porch.

"So it's yours' a hippy attire woman," called out. "It's a regular occurrence with the walkers."

Hurrying to catch my tramping buddy, contemplating a downhill side track to a nearby marina and catch a water-taxi. 'Yea, I could hop on the next boat going to Bark bay which was six hours walk. Relax, eat and read, watch the trampers come through in the late afternoon.'

Walking in the opposite direction, a girl asked, "are you Sean?"

"Yes, that's right."

"Simon said he'll wait at the Anchorage hut, where you can have lunch."

"How far is that?" I asked.

"You'll make it in about two hours."

"That's great," a thank you handshake.

Meeting other ramblers, exchanging pleasantries, finally turning a corner, a voice rang out. "Oi, oi" Simon was sitting in a shaded area with three Austrian women, eating fruit and homemade sandwiches.

"We bought a car in Auckland from Irish guys," one of the women informed excitely.

"Has the engine seized yet," I joked.

"No, no they were so nice. We still have the car, it was a bargain. We will sell it in Christchurch, just before we leave the country."

The normal routine is to check the notice board in hostels for automobiles. Drive around the country, then sell it to other travellers before leaving. Not everyone gets a fair deal. One Dutch couple I knew, their engine cracked two days after their purchase.

We passed through rugged bush areas overlooking white sandy beaches with clear blue waters. It was winter, walkers were minimal. At Bark bay a total of seven checked into the local hut. The bunks were hard wooden frames, just my sleeping bag as a cushion. There were no shops to buy food, this is a wilderness. By day two we had three packs of noodles between us, rabbit food.

"We can eat grass for lunch," I suggested. Our track continued to hug the coastline, perfect in warmer weather for camping.

'Boiling vegetables and frying fish with miniature gas cylinders in such a romantic setting,' wishful thinking for us losers. By mid-afternoon I was hungry and getting irritated.

"That's it, let's get a water-taxi back. We've seen enough, the food cupboard is empty," I suggested as we walked towards a beach where one boat was just pulling in. Simon agreed without hesitation. The ride was bumpy, stopping briefly for a closer view of seals, clamouring on rocks.

At the hostel I had new roommates, Shay and Vinny from Donegal [Ireland], arriving on the next 'magic bus' coming through. We hit a Karaoke contest, each of us taking the stage just once. The winner, vocalized five times, he accumulated the most points, we didn't know the rules.

The following day we continued south on the west coast of the South Island.

'Oooh, there's gold in them hills nowwww,' a comical voice rang out. Cowboys arrived before us, about one hundred and thirty years before us. They rode into town to seek their fortune, it sounds romantic, but we got a brief taste of the hardships. In the small town of Blackball we tried gold panning. Using a sieve, separating the gold grains from the sand with the help of cold water, I managed about seven grams, a value of, well nothing really. For sure a century ago it was back breaking labour, digging in the hills, many with limited success. This was a lunchtime stop, before arriving in Greymouth, which had a historical industrial feel. Perhaps in days gone-by it was thriving because of the now redundant coal nines, the largest town, down the west coast.

We stayed at Noah's ark backpackers, which once was a monastery, remains of gothic existed. Each room had an animal theme. Paul's snoring becoming increasingly irritating. The trampoline and table tennis were items for competitors. The Railway hotel had a cheap buffet, 'so that will do us,' always looking for an economical night. Simon was giving a flamboyant show on the pool table, partnering the big man, Paul, high-fives and victory roars after each game. Tanya and I put the brakes on that, just for the bragging rights, leaving them with four balls. Cruising past our next three opponents, it was an unlikely duo. Tanya was ex-British army, we both agreed a dividing line in Ireland was not necessary.

A lively bar became more animated with another Karaoke getting into full swing, there was no shortage of contestants. 'Love me do.' 'Can't get you out of my head,' 'Dancing queen,' 'Return to sender,' 'Wonderwall,' all sprayed out from the speakers with exceptional quality. In my opinion, choose a song that you know the words. No need to stand like a stiff, continuously staring at the television monitor, add a little choreography.

"The stage movement tipped the balance in your favour," said the owner as he placed a bottle of wine and a tee-shirt in my lap. My voice certainly lacks the potency for an audition, never made the church choir or the singing class at primary school.

The real performance of the night was a demonstration by the proprietors on how to down a beer. A full pint glass of lager placed on a table, drink without touching the glass with their hands. Slowly slurping, then sucking the beaker around their mouths. Moving into a kneeling position, lifting their heads backwards, not a drop was spilled, continuing until the glass is empty. A simultaneous act by husband and wife, a breadth taking enactment, quite literally, a standing ovation followed.

As we travelled further south in the 1965 triumph, half-way down the west coast is one of this country's astonishing attractions. The glaziers, 'Franz Josef,' named after an Austrian emperor by his fellow countryman Julius Haast, an explorer. 'Fox glazier' is the other ice river, named after a New Zealand prime minister. Nowhere else in the world have glaziers advanced so close to the sea at this latitude.

The reasons for this are, rain falls as snow, which develops into crystals, then form into clear ice. The ice accumulates in large zones, so there are huge amounts to push down the valley. The glaziers are steep, so the ice can travel a long way before melting. Easy for Metrological people to grasp, for the masses we nod and accept as it's been explained.

Football continues when it rains. Tennis can get rain-delayed for a couple of hours, Baseball for one night, Cricket for a day. But we had four days of bloody waiting. Watching the drops fall, no glazier tours in the wet. Produce your own entertainment, a walk through the roads parallel to the ice river, browse the information centre, lie in bed like a hatching hen and read. Play cards or games the hostel has to offer. When you are tired of been sensible, hit the high-stool.

Special footwear with prong grips were necessary, the boots were your saviour, gingerly threading on planks across deep crevasses of thirty feet. Narrow paths with steep edges, stepping sideways through the ice tunnels.
Sarah, one group member took a tumble scratching her face in three places. A time out, sympathy extended. It was a fantastic walk, up-stream on this ice river, everyone was vulnerable. Downhill was trickier as one would expect, blue ice formations, large enough to squeeze through. This is pure natural, not justifiable with photos. It was worth the wait of four days.

****

Somewhere north of a town called Wanaka the connection with the '1965 triumph' would begin to terminate. It stumbled and stuttered on the ascent of a steep hill, two further attempts would be unsuccessful. Two cars stopped to offer assistance.
"If it doesn't go up this hill, you guys have no chance at the next one," introducing himself as Phil.
"There are hills for the next couple of miles, I know this area," Phil offered to take our luggage.
"Try it without the extra weigh and no passengers."
It didn't make a difference, stalling in low gear. Not enough horsepower, the engine had lost its stamina. Like a pensioner who is healthy and rides his bicycle, but some climbs are too strenuous. We returned to the nearest village, Haast where we kipped for the night, a population of less than three hundred. We give the keys of the triumph to the hostel owner.
"It's all yours miss, use it for errands. Pass it to folks going north, just avoid big hills."
Not easy in this country.

The views as we descended into Queenstown with a shuttle service are magnificent, a population of over seven thousand. It's built on the shores of Lake Wakatipu, surely a top-five picturesque town on this planet.

Bungee jumping, mentioned only about one thousand times by Simon, he had completed five in Australia. Now he was out to impress, booking a jump at the Nevis highway and encouraging others to duplicate. Leaping from a gondola in a remote gorge with the Nevis River underneath. Catapulting up and down, with the second ascent you release a rip-cord and swing into an upright position. Now you can be winched back up into the cable car. Of the four who set out to complete the task, two refused.

Meanwhile, simultaneously I'm on my way to Kawarau bridge. Everyone feeling anxious, lost in their thoughts, the bus is quiet, very quiet.

"No use worrying about it," the driver calling out over his microphone, nervous laughter breaking the silence.

Preparation for the jump, starts with details been logged, weight is most important for the ropes resistance. I paced back and forth on the bridge, six people before me. I asked a couple could I go ahead of them, wanting to keep waiting time to a minimal, they refused. I pleaded, to no avail. Fear was running through my bones. The Nevis highway gang suddenly arrived, making jokes, tantalizing comments. My mouth was dry, I couldn't muster a response. Taking deep breadths to ease the tension, my heart was pounding.

'Let's duck this guy in the water,' as a staff member wraps a towel around my ankles to cushion the elastic rope.

"No you don't," trying to look calm.

"Yea, you need to get wet," his companion backing him up.

"My skin is allergic to river water," now becoming more worried.

"We've heard that before."

"Stand-up and ease yourself to the edge of the platform," I was instructed. "You're o.k., it'll be short of the water," I was assured. Looking at them, shaking my head, too late for any adjustments.

"Don't look down," someone said.

A short pause and I was gone. No stomach sensations, because it's head, not feet, first. No sudden jerk as I sprung back up, relieved and elated I managed a few roars. About the sixth motion, springing up and down, I was low enough to grab an oar extended to me by the boatman, pulling me aboard.

"Now that wasn't too bad," as he eased me into the rubber dingy. Jubilant and adrenaline flowing, without hesitation I wanted a second jump. This time a ducking, exactly what the instructor informed, just my head and shoulders getting wet and nothing else. Breaking the water perfectly with my hands, head tucked in.

A steady flow of jumpers for the last hour, including the 'bungee king,' Simon. One girl stood on the platform for more than ten minutes before leaping. If you refuse, the payment is not refunded, they offer other activities. Another girl, her tee-shirt almost came off, wrapped around her shoulders, flesh been exposed, cheers rang out. She refused the video of her jump.

"How can I show this to my family," she shrugged.

One can spend too much money in Queenstown, with all the catchy tempting advertisements on adventures.

Motor scrambling on the dirt tracks in the mountains, way above the residents was worth the effort. We were given old clothing, rubber boots and gloves. A wet muddy path, deep puddles of water in unsuspecting areas. Six in our group, each one involved in separate tumbles, speed on tight bends been the common reason. Queenstown will test your nerves, it's full of adrenaline lunatics.

I awoke early on a cold, frosty morning, shuttling between my dormitory room, the kitchen and the lounge. Stuffing my backpack, cooking breakfast and catching the re-run of the rugby world cup semi-final match, New Zealand verses France. It had been played three hours earlier in the U.K. New Zealand All-Blacks created a comfortable lead. My attention shifted to other things, but something would happen that would result in nationwide mourning. Deep into the second-half as I checked on the latest score, I can still hear the commentators' voice echoing.

'Is there a shock in the making as the French keep possession.'

The television room suddenly became crowded, as we waited for the 7:30a.m bus pick-up to Christchurch. The mighty All-Blacks would be defeated.

In past years New Zealand has strongly and rightly criticized the French for nuclear testing in the South-Pacific Ocean. Now once again France were causing turmoil for the Kiwis, this time on the sports field. Throughout the day our driver was hearing the jibes.

"We're going for lunch, do you want French-fries."

"They have great wine in that restaurant, it's French."

Christchurch was the departing point for many in our group.

Destinations varied, the west coast of North America, South America and south-east Asia. Pacific islands, mainly Fiji and Western Samoa. Sydney was on the horizon for me. I guess we should be 'thankful' for our ability to see, enjoy and experience far-flung places.

Christchurch is an English-style city. Small boats are on offer for a gentle ride down the Avon River. Highly manicured gardens dominate the suburbs, hedges and lawns perfectly trimmed. At first instance a sense of stuffy conservatism, but this soon changed.

"Go see the wizard at lunchtime," was the advice of the hostel receptionist.

The wizard dressed to his character name.

A witches hat, long black cloak, long grey hair with matching beard, looking seventy but I think he was much younger.

A comedian, who was gabbing about northern hemisphere countries dominating the globe. He displayed a reverse, upside-down map of the world, now New Zealand was on top. Proud that it is a member of the British commonwealth, he didn't like American dominance. He went into a charade about the sexes;

"Men can live without women. They can go to war. Survive in the desert, in harsh conditions, in isolated regions. A man doesn't need much. He can go into the wilderness and stay for many days. Pitch his tent, sleep in ramshackle huts or in the bushes if he must. Women cannot survive without men. They want five-star luxury accommodation. Sleeping rough would be unthinkable. They don't go anywhere without their chemicals."

Gesturing to the males in the audience, he continued, "how much space do you have in the bathroom?"

"Just enough for a tooth brush and a razor, right. Women have all those sprays, how much damage is this to the environment."

By now we were cheering and clapping on every line.

Cathedral square is the wizard's play ground.

I paid a visit to the Shackel household, in a leafy posh-looking suburban street. Margaret, been most welcoming, contacting Mary, back home after a number of years overseas and the easy-going Josefa to be my Friday night escorts. A past college haunt bar was their choice. At first glance, the locals give an intimidating impression, long-haired beefy biker crowd. This was mythical, receiving a number of friendly exchanges and more when they realized my nationality. The band rolled out rock and soft-rock hits, we mixed freely in the smoke filled pub.

The following day, an afternoon with amicable and nonchalant attractive hostel folk, Anna, with an Asian background and Shelly, blond and casual. We educated ourselves with history and geography explanations; stories of voyages, charts and maps at the Antarctic museum.

Snow and cave rooms with freezing temperatures, a three-way project built by the locals, Italy and America. It was here I learned why there is a hole in the ozone lair above New Zealand and Australia. Sparsely populated countries, it can't be fuel omissions from traffic. It came from gases in the atmosphere blown north from the South Pole.

We sampled the nightlife at Oxford terrace, I encountered a wedding crew.

"I travelled through your country," Jake reminisced, shaking my hand.

"I visited two buddies, ex-house mates from when I lived in London. Irish mothers are great, a big breakfast every morning."

I bought a round of beers, one guy was refusing.

"Never refuse a drink from an Irishman," another commented.

"You dress like a military commander," I joked.

The 'refusal man' was not laughing. Quickly changing the subject to rugby, that loosened him up.

The 'wedding crew' invited me to join them at a local festival which was kicking-off two days later. But my gallivanting was put on hold, an infection in both ears set-in. I don't know how it came about, but it did. Excruciating pain, extra strong antibiotics, six days in bed. Despite my sickness I had more laughs in New Zealand than any other country. So I say "thank you to all."

Braised lamb with marjoram, apples and golden syrup

Ingredients:
8 lamb shoulder chops, well trimmed.
2 onions, peeled and quartered.
1 leek, trimmed, washed and sliced thickly.
2 apples, cored and sliced thickly.
2 carrots, peeled and sliced.
2-3 tbsp. chopped fresh marjoram or oregano.
2 cups vegetable stock.
1 tbsp. golden syrup or maple syrup.

Method:
Heat a dash of oil in a frying pan and brown the lamb chops well.
Transfer to a casserole.
Add a dash more oil to the pan and brown the onions, leek and apple slices.
Scatter over the lamb chops with the carrots and marjoram or oregano.

Season well with salt and pepper and pour the stock over.

Cover and cook at 160 degrees for 1¼ -1½ hours or until the lamb chops and vegetables are tender.

Carefully pour the cooking juices into a saucepan, leaving the chops and vegetables in the casserole for now. Mix the corn flour with enough water to make a smooth paste and stir into the cooking juices.
Cook, stirring over a moderate heat until thickened. Add the golden-syrup or maple syrup, season and pour back over the chops and vegetables in the casserole dish. Mix well and serve with plenty of mashed potatoes.

Australia

Australia, land of open vastness, but also bush, heavy thick bush. Red rock and bright coloured sand landscapes. Endless beaches, picturesque harbours, mining towns, cattle ranches and Aborigine societies. Easy-going communities, where men talk like they are gods' gift to women, 'A raw deal for a Sheila I'd say.'

A fair skin emigrant will certainly age more quickly. If your complexion can weather the potent rays, thank your parents for a healthy concoction.

At Kingsford-Smith airport in Sydney [that name doesn't sound right, a bit too-stuffy] I was opting for a bus. Well a passenger ferry boat would have been a more scenic route from New Zealand, if only there was one. Perhaps a stowaway on a cargo ship may have been possible, making an entry at Botany Bay, like the thousands from Europe who made the arduous voyage many years before.

"Where ya going mate?" asked a bus company employee, dressed casually in shorts.

"Coogee beach, this is the address," producing a slip of paper.

"Have ya got a reservation mate?"

"Well, no."

"No worries mate, we'll check it for ya."

A few minutes later, "they have room at that hostel, take this bus mate," informing the driver of my drop off point. That's Australia, helping without a fuss.

I was quietly excited, there to meet the Hughes family, our next door neighbours in Ireland who had immigrated to the land down under. On the day of their departure, the neighbourhood bid them farewell, in which, as a naive primary school kid, watched the flow of tears, now on their territory, a reunion I day-dreamed of periodically.

A job came quickly with an Electrical firm, Tony Hughes using his influence. An early rise at 5:15a.m., for the seven o'clock start. The 3:30p.m. finish, forty-five minutes later strolling on a semi-crowded beach. Other times I'd stretch-out in Hyde Park, downtown. It was summer and good weather never fails. Christmas was approaching, but this year was different, the beginning of a new millennium would follow.

Australia is a generous country……….with holidays, granting more than Europe and streaks ahead of America. The hostel was predominately English, sharing a room with Simon, a bricklayer from Fiji. For the past nine years he floated between Melbourne and Sydney, the two largest cities in this country. A mild mannered character that enjoyed smoking rollies with a dash of weed of course. Tel from Canada and Tony from Leeds, with his distinctive Yorkshire accent became my buddies, positive personalities, never shy to charm.

Coogee is a district in the Eastern suburbs which has a number of majestic seaside communities, Bondi beach, the most famous has a prominent Irish base. A Saturday night visit to the Cock N' Bull was confirmation of this. Joe, another Canadian residing in more expensive accommodation became the fourth member of our group. 'The quiet man,' I labelled him, that changed to the 'invisible man.' He kept doing disappearing acts, I thought he was having quick puffs of something illegal.

Eating dinner one evening in the hostel television room, Tel and Tony arrived in. "Hay what's going on lads."

"Ah you missed the free-bee last night," Tony gushed excitedly.

"What happened, a keg of beer fell off a truck," I shot back.

"Better than that, we wined in elegant company," Tony teasing.

"I have friends from back home, in town. So we made arrangements to meet them," explained Tel. "But we went to the wrong bar, it was like a restaurant, a bit posh. As soon as we walked-in, drinks were thrust into our hands. One lady introduced herself, saying her husband owned the company. Now what department do you hale from? she asked. Advertising, I answered taking a chance. Excellent, excellent, don't be shy, drink and be merry, we had a good year, she beamed."

"Good stuff, you swindlers, didn't they notice."

"We realized it was a fashion magazine shindig. Some people would say, 'I don't know you.' So I'd introduce myself as a photographer from Canada and would be joining the company in the new year," Tel basking on his bullshit.

"I was doing maintenance at the home of the company boss and Joe was my helper," Tony blurting his angle.

"Tel was the one hooking things up, he sniffled three phone

numbers."

"So is there any company parties tonight," I asked.

"We'll be in-the-mix, come with us. Actually I'm making another attempt to meet my home-boys tonight."

Tel's buddies were in jovial mood when we arrived at 'Cheers bar' in downtown George Street, looking like they had a three-hour head-start on us.

After a few games of pool with the Europeans trouncing the Maple Leafs, Darling harbour was mentioned.

Crossing a pedestrian bridge, Darling harbour, what a name, looked beautifully constructed. A socializing district, newly developed trendy theme. We entered one establishment with a snobbish sentient, a broad doorman blocked our path.

"There's a private party guys, no admittance." Several men mingled in a hallway, others on a balcony.

"They should loosen their ties, like they are enjoying themselves," Tel quipped. We proceeded to a garden-style architecture, penetrating the sociable and salubrious masses. Tony and Tel seemed to be jockeying for pole position with an attractive blonde.

"What's going on here," I said loudly with a grin to a group under a tree with a circular table.

"Sure there laddie, to be sure," a short fat guy shot back in a bad imitation.

"Well I'm not sure at all," shaking his hand.

"It's the silly season Ey-rish," making room for me, his taller companion enthused. The Aussies are generally open to strangers, this was no different, an accountancy firm on their festive season booze-up, as it was Christmas week.

I asked about the recent election on the country becoming a republic. [Two months previous this nation rejected in a national referendum to become a Republic. So they keep with the tradition of been in the British Commonwealth].

"We want to become independent totally," introducing herself as Yvonne, throwing out all the names surrounding me.

"Wait a minute," the fat guy interrupted, "Britishness' is part of our history, culture, we should not give that up."

Comments began flowing from all angles.

"We need a strong ally, Indonesia is not far away, they could be a threat to us," Phil making his contribution.

I looked around, siblings Tom and Janet began arguing. Tom motioned for me to come closer.

"She voted against a republic because she wants to work in London. Ya see Sean, all these younger knuckleheads are thinking only of the work visa for the U.K."

"This is my brother, he's an ass."

"Don't let her ear-bash you," Tom been sarcastic.

"Hay Tom get another round in, don't forget that man," pointing at me, Phil shouted over everyone. Then he whispered to me, "we've got a company credit card."

A guy called Scott stepped forward, "I can't believe there are so many tossers in this country, voting against a republic"

"I think I asked the wrong question, stirring up emotions," I shrugged. "It's fair dinkan mate, it's a major issue," Phil back-slapping me.

Tony and Tel re-appeared, I think they cancelled each other out with that Barbie, one blaming the other.

The lads listened to the loud debating, not their character to stay quiet on the sidelines.

"You gotta change your national flag, put a kangaroo on it, something parochial," Tel, never shy to provoke.

"We have the southern star," fat-boy informed, gesturing for support.

"Put a croc on it, along with Dundee and his buddy Wally," Tony suggested, half the group cheering in support.

"O.K., we'll eliminate the southern star," Janet offered.

Tel explained, "take a leaf out of our book but make sure it's not maple." Some of the Aussies looked puzzled.

"I'm from Canada, we're a part of the Commonwealth but our flag doesn't reflect this."

So of course that started another chain of comments.

****

I arrived forty minutes late at the construction site the following morning on two hours kip.

"Good afternoon," the foreman shouted as he studied scaled drawings, then handing me a notice for the company festive party.

"Be on time for that," with a wry smile.

Andy, a Limerick native would be the stewardship, long-time local resident introducing our group at the Christmas piss-up, two days later. Lots of handshakes and well wishes, the alcohol flowed, the food trays emptied at a slower pace.

"Hay Andy, who's that?" I asked, pointing to a tall six-feet plus guy.

"That's Shultzie."

It had to be him I was thinking.

I asked Shultzie, if he was in Kathmandu [Nepal] a year earlier.

"I was," raising his eyebrows.

"I met you there, briefly, with Lee,"

Thinking for a moment, "Ooooh shit, Shauuuun. I don't believe it, how the bloody hell are you mate."

His image had changed from the carefree long hair and beard to a kojak look.

"We got done in India, robbed on one of those train journeys."

"No way, what happened, did you fall asleep?" I curiously asked.

"You would not believe it mate. I think it was a Scandinavian chic, it had to be her. I was glad to reach London and start working. My girlfriend and I were sharing a compartment with her. I went to the bathroom at one stage, my girlfriend was sleeping. I think that's when she searched the bags. When we reached our destination this sneaky chic was rude. She didn't want any help from us, to share a taxi, finding accommodation.

She shouted, 'I want to be alone, get away.'

Later when I booked into a small hotel, I noticed my wallet was missing, she hurt us badly mate."

Eighteen months earlier I had met Shultzie in Nepal. A group of people had congregated to say their goodbyes. We had common friends, addresses and e-mails were exchanged. I talked with Shultzie three times on the phone, while he was in London but we didn't meet.

So here we were working for the same company in this guy's hometown.

Joanie, probably the most mature and stable, but highly popular backpacker in the hostel, organized a Christmas day buffet. Money was chipped-in, we promised to help with the preparations. But that was broken after a few early evening beers in the local Coogee Bay hotel [C.B.H.]. We headed downtown, well it's Christmas Eve after all, the second best partying day of the year after March 17th. Strolling on the main artery, George Street, a schooner here and there.

Popping into the large department stores in search of Santa hats, we came up empty, all sold out. I offered to buy the Santa hats two employees were wearing. They passed over a box from under the counter, rummaging through, we found three hats.

Our next 'port of call' was the Mercantile at the 'Rocks' in Circular Quay, right next to Sydney harbour bridge, the busiest establishment we encountered, packed to the rafters, actually

Tel nudged me, "one can always rely on an Irish bar for action."

'White Christmas' by Bing Crosby and Bowie, Slade's festive hit, 'Fairytale of New York' by the Pogues were all ringing out.

Then 'We don't wanna go home' by a guy called Martin. A catchy song about the twelve-month work-visa that is issued to Irish nationals. When it has expired, many reluctantly walk to the departure gates after one year down under. But thankfully that has changed, a compliment to this country.

The morning of December 25th. brings the greatest joyous moments for many. When some Anglo-Saxons and large quantities of alcohol mix, it can be a different story. I was awakened by loud stomping, doors banging, a female crying.

"I hate you, stay away from me."

The commotion seemed to continue downstairs. This is a time of year that you like to be on your best behaviour. I ventured to the kitchen to make coffee. One guest Deano was consoling a sobbing girl in the television room. Minutes later he was sizing-up to Alfie in the hallway.

"Come-on hit me, I'll tie my hands behind my back. Let's see how tough you are now," Deano inciting.

I intervened, "hi lads it's Christmas, calm down."

"This guy likes to hit women," Deano pointing his finger.

Alfie looked sheepishly bowing his head, retreating behind me into the kitchen.

The caretaker of the hostel unselfishly arrived on this special holiday to do a quick cleaning for us slobs. Deano was quick to blabber the unfortunate incident to the cleaning lady as she checked the toilets. Without hesitation, Alfie was chucked out, apparently he slapped his girlfriend for snogging another guy. Of course Deano wasn't satisfied, continuing to ridicule Alfie as he prepared to leave.

Alfie was taking no guff this time, grabbing a sweeping brush, gearing-up for a confrontation. Sleepy heads began emerging from the rooms, the cavalry had arrived creating a crowded hallway. Deano retreating for a smoke to the backyard, Alfie slowly exiting the front door. Searching for a vacancy in Sydney would be a major headache, rooms were scarce as travellers were pouring-in for the holidays.

A buffet was prepared, many dishes of salads, vegetables, fruits, cold meats, cocktail sausages, french and garlic bread and of course turkey, full marks to Joanie for her efforts.

It was a damp wet morning.

"Hay Sean we've flown twelve thousand miles to the southern hemisphere and we get bloody English weather," Tony giggling as we surveyed the cloudy skies on the rear balcony.

"We should have followed the swallows and went to Africa," I replied.

By mid-day the sun-rays were shinning through. So we were bustling and fumbling on the shores of the South-Pacific, first football, then volleyball, one hundred yards from our residence. Less famous than Bondi to the north, more attractive than Botany Bay to the south, Coogee was our base camp. My first Christmas in summer weather, a break with tradition, the contrast is bliss.

Tel very kindly donated a hesky of fruit punch which had a potent kick. Let settle over night, a mixture of fruits prepared at a local delicatessen topped with vodka and gin. We began dipping into at breakfast, by mid-afternoon as I chased a loose ball in the football match my anatomy was floating, taking a breather, resting my buttocks on a cooler. Not realizing it was the hesky containing the fruit punch, the bulk of it already consumed. Five seconds later it collapsed under my weight, somehow I managed to salvage most of the ingredients, pouring them into another cooler. I wanted the ground to open and swallow me, feeling like the biggest idiot on the beach. Luckily many of our group were still playing football and didn't notice. But a few of the populace did eye-witness, laughing at

my expense. I shrugged and chuckled amongst the snickering group.
"We'll take a commercial break, back in five minutes for the next
trick," I announced.

A taxi to the suburbs in the early evening had me mingling with an
ex-patriot community. Dominated by Irish with a sprinkle of English
and Aussies. Nidgza, the perfect host, letting the craic flow.

Nobody was concerned about an early rise for work as the
entertainment continued into the small hours, many on a ten-day
break.

****

New Years Eve would bring the new millennium, the extra hype was
expected, bars and restaurants offering special parties. The hostel
gang opted for the obvious, head for Circular Quay and watch the
fireworks on Sydney harbour bridge, this is perfect for the masses,
for there are many vantage points on either side of the bay. Sydney
harbour is one of the finest in this world, it stretches more than
twenty kilometres to join the Parramatta River. With many
developed bays and coves, a mix of residential and commercial. We
set out our stall by 6p.m., in an already crowded quayside. Eighty
degree temperatures, national brews stashed in coolers. The
occasional time-out to a burger stand, 'a balanced consumption
helps, right.'

I bought a bushy purple wig, not that I had a variety of choice, tinted
blue the only other colour the vendor had on display. Anyway, who
cares, 'game for a laugh' is the tone. Tony followed suit when he
seen me flirting with a bunch of women dressed in dazzling silky
outfits.

"Hay Tony, just craving for attention," I teased.

"I spent weeks debating where to celebrate this one night, I'm not
about to drift along quietly," he replied.

With the evening growing darker, a spectacular fireworks display
kicked-off at 9 p.m. This, so adults with children didn't have to wait
until midnight for the main event, good insight by the authorities.

Barry, a Dubliner, Brad, a local, Tel, Joe, [the 'invisible man'] and
me mingled with a group from Wooloomooloo, a district in Sydney.

"Where did that name come from," I asked.

Nobody had an educational answer.

"If I lived in that area, I'd change the name. So you guys are the Wooloomooloo boot crew."

All were dressed in black high heeled boots with green and yellow clothing, the Aussie colours.

We made constant jokes, "Lu, lu Willoomooloo. I have to go to the loo in Wooloomooloo." What a name to poke fun at, our new friends enjoyed our humour. At midnight the organizers didn't disappoint, the famous harbour bridge was turned into a magnificent sea of lights, sparks and flames, constant cheers echoed across the bay. Jubilation occurring all around, our Wooloomooloo buddies extending invitations to continue the craic in their local district. That changed to the Cross,' a better bet for late opening. The party resumed at the 'Bourbon,' live music keeping the adrenaline flowing.

At sunrise we were on Coogee beach for first light of the new Millennium, a cold wind blowing with a light drizzle, not unlike a winter morning back in Europe. Hundreds thronged the shore, many in small huddles and shivering.

The New Year brought changes. Good times can get better............. for the chosen few. The 'Invisible man' went off to Tahiti, an island in the Pacific Ocean. Tel and Tony headed for Thailand. For me, well, I also moved.................... about four miles, to Surrey hills and went back to work.

Now I had just a seven-minute walk to the Central railway station, feeling blessed and fortunate that my salary allowed me to live just a stroll from downtown. Certainly this would not be possible in other westernized countries, a six figure income would be necessary. At my job I was transferred to a team with a contract in the headquarters of a major bank. Data cable runs could only be completed after the bank closed. A 6p.m start, an awkward 4a.m. finish. Many of our group, Irish and British lads were on a working holiday.

"We're not here for a long time, we're here for a good time," Liam humorously speaking for the visitors. I could walk home in twenty-five minutes. But a middle-of-the-night social drink with my workmates was not out of the question. Twenty-four hour bars in Oxford Street were tested, popular with the gay community as cross-dressers flirted with heterosexual drunks, late night customers having no deadline. It was entertaining for us, tired but sober.

"Maybe they're all together and just playing out a fantasy," Don observing coming back from the bar with a fresh pint.

"The more gays the better, that leaves plenty of women for us single guys," Sam jumping-in.

"But it doesn't matter, you're married," Ronnie laughing.

"I'm not, not yet anyway."

Ronnie nudging me, "he's living with someone for three years, so it's the same thing, right."

January can be a miserable month in the northern hemisphere; Santa Claus has returned to the north-Pole. The credit card bills have replaced the joyous Christmas mail. Below freezing temperatures is the normal weather bulletin. Darkness falls early, the neighbours are hibernating. Down under it's mid-Summer, the bank account needs patient stabilizing, but life flows piously. Cricket tests, crowded beaches, busy sports facilities. Walkers, joggers and cyclists populate the coastal pathways.

The face of this country's population is changing. In the past there was a steady influx of Irish and British immigrants. The Italians, Greeks and Yugoslavs arrived in droves. With a national count of eighteen million, sustainability is buckling. So the doors have opened to Asian countries. Australia, not much smaller than America, many habitants reside on coastal areas. But in recent years large numbers of Irish and British residents are migrating to these shores again, who could blame them with a stable economy and good weather.

One day I took the train to Millets Point station on the north shore, then I walked back across Sydney Harbour Bridge. A security guard watching for disorderly activity informed me that there are on average, six suicide attempts from the bridge each year.

"If I see any problems I will call the emergency services immediately."

"So they jump down into the water and drown," I quizzed.

"That's the general idea, most are men. I have stopped some, managed to talk to them until the police get here."

"But they could still jump with the police here."

"Yea mate, but once someone starts pleading with them, they

normally change their mind."

The harbour looked clean and fresh, no cargo ships in this area. Down below is Circular Quay, the docking port for passenger ferries to places like Manly beach, Britta's bay and Watsons bay. Also one of the most recognizable structures in the western world, the Sydney Opera House. A triangular and shell like shape exterior, dramatically situated on the edge of Circular Quay. One million Swedish shaped white tiles, I counted them, no kidding.

Tony Hughes took me to his dear father's resting place. It's a magnificent hillside cemetery in Waverly, overlooking the Pacific Ocean. In the middle of these spiritual grounds is a memorial dedicated to the 'Wicklow Chief,' Michael Dwyer, an Irish Republican. He was laid to rest here in 1825, his wife is also buried here. Other Irish names are inscribed, including the ten hunger strikers who died in the H-Blocks prison protests in Belfast, in the early 1980's.

This is significant for me and could be for others who attended my local Blackrock Primary school. In our final year it was a necessity to learn the poem, 'Michael Dwyer.' Thirteen verses, and you better know them, with a stern teacher testing you. I can still remember some of them. Michael Dwyer fought against the British in the Wicklow Mountains in the 1798 rebellion. He managed to elude the British military with the help of local sympathizers. Many people were killed protecting him, so eventually he negotiated a deal with the British for safe passage to America. But his enemies reneged on the agreement and put him in Kilmainham jail in Dublin for two years. Then they sent him to a British colony, Australia.

He was given the free settlers status. He was given one hundred acres of land, but he soon had problems with the authorities. Accused of planning to overthrow the government for making statements that all Irishmen in Australia should be free. He was acquitted with the help of the chief of Sydney police, who spoke on his behalf that he was not a threat. But his troubles were not finished. Governor Bligh, disregarded the trial and ordered another. Dwyer was sent to 'Van Diemans land' [Tasmania]. A year later the governor was overthrown. The new governor, George Johnson reinstated Michael Dwyer's freedom. He later became head of police in Liverpool, a suburb of Sydney. All that for seeking emancipation in his own country.

Ireland can be a single island regardless of it's name. All citizens of the world are welcome, to do business, visit for a holiday or live there if they have the correct official papers, but not to takeover.

The electricians union had a policy, two hours were stopped in my wages every week, that accumulates to eight hours [one day] after four weeks. These days were called 'roster days.' It was optional when you could take these days off. Allowing my roster days to accumulate plus other holidays, I went off on a ten-day break to the centre of the country in March.

As one stares down from thirty thousand feet, a vast open space of deserted land, green fields are rare. Yellow and red earth is most common. Three hours after our ascendancy, this country's greatest attraction came into view. A monstrous rock, reddish in colour rising above the bush flatland of the 'Australian outback.' Ayres rock, known to the Aborigines as Ulluru. Nearby, a runway adjacent to a small terminal easily recognized with little sign of habitation around. Free transport is provided from the miniature airport to the Ayres rock resort, a collection of hotels, a hostel and camp site.

I immediately made an acquaintance, Graham, originally from the borders of north Wales and Merseyside in Britain, a top-ten character to chill-out with. He had been to Ireland many times, working as a mechanic on a racing team in the car rallies. Now he was employed in the outback on a cattle farm, it had a labour force of forty-five. There were many trucks to service, plus four helicopters. Horses are also used for herding cattle on the parochial pastures. But this is a ranch that is bigger than some countries.

"Every three months I take a break, Jack. Too much isolation in the outback, I have to get away, let's have a game of pool."

Graham was normally in the vicinity of the bar, his social life a feast or a famine it seemed.

I had booked into the men's dorm room, with twenty-eight beds, perhaps late night drinks will be necessary as sleeping pills. The room was divided into seven bays, thankfully it wasn't high season, so grunts and snores were minimal.

Sunrise or sunsets are the ideal times to visit Ayres rock. Missing my early morning bus pick-up to the rock, I hitched a ride with

Germans, arriving on time to catch a new day, beginning with the rock changing from a deep red colour to orange. Plenty of mug shots used by the international gathering. The entrance to the summit was closed:

"too windy, too dangerous," the park authorities informed.

I noticed plaques posted in memory of those who lost their lives attempting to reach the top. So a walk around the perimeter would absorb a taste of this sacred area for the Aborigines, lots of dry sand, bush and stone.

The following morning I was able to scramble up the rock, a continuous chain linked with steel poles every two meters for assistance, friendly banter with other climbers.

Challenging, "I'll race you to the top," with mainly those who were panting heavily. The climb is a gradual slope, the surface surprisingly smooth. A magnificent view the higher one goes, red sand, green bush, large peak formations in the distance, the Oslos on one side, Connors rock' on the other. A small monument marks the summit, where everyone poses for their photo shoots. To add something extra I introduced my '1970's Afro' wig. Giggles all around as I lay on the ground, acting the clown. It was passed around to different heads, each with an individual pose. The wig occupies a bit of room in my backpack but it's worth a laugh whenever I'm brave enough to pull it out.

Start early, it's imperative to reach the top of the rock, climbing in the shade. On the descent the sun much higher in the sky, the flies buzz in abundance around your sweaty forehead, in their thirsty quest for moisture.

By now I was part of a gang of eight, chatting lightly on the descent. Cracking jokes with others arriving late in their pursuit to reach the top.

"I'm sorry it's closed up there now."

A frustrating disappointed expression coming back at me.

"Only joking."

"You better hurry the bar is still open, make sure you have the right change," I said to another group.

"It doesn't say it in my guide book," an Israeli responded.

"Check again," someone said amid loud laughter.

We were in the Northern Territory, home to over three hundred thousand Aborigines. Each state in Australia has its own provincial government, except the Northern territory. The Aborigines have been looking for a public apology from the Australian government for several reasons. The Aborigine way of life is a major contrast to the Caucasian community. The outdoors is important to them, going walkabout, disappearing into the outback for days.

That evening at the hostel bar I talked with a family of four. "We run a store in an Aborigine community four hours drive from here, near the state border of Western Australia. The Aborigines and alcohol don't mix favourably, so it's a dry town," the father speaking frankly. Every two months they have a five-day break, including Graham and myself in their next round of drinks. Minutes later I was shaking hands with an attractive miss Kearney from Castlebellingham, a town four miles from my mum's house in Ireland, an enjoyable spontaneous moment.

The following day I took a ride with Graham to Alice, 'who the f--- is Alice,' as the song goes. A seven-hour journey to Alice Springs, what a name. Through the outback, long straight roads. Traffic was sparse, nine vehicles came in the opposite direction, five trucks and four cars. Drivers waving, dry landscapes, no chance of habitation. There is simply almost no rain.
A pit-stop at an isolated petrol station, to fill-up and stretch our legs. A Danish couple with a broken axel on their Combi van, the interior, a maze of clothing and camping material. I seen cleaner scrap yards, but their free-spirit was shining through. Nearby is Connors rock, towering the barren countryside, a few days earlier we viewed it on the horizon from Ayres rock, it had taken four hours driving to be in it's proximity.
Just one night in Alice, a town of 27,000 people, a mixture of western and aboriginal influences. This town originally a telegraph base, halfway between Adelaide on the south coast and Darwin in the north. It began to grow when gold was discovered in Arltunga, 100k.m. east, but currently it depends mainly on tourism.
The next day I'm looking down on the vast 'Aussie outback,' flying south to Melbourne for the Australian Grand Prix.
Albert Park is closed to public traffic, re-arranged for this car race

event. Beverage and food tents spread across the course, miniature expeditions of the current racing teams. Schumacher the comfortable winner as the drivers whiz-by, now you see them, now you don't. A noisy sport, ear plugs are distributed. In the aftermath the track is open to the public, long stretches of skid marks on every corner. Tow trucks passed through with vehicles decked in brightly coloured advertisements which didn't complete the race. The red Ferrari flags were popping-up in celebration of victory.

Prior to my arrival, I had literally made dozens of phone calls requesting a room. Receiving a repetitive response of 'sorry, we have no vacancies,' my dear friend Ingri coming to the rescue. Her family, local residents of Melbourne were perfect hosts. No elaborate changes, just slide right-in and be a clan member.

A few days later was the Saint Patrick's day 'Irish holiday,' Port Melbourne was the word. Squeezing onto a packed tram, the locals were flocking to the emerald bars. Minutes earlier a frantic eleventh-hour search for green hair spray proved fruitful, as the shops were closing. I teamed-up with Gerry, Kieran and Joe, Irish friends living in Sydney. A line longer than a flight path greeted us at Sullivan's, an eight-foot high wire fence to prevent a sneaking entry. Standing around for twenty minutes the queue hadn't moved. "It's feckin madness this line, some of them won't get-in until after midnight, what do youz think lads," Gerry observing.

"Make a phone call, tell them there is a device hidden under a table. They'll have to evacuate the place, then we'll be in with the all clear," Kieran suggested.

"This country has no real enemies," Gerry shrugged.

"Except for a few Kiwi's," Kieran shot back.

"Let's check-out that joint across the street, it'll get the over-flow crowd," I pointed-out.

First round was on the house, now that's the way to treat customers. One Aussie kept buying us green jello shots, I think she had an eye for Kieran, but he fell asleep, standing against a pillar. Joe was awarded a bottle of whiskey for singing an Irish number, 'The fields of Athenry.'

I stepped forward to give 'The Wild Rover,' a blast, forgetting the words, I was continuously jeered all night.

Then I got mixed-in with a group who were big Pogues fans [Irish traditional rock band]. They were challenging me on how many of their songs I could name. These folks hadn't a note in their heads, but they were given it their best shot.

As we strolled along the nearby waterfront looking for a taxi I noticed the 'Spirit of Tasmania,' a huge ferry docked and waiting for it's next crossing of the Bess Strait to the island of Tasmania.

I managed to track down Mike 'Stack' McConnell, opponents at juvenile football in the primary school yard.

"It's not an issue where you come from, everyone just mixes in this country," the big man happily residing down under.

Melbourne has the coldest climate of Australian cities, no reflection on the people who are warm. A reunion with local acquaintances Kate, Melissa and the affable Allan Richards in the popular seaside area of St. Kilda. Clear blue skies but a chilly wind influenced our decision not to hit the beach. Instead, the bars on Fitzroy street were a unanimous choice, which is wide enough for traffic of cars, bicycles and tram lines. My buddies have strong stamina to socialize, but a few timeouts for food, obviously the Aussies were feeling the pace, even on home soil, of course they would never concede to that. Later in the evening we head for the rugby league match between Melbourne and Parramatta from Sydney. With ten minutes remaining in the game I bet with Kate that Parramatta who had a narrow lead, would hold out. The home side managed a late score and clinch victory, I wanted her to win anyway.

Returning to my job in Sydney, I settled-in to a disciplined routine. My neighbours on Cleveland street, were frequent callers, we played tennis and football under the floodlights in the cool evenings as winter approached, entertaining with workmates on the weekends. But that comfortable lifestyle would be severely disrupted, I received that dreaded phone call on a family matter, my father had passed-away. A message that is almost inevitable, but always believing it's light-years away. Deeply disturbed I would limp out of this country, heading for passport control.

Aussie Meat Pie

Ingredients:
1 lb chuck or blade steak
2 tablespoons flour
Freshly ground black pepper
1 tsp. salt
½ cup water
12 oz packet frozen puff pastry, thawed.
Beaten egg to glaze.

Directions:
1. Trim gristle and fat from steak, cut into thin shreds, then chop finely. Dust with flour, salt and pepper and place in the top of a double boiler or pudding pan.
2. Place enough boiling water to come halfway up sides of bowl, Simmer for two hours or until the meat is very tender. Replace water in saucepan as necessary to maintain level.
3. Allow to cool completely.
4. Roll out pastry dough thin and cut ¾ of it to fit individual, round, or square pie tins. Line tins with dough, and fill about ¾ full with meat filling. Cut lids from remaining dough, dampen edges and put into place.
5. Cut a vent in the top of each pie for steam to escape. Chill for 15 minutes and then brush with beaten egg. Bake in preheated oven [200c] for 25 minutes or until pastry is puffed and golden.
Serve with tomato sauce [ketchup].

Ear Cleaning- India.

India-Nepal border.

Somewhere between Udaipur and New Delhi.

Trekking in the Himalayas, Nepal.

Taj Mahal, India.

Red Square, Kremlin, Moscow.

The 'Madres of Plaza de Mayo' in Buenos Aires, Argentina.
Protesting about their missing children.

San Telmo, Buenos Aires, Argentina.

Class 6, Nepal.

Favourite people, Rica and Sea-Horse, A.C.B. Auckland, N.Z.

About the writer:
Sean Breen grew up in the seaside area of Blackrock, near
Dundalk on the east coast of Ireland.
Home is where I hang my hat,
Would you invite me in for a cup of tea?
No sugar.
I'll make sure it will not be dull.
Long term, he has lived in
New York and London.

Check out: www.facebook.com/1WayTicket.Book.

mytravelblog.org/jacktravel or mytb.org/jacktravel.

Feel free to leave a message at: jackpassxyz@gmail.com

Book cover and interior design:
Andrew Breen
andrewbreen_18@hotmail.com

Printed in Great Britain
by Amazon